but go alone —— You cannot
learn to walk without tumbles and
knocks and bruises, but you will
never learn to walk so long as there
are props.               The props of art
are — on the one hand — the
slavish imitation of old work — no
matter what date or from what country
—— and on the other hand the
absurd and false idea — that there
can be any living emotion expressed
in work scientifically proportioned
according to antient principals —
but clothed in the thin fantasy of
the authors own fancy.
The artists motto should be
I care not the least for theories
for this or that dogma — so far
as the practise of art is concerned
—— but take my stand on what
I myself consider my personal ideal.
——— and I am sure that
no one of any gifts of reasoning —
will question the value of a high ideal
—— a strong ambitious conviction —

# CHARLES RENNIE MACKINTOSH
# THE ARCHITECTURAL PAPERS

# CHARLES RENNIE MACKINTOSH THE ARCHITECTURAL PAPERS

*edited by Pamela Robertson*

*The MIT Press, Cambridge, Massachusetts*

First MIT Press Edition, 1990
© 1990 The University of Glasgow

Published in Great Britain by White Cockade Publishing
in association with The Hunterian Art Gallery, University of Glasgow.

Library of Congress Cataloging-in-Publication Data

Mackintosh, Charles Rennie, 1868-1928.
    The architectural papers / Charles Rennie Mackintosh / edited by
  Pamela Robertson. – 1st MIT Press ed.
      p.  cm.
  Includes bibliographical references and index.
  ISBN 0-262-18142-8
  1. Mackintosh, Charles Rennie, 1868-1928–Archives.
I. Robertson, Pamela, 1955- . II. Title.
Z6616.M176M2 1990
[NA997]
720–dc20
                                    90-7285
                                       CIP

Designed by Gerald Cinamon, Cinamon and Kitzinger.
Typeset in 10 on $12\frac{1}{2}$ point Photina at the
Oxford University Computing Service.
Printed and bound in Great Britain at The Alden Press, Oxford.

Endpapers: Two pages from Mackintosh's last paper, 'Seemliness'
(© Hunterian Art Gallery)
Opposite title page: Charles Rennie Mackintosh (1868-1928) *c.* 1900
(© Annan)

The production of this volume has been sponsored by SBT Keppie,
architects and planning consultants.

THE CONTRIBUTORS

PAMELA ROBERTSON has been since 1977 Curator of the Mackintosh Collection at the Hunterian Gallery, University of Glasgow, the major collection and archival resource for the work of Charles Rennie Mackintosh. Since completing in 1981 the installation of The Mackintosh House interiors in the Gallery she has researched and mounted regular exhibitions on the work of Mackintosh and his contemporaries.

JAMES MACAULAY is Senior Lecturer in Architectural History at the Mackintosh School of Architecture, Glasgow. A past Chairman of the Society of Architectural Historians of Great Britain and of the Architectural Heritage Society of Scotland, his publications include *The Gothic Revival, 1745-1845* (1975) and *The Classical Country House in Scotland, 1660-1800* (1987).

ROBERT MACLEOD, Canadian born, has practised and taught architecture for many years, and is currently Professor of Architecture at Brighton Polytechnic. He is the author of *Charles Rennie Mackintosh: Architect and Artist* (1968, 2nd edn 1983) and *Style and Society: Architectural Ideology in Britain* (1971).

DAVID WALKER is the Principal Inspector of the Historic Buildings and Monuments, Scottish Development Office. With Andor Gomme he wrote *The Architecture of Glasgow* (1968, 2nd edn 1987), and, a recognised authority, has published widely on the work of Mackintosh and his Scottish contemporaries.

FRANK ARNEIL WALKER trained as an architect and from 1969 has taught architectural design and history at the University of Strathclyde, where he is now a Reader. His wide-ranging studies of nineteenth and early twentieth century British and Central European architecture have been extensively published in the architectural press.

# Contents

# *Preface*

This volume presents for the first time, and in a fully-edited form, the only known architectural writings of Charles Rennie Mackintosh. The seven manuscripts form part of the Mackintosh Estate, which passed to the University of Glasgow in 1946 with the consent of the residuary legatee, Sylvan MacNair, and now forms the nucleus of the Mackintosh Collection housed in the Hunterian Art Gallery.

1990, Glasgow's year as 'European City of Culture', is an appropriate time to publish this material. Mackintosh's internationally recognised achievements – in particular his contribution to the architectural heritage of his native city – were undoubtedly major factors in Glasgow's successful bid for this accolade.

Many individuals and institutions have contributed to the appearance of this volume and my thanks are due to all, above all to the contributors who have provided copy and erudition with unfailing courtesy and efficiency. I am grateful to Joan Hughson for the initial transcription of the Mackintosh texts and to Denise Perry and Margaret Stewart for their forbearance in their final preparation. Valued advice was provided by Chris Allan and Martin Hopkinson, my colleagues at the Hunterian, by Robert Gibbs of the History of Art Department, University of Glasgow, Professor Timothy Miles of the Dyslexia Unit, University of Bangor, and by Roger Billcliffe. Thomas Howarth was, as ever, generous both with his wide knowledge of matters Mackintosh and with encouragement for the project. A heart-felt thank you also to Perilla Kinchin of White Cockade Publishing whose scrupulous attention to detail has finely polished the rough manuscripts.

The Glasgow Institute of Architects kindly granted permission to publish for the first time correspondence and a memoir relating to Mackintosh's Italian tour. Many copyright owners and owners of original material have generously allowed their works to be illustrated, in particular Dr Thomas Howarth, Wilma Paterson, the Mitchell Library Glasgow, the Royal Commission on the Historical Monuments of England, and Glasgow School of Art, and also Glasgow Art Gallery and Museum, The Charles Rennie Mackintosh Society, Renfrew District Council, and the Royal Commission on Ancient Monuments Scotland.

Generous financial assistance towards publication costs has been provided by SBT Keppie, architects and planning consultants. Their support is particularly appreciated and apposite as SBT Keppie now incorporates Keppie Henderson, formerly John Honeyman & Keppie, the practice with which Mackintosh was associated for nearly twenty-five years, from 1889-1913, rising from junior draughtsman to partner.

Pamela Robertson

# *Chronology*

This brief chronology dates the beginning of Mackintosh's involvement, at design stage, with his major projects. Certain of these were completed in subsequent stages or over a period of years. For fuller chronologies see Howarth and Kimura, cited in the Bibliography. A distinction is made between competition entries and competition designs: the former were for commissions, the latter for awards. It is notable that Mackintosh's only successful competition entry was for the Glasgow School of Art.

1868  Born in Glasgow, 7 June.

1875  Reid's Public School, Glasgow.

1877  Allan Glen's High School, Glasgow.

1884  Apprenticed to John Hutchison, Glasgow. Begins evening classes at Glasgow School of Art.

1885  Francis Newbery appointed Headmaster of Glasgow School of Art.

1887  First of five volumes of D. MacGibbon and T. Ross, *The Castellated and Domestic Architecture of Scotland* – publication completed in 1892.

1888  Mountain Chapel, and Town House in a Terrace competition designs.

1889  Joins Honeyman & Keppie as a junior draughtsman. Presbyterian Church competition design.

1890  Science and Art Museum competition design. Public Hall competition design. Wins Alexander Thomson Travelling Studentship. Redclyffe, Glasgow.

1891  Scotch Baronial Architecture Lecture.
Tour of Italy, April to July: Diary of an Italian Tour.
A Chapter House competition design. W. R. Lethaby, *Architecture, Mysticism and Myth*.

1892  Glasgow Art Gallery competition entry.
A Tour in Italy Lecture.
Manchester Technical Schools competition entry. A Railway Terminus competition design.

*c*. 1892  Elizabethan Architecture Lecture.
Architecture Lecture.

1893  Glasgow Art Club interiors.
Architecture Lecture.

1894  Sketching trip to the Cotswolds.

1895   Glasgow Herald Building tower. Queen Margaret College, University of Glasgow. Martyrs' Public School, Glasgow.

1896   Glasgow School of Art competition entry. Buchanan Street Tea Rooms, Glasgow, murals. Exhibits at Fifth Arts and Crafts Exhibition, London.

1897   Queen's Cross Church, Glasgow. Argyle Street Tea Rooms, Glasgow, furniture.

1898   National Bank of Scotland competition entry. Glasgow International Exhibition buildings competition entry.

1900   Windyhill, Kilmacolm. Ingram Street Tea Rooms, Glasgow, interiors. 120 Mains Street, Glasgow, interiors. Exhibits at Eighth Vienna Secession Exhibition. Marries Margaret Macdonald.

1901   House for an Art Lover competition design. Daily Record Building, Glasgow. Liverpool Cathedral competition entry. Becomes a partner in Honeyman & Keppie.

1902   Liverpool Cathedral competition entry. The Hill House, Helensburgh. Exhibits at the International Exhibition of Modern Decorative Art, Turin. SEEMLINESS Lecture.

1903   Willow Tea Rooms, Glasgow.

1904   Scotland Street School, Glasgow.

1906   Glasgow School of Art second phase. Mosside, Kilmacolm. Auchinibert, Killearn.

1913   Resigns from Honeyman, Keppie & Mackintosh.

1914   Moves to Walberswick, Suffolk.

1915   Moves to London.

1916   78 Derngate, Northampton, interiors.

1917   Willow Tea Rooms, Glasgow, interiors.

1920   London studio designs.

1923   Moves to the South of France.

1927   Returns to London.

1928   Dies in London, 10 December.

Elizabethan Architecture.

Scotch Baronial Architecture.

1. Pages from Mackintosh's architectural papers

PAMELA ROBERTSON

# General Introduction

Preserved among Mackintosh's effects at the time of his death was a bundle of manuscripts comprising six lecture scripts and a diary. Obviously valued by their author, they constitute Mackintosh's only surviving writings on architecture. Possibly others have not survived, but it is clear that Mackintosh was not by inclination a prolific writer. The manuscripts, which are wide-ranging both in subject and in source, document Mackintosh's evolving perceptions of architecture in a professional and aesthetic context. Beginning with general analyses of specific national architectures – Scottish, Italian and English Elizabethan – Mackintosh progresses to more theoretical considerations of architecture, concluding with 'Seemliness', the most personal and independent of his statements on architecture, art and design.

The papers span the period 1891 to 1902, covering Mackintosh's formative years. By the time of his first lecture in 1891, Mackintosh had completed his five-year apprenticeship in Glasgow with John Hutchison and had served two years as a junior draughtsman with Honeyman & Keppie. From 1884 he had attended evening classes in Architecture and Building Construction at Glasgow School of Art. At that time the study of architectural theory and history played little part in the curricula of these courses. Such topics were dealt with within the forum of the Glasgow Architectural Association set up by the junior members of the profession in 1877, and it was to this group that Mackintosh's first two lectures, 'Scotch Baronial Architecture' and 'A Tour in Italy', were given. The invitation to Mackintosh in 1891 reflects his success in student examinations and competitions, including the prestigious Alexander Thomson Studentship of 1890. His was a name to be watched. By the time of the last lecture, 'Seemliness', in 1902 Mackintosh's career was in full stream, and he was able to present, as Robert MacLeod shows, 'a manifesto of his attitude to his art'. Yet contained within 'Seemliness' are intimations of the premature stifling of that career, hints at conflicts within both Honeyman & Keppie and Glasgow's architectural circles. As early as 1892 Mackintosh had condemned the indiscriminate pursuit of fame: 'by an excessive & unsatiable thirst after it they will come to have vulgar views, they will degrade their style & their taste will be entirely corrupted' [E 40]. In 'Seemliness' he continued the crusade: 'The man with no convictions – no ideals in art, – no desire to do something personal something his own, no longing to do something that will leave the world richer his fellows happier is no artist. The artist who sinks his personal convictions – who lives not up to his ideals is no man' [G 7]. The consequences of his uncompromising stance were touched on in a letter written the following year, 1903, to Hermann Muthesius. Mackintosh, deeply depressed, writes of 'antagonisms and undeserved ridicule ... feelings of despondency and despair'.[1]

Though Mackintosh's persona remains tantalisingly enigmatic, certain characteristics are clearly evident. His passionate nationalism reverberates through 'Scotch Baronial Architecture', a nationalism which perhaps tied him to Glasgow to the detriment of his career. The Italian papers exude the enthusiasm and energy (and humour) of a gifted and responsive student confronted for the first time with the architectural wonders of Italy. But the most consistent quality threading through the writings is Mackintosh's uncompromising pursuit of the ideals and integrity of architecture, an exacting credo apparent also in practice.

Tantalisingly also the papers contain no reference to Mackintosh's work and only passing reference to that of contemporary architects. But though not specific to his own designs, they are specific to current topical issues. The second half of the nineteenth century was a volatile period for the architectural profession as Mackintosh was clearly aware, pronouncing it 'a difficult task to read a history from the architecture of this nation at the present time' [E 36]. Major developments in technology and materials were accompanied by demands for unprecedented building types. These upheavals were compounded by internal arguments as to the structure of the profession and the status of architecture. Many of these issues were addressed in Mackintosh's lectures.

To the major technological developments Mackintosh's was an essentially conservative response. Of the possibilities offered by ferro-vitreous structures, for instance, he wrote: 'These two comparatively modern materials iron & glass though eminently suitable for many purposes will never worthily take the place of stone, because of this defect the want of mass. With the advent of the Crystal Palace and the many rosetinted hallucinations of that period arose the belief in the invention of a new style. At last common sence it was shouted prevails – no more connection with the works of the past – no more deference to the ideas of artists poets, or even the principals of beauty in Nature: for now we can pile up the hugest buildings with the least possible means of support, and that on most economical principals as design can be turned out of the foundry by repetition without limit, to the minimising of intellectual labor and so also to the payment of it. But time has passed, and practical experience has shown that apart altogether from any defect in stability or actual comfort the want of appearance of stability is fatal to the introduction of such a style for either domestic, civil or ecclisiastical buildings.' [E 16-17] [2]

The debate over training methods had been nationally addressed by the 1887 R.I.B.A. conference which devoted an entire session to the Education of Architects. Discussions subsequently filled the professional press as advo-

2. Mackintosh (standing right) *c.* 1890, with other Honeyman & Keppie staff, including J. H. MacNair (standing centre), Alexander McGibbon (seated centre) and Charles Whitelaw (seated right).

cates of a regulated syllabus and examination system challenged the established informal methods of articled pupillage. Mackintosh implicitly supported the latter system, of which he was a product, condemning 'the stupid forms of education – which stifles the intellect paralizes the ambition and kills emotion' [G 11], supporting the 'advocates of individuality, freedom of thought and personal expression' against 'the advocates of tradition and authority' [G 2]. Concomitant with the education debate was the attempt to introduce registration of architects by statute in 1891. Reaction from the profession was swift and took the form of a series of essays published that year, *Architecture: A Profession or an Art*, edited by Norman Shaw and T. G. Jackson. These essays, by among others Prior, Lethaby, Bodley and the editors, raised important issues about the respective roles of architect, builder and craftsman, and the relationship between architecture and building, issues which became recurring themes in Mackintosh's later writings as he searched for a comprehensive definition of true architecture. Mackintosh consistently maintained a distinction between architecture and building, and took several swipes at the view that architecture was subordinate to painting and sculpture. By 1893 he concluded that architecture had to involve all of the arts and handicrafts: 'To get true architecture the architect must be one of a body of artists posessing an intimate knowledge of the crafts, and no less on the other hand the painter & sculptor & other craftsmen must be in direct touch & sympathy with architecture.' [F 24]

In his search for a satisfactory definition of architecture, Mackintosh considered various combinations of attributes: strength, usefulness and beauty; the needs and desires of men, the structure and needs of materials, nature; form, colour, proportion, soul. His initial explorations in the first three lectures however were of the development of national architectures, in which Mackintosh later recognised parallels with contemporary theories of human evolution. 'Behind every style of architecture there is an earlier style in which the germ of every form is to be found except such alterations as may be traced to new conditions or directly innovatory thought in religion, all is the slow change of growth' [F 8-9]. Once this evolution was interrupted by the importation of exotic styles, the integrity of native architecture was forfeited. Scottish Baronial had been debased by the importation of English Elizabethan; Elizabethan in turn was corrupted by Inigo Jones' Classical revival. On the same basis Mackintosh regarded contemporary historicism as valueless. 'It is absurd to think it is the duty of the modern architect to make believe he is living 4 – 5 – 6 hundred or even 1000 years ago – and that his mission is to exercise on the forms found associated with a certain decade.' [F 20-1]. This was uninhibited outspokenness, as his immediate target comprised the majority of the Glasgow architectural establishment, including his principal John Honeyman. Mackintosh's interest in these uncorrupted native architectures was concentrated on their responsiveness to changing needs and requirements. Here there were important lessons for his own generation, lessons passed on in his subsequent lectures. In 1893 he emphasised that 'all great & living architecture has been the direct expression, of the needs & beliefs of man at the time of its creation, and how if we would have great architecture created this should still be so' [F 19]. Almost a decade later the same message was underlined. A fundamental responsibility for architects was 'the task of clothing in grace and beauty the new forms and conditions that modern developements of life — social – commercial and religious insist upon' [G 8].

His analyses of Scottish, Italian and Elizabethan architecture reveal Mackintosh's sensitivity to architectural qualities which were to become characteristics of his mature designs. Of Scottish Baronial he singled out its 'beauty of external outline grouping of parts boldness freeness & variety of conception' [A 11]. The Florentine palaces impressed with their 'beautiful simplicity, the large masses of plain masonry & small windows, surmounted by tremendeous cornices beautifully designed' [C 26-7]. The account of Elizabethan architecture, though less engaged perhaps because at that time

3. David MacGibbon (1831-1902), photographed *c.* 1901
4. Thomas Ross (1839-1930), a portrait by W. H. Kerr, 1893

he lacked first-hand knowledge, expresses admiration for its 'care for archi-tectural effect', sound and truthful construction and 'appropriateness in design' [D 19], and specifically its use of windows, woodwork and fireplaces.

Mackintosh's respect for the buildings of the past was expressed through his interest in vernacular architecture – the humble Scottish cottage, the Italian brick house or Elizabethan grange, farmhouse and cottage – examples of which were recorded in his sketchbooks and cited in the lec-tures. His enthusiasm was not an isolated phenomenon. Fuelled by a rereading of early Ruskin, English Arts and Crafts architects were rediscovering the beauty of vernacular buildings as documents in stone bearing the hand-writing of a craftsman's touch. It is significant that Mackintosh's first sketching trip in Britain outside Scotland was to the rediscovered and newly-fêted Cotswolds in 1894. Undoubtedly this interest influenced his frequent references to the work of the 'falcefying restorationist' [E 2]. The only occasion on which Mackintosh went into print was on this subject, in a discussion of the restoration of three churches in Wareham, Dorset, pub-lished in *The British Architect* of November 1895.[3] He toed a clear Society for the Protection of Ancient Buildings line, undoubtedly impressed on him by Honeyman, an active S.P.A.B. member from 1877-88. Mackintosh claimed that St Mary and Holy Trinity had been ruined by 'ignorance and restoration – they usually go together', while at St Martin's he concluded 'a very small sum judiciously spent from time to time is all that is required to make it for all time one of the most interesting churches in the neighbourhood'.

Despite his protestation in 1893 that 'my knowledge of books is only that of the general reader' [F 2], the catalogue of Mackintosh's largely unacknowledged sources is lengthy. In particular he raided David MacGibbon and Thomas Ross, W. R. Lethaby, Ruskin and James Fergusson. The fact that, in common with other students with deadlines, Mackintosh 'borrowed' extensively and expounded received opinion is less significant than the content of what he lifted. With the first two sources, Mackintosh reveals himself fully *au fait* with the latest architectural research and theory. The final volumes of MacGibbon and Ross's pioneering and definitive study *The Castellated and Domestic Architecture of Scotland* were yet to come off the press as Mackintosh plundered its published parts in 1891 and possibly cribbed from MacGibbon's lecture at the 1889 Edinburgh Art Congress.[4] Lethaby's *Archi-*

5. W. R. Lethaby, *Architecture, Mysticism and Myth*
Despite the date given here it has been established by Godfrey Rubens that this influential book appeared at the end of 1891.

ARCHITECTVRE
MYSTICISM AND
MYTH.  *By W. R. Lethaby*
*with illustrations by the Author*

' *Are there symbols which may be called constant; proper to all races, all societies, and all countries?* '  César Daly.

1 8 9 2
London: Percival & Co.

*tecture, Mysticism and Myth* appeared at the end of 1891. A controversial book, it mystified much of the architectural and lay press. *The Times* commented drily: 'If architects are to write so obscurely as Mr Lethaby writes, we cannot but rejoice that writers on architecture have not too often been architects.'[5] But as Godfrey Rubens noted it was Mackintosh's contemporaries in the Architectural Association, the younger members of the profession, who responded most enthusiastically. They saw in its pages 'the germ of all noble buildings in the future and we earnestly hope that the appearance of this book is itself a sign of the ripeness of the times and that it comes to an expectant world able and willing to make use of the ideas it contains.'[6] Lethaby's introduction, as David Walker outlines, provided the central passages of Mackintosh's 1893 paper on Architecture. In Lethaby's text Mackintosh found radical definitions of architecture and craftsmanship and their interrelationship, in some instances resolving ideas outlined in his own earlier writings. Lethaby provided confirmation of Mackintosh's distinction between building and architecture. Building was 'but the vehicle of architecture, which is the thought behind form'.[7] Architecture was the 'commune of the crafts', a concept anticipated in Mackintosh's praise of Scottish Baronial in which 'many examples still remaining show how all the arts were united in one building' [A 11]: this view was reinforced for Mackintosh by his Italian trip and is implicit in his study of Elizabethan interior design.

Mackintosh's reading was not wholly uncritical. He made a telling adjustment to Lethaby's statement 'If we trace the artistic forms of things, made by man, to their origin, we find a direct imitation of nature.'[8] Mackintosh's text reads: 'If we trace the artistic form of things made by man to their origin, we find a direct inspiration from if not a direct imitation of nature.' [F 12]. Through the second half of the nineteenth century, a new school of thought, founded on the influential writings of Pugin and followed by those of Henry Cole, Owen Jones, Richard Redgrave, Christopher Dresser and others, had contributed to an important shift of emphasis, in the training of designers, away from the study of the human figure to the study of nature. Opinion varied however as to whether nature was to be imitated or creatively interpreted. Mackintosh was dismissive of the former approach, condemning the 'many indiscriminating admirers of nature, who unable to deduct a principal, would attempt a childish mimicry' [E 19]. Later in the 1893 paper he is more outspoken: 'the servile imitation of nature is the work of small minded men' [F 27]. His own work shows how in practice he interpreted the potential of conventionalised plant forms for ornament and absorbed the abstract principles of their structure in his designs.

The definition of architecture as a commune of the crafts, with its implicit integrity of concept and execution, was a cornerstone of Mackintosh's theory and practice. It was a point of view vigorously argued by the influential writer and architect John Dando Sedding, of whom Muthesius wrote that

6. John Dando Sedding (1838-91), photographed *c.* 1887
7. C. R. Mackintosh: 'There is hope in honest error . . .' (1901)

he formed 'the first bridge between the architects' camp and that of handi-
craft proper'.[9] Overlooked today, Sedding was unquestionably a significant
figure for Mackintosh.[10] He is cited in Mackintosh's short list of important
contemporary architects alongside Shaw, Bentley, Belcher, Bodley and
Stokes. His aphorism 'There is hope in honest error, none in the icy perfection of the mere stylist' became a personal motto for Mackintosh. The common ground between the two is apparent from Lethaby's obituary after
Sedding's premature death in 1891, in which he concludes that Sedding's
work was characterised by 'A critical distinction between what is native and
what is exotic: Separation between the living and the dead: Saturation with
the spirit of nature, the source of all art, and the canvas, as it were, on which
architecture must be painted, so that in time it becomes almost a part of
nature.' That Mackintosh studied this obituary carefully is apparent from
his subsequent borrowing of two passages contained within it.[11]

In the 1880s and 1890s, many of the Arts and Crafts architects, including Sedding and Lethaby, reread the works of Ruskin, finding new relevance
in their texts. Indeed Ruskin had encouraged Sedding, writing to him: 'If
you would be a real architect you must always have either pencil or chisel in
your hand.'[12] Mackintosh also turned to Ruskin, though in common with
many from the architectural profession, he was by no means an uncritical
reader. Among his papers is a laboriously transcribed copy of H. H.
Statham's scathing review of the 1888 edition of *The Stones of Venice*[13] – a
rogue survival from an undoubtedly large reference library assembled by

Mackintosh – from which Mackintosh subsequently quoted in his first paper on 'Architecture' [E 7]. There were many areas of fundamental disagreement between Mackintosh and Ruskin: Ruskin's dislike for English Perpendicular, Elizabethan architecture and post fifteenth century Italian architecture particularly the work of Palladio; Ruskin's naturalistic ornament; his championing of painting and sculpture over architecture; his belief that decoration should be constructed, not construction decorated. There was however much common ground: shared reservations over new technology and materials; delight in the surface ornamentation, polychromy, light and atmosphere of Italian architecture; emphasis on the close observation of nature; the importance of craftsmanship; the importance of truth and honesty. The concept of 'truth' was a recurrent theme for Mackintosh, applied, on a practical level, to the specifics of function and material, and, on a philosophical level, to his personal belief in the primacy of truth to one's ideals. One central aspect of Ruskin's later writings however drew no response from Mackintosh – his moral concern over the social consequences of industrialisation. Such anxieties appear not to have impinged on Mackintosh, despite the fact that he lived in one of Britain's most heavily industrialised cities, and had worked in 1890-1 on housing for the City of Glasgow Improvement Trust.

8. John Ruskin (1819-1900), at Brantwood, Coniston in 1894

Mackintosh's other principal source was James Fergusson. Now largely dismissed, Fergusson was a major and prolific historian and theorist of the period. His works were prescribed reading for the R.I.B.A. standard examination introduced in 1889. Mackintosh draws on Fergusson's historical surveys, abstracting in particular his analysis of Transitional or Elizabethan architecture, as James Macaulay illustrates. Mackintosh is less respectful of Fergusson's theoretical writings, dismissing specifically one of his more far-fetched categorisations, 'Phonetic' architecture [E 37].

Another significant but less easily documented influence must have been Mackintosh's friend and mentor Francis Newbery, Director of the Glasgow School of Art.[14] According to Jessie Newbery it was Mackintosh's Italian sketches which first drew Newbery's attention to his gifted student.[15] From

9. Francis H. Newbery (1853-1946), *c.* 1898
10. Edward William Godwin (1833-1886), *c.* 1880

his arrival in Glasgow in 1885, Newbery actively promoted the decorative arts. He brought leading figures of the Arts and Crafts Movement to the school to lecture and examine, transferred the second Arts and Crafts Society exhibition to Glasgow in 1890, and in 1892 opened a series of decorative art studios at the School. A prolific lecturer, he addressed what were key issues for Mackintosh. His titles included 'The Training of Architectural Students' (1887), 'The Place of Art Schools in the Economy of Applied Art' (1889), 'Impressionism in Architecture' (1890) and 'The Artist in the Architect' (1891). In the first, published by the Philosophical Society of Glasgow in 1889, Newbery quoted Ruskin's aphorism from the opening lines of *The Seven Lamps*: 'Architecture is the art which so disposes and adorns the edifices raised by man, for whatsoever uses, that the sight of them contributes to his mental health, power and pleasure.'[16] This passage was to be the central theme of Mackintosh's first lecture on 'Architecture'. In the same paper, Newbery expresses admiration for Palladio, 'whose efforts and learned treatises have made classic architecture our most precious heirloom'[17] – a point of view which may help to explain Mackintosh's otherwise unexpected enthusiasm in Italy for Palladio's classicism. Indeed in 1893 Mackintosh quotes from a Newbery lecture on the education of artists [F 23].

Mackintosh's passionate appeal for artistic independence from fashion and style closely echoes the radical pleas of one of the most innovative architects of the previous generation, E. W. Godwin. *The British Architect* of 1878 summarised a lecture in which Godwin reviewed his own work. The published account discloses a significant shift from Godwin's stance earlier in his career as a committed and highly successful Gothicist: 'Be archaeologists that was to say, to know all about the past; study Greek, Gothic, Renaissance, the Roman and later developments, study it in all its different phases and countries, but don't take up any one and say, "This is my line of departure; I will work on this line," because, after they had worked for a time the fashion would change . . . . He [Godwin] asked his audience to be independent of fashions by simply being architects and artists, taking up work and doing it as their own. Study all; take what good they could from every country and every age; but work in no particular style. If asked what style their work was, to say – "It is my own".'[18] Mackintosh breathed the same passion into his last lecture, 'Seemliness': 'you must be independant – Independant independant, dont talk so much – but do more – go your own way and let your neighbour go his. Don't meddle with other peoples ideas when you have all your work cut out of you in trying to express your own — Shake off all the props – the props tradition and authority offer you – and go alone crawl – stumble – stagger – but go alone' [G 9-10]. As Godwin's revolutionary late studio designs and Mackintosh's mature work demonstrate, both found solutions in the abstract principles of architecture. For Godwin 'Much good architecture or building depends almost wholly on its masses and disposition of light and shade: its details – mouldings, carvings and so on – give it a texture as it were and a special interest to near views of bits or pieces of the work; but the foremost beauty and charm of building as building are always to be found in the measure, the balance, the allotment of its lights and shades.'[19] Some ten years later Mackintosh concurred: 'the building in grouping may be artistic and truly architectural and yet not have a single cornice or moulding, politeness in building that is Archi may be obtained without unnecessary feature but not without unnecessary design' [E 7a]. Though championing creative individuality, Mackintosh expressed a profound respect for his architectural heritage: 'We mean to stand to architecture in its widest sense – we plant our feet in traditional tracts, we will not relinquish one item of the time honoured programme of our art as practiced in days of old.' [F 30].

As Robert Macleod argues, Mackintosh's position in 'Seemliness', his 'urge towards expressive individuality', contained the seeds of his ultimate failure. No further papers by Mackintosh exist to document subsequent developments in his thinking, but the facts of his later career suggest that, unlike his long-standing friend and supporter Hermann Muthesius with the German Werkbund, or Lethaby and Mackintosh's last patron Bassett-Lowke with the Design and Industry Association, or his great contemporary Frank Lloyd Wright, Mackintosh failed to embrace the collectivism of indus- trialised labour and the potential of the new technology. With his un- equivocal acceptance of utility and function, of the need to respond to 'the new forms and conditions that modern developements of life — social – commercial and religious insist upon' [G 8], of the need for independence from historicism, Mackintosh's intellectual standpoint looks forward to the Modern Movement. But his respect for tradition, for craftsmanship, for nature, ally him with the Arts and Crafts movement and its mediaeval antecedents. Mackintosh's architectural writings, like his buildings, present two configurations – one rooted in the past, the other heralding the future. The manuscripts are founded on his passionate commitment to his art. Though in large part derivative, their intention is neither to flaunt know- ledge acquired at second-hand nor to present superficially extracted received opinion. Rather, rough and unpolished, compiled around the demands of a busy architectural practice, the papers constitute Mackintosh's honest and consistent and often idealistic attempt to crystallise a philosophical basis for his work.

NOTES

1. Letter from Mackintosh to Hermann Muthesius, 27 March 1903 (Private Coll.).
2. Mackintosh's idiosyncratic spelling and punctuation are discussed in the 'Note on the Mackintosh Texts' below.
3. 'Wareham and its Churches', *British Architect* 44 (1895) pp. 326-7.
4. 'David McGibbon [*sic*] read a paper on "The Characteristics of Scottish National Architecture." He said the most prominent and important characteristics of the Scottish national style of architecture were – (1) that there was a Scottish style; (2) that from the point of view of economy or convenience it accomplished its purpose; and (3) that it was effective and picturesque.' *British Architect* 32 (1889) p. 337.
5. *The Times*, 31 Dec. 1891, p. 4, quoted in Godfrey Rubens' introduction to W. R. Lethaby, *Architecture, Mysticism and Myth* (repr., London 1974) p. xi.
6. See Rubens (n. 5) p. xiii.
7. W. R. Lethaby, *Architecture, Mysticism and Myth* (London 1891) p. 1: quoted by Mackintosh [F 3].
8. Lethaby (n. 7) p. 4.
9. Hermann Muthesius, *The English House* (Eng. edn, London 1979) p. 37.

10. Sedding merits re-examination. The only current account is in Alastair Service, *Edwardian Architecture and its Origins* (London 1975) pp. 259 79, with a reprint of an 1897 review of Sedding's work.

11. W. R. Lethaby, 'J. D. Sedding', *Builder* 61 (1891) pp. 270-1. Mackintosh's quotations are at F 20 and 21.

12. Michael Brooks, *John Ruskin and Victorian Architecture* (New Brunswick & London 1987) p. 264.

13. Coll. H.A.G.

14. Newbery also merits examination. For a useful outline see Isobel Spencer, 'Francis Newbery and the Glasgow Style', *Apollo* 98 (1973) pp. 286-93.

15. Jessie Newbery, *Mackintosh Memorial Exhibition* (Glasgow 1933) catalogue foreword, p. 1.

16. Francis H. Newbery, 'On the training of architectural students', *Proceedings of the Philosophical Society of Glasgow* 19 (1889) p. 177.

17. Newbery (n. 16) p. 183.

18. E. W. Godwin, 'On some buildings I have designed', *British Architect* 10 (1878) p. 211.

19. E. W. Godwin, 'To our student readers', *British Architect* 14 (1880) p. 95.

# Note on the Mackintosh Texts

Mackintosh's manuscripts were never intended for publication, and it might seem an obstacle to easy comprehension as well as a disservice to his reputation to present them here as faithful transcriptions. His unorthodox spelling, erratic punctuation and clumsy syntax are immediately obvious, and recur throughout the texts. However it was judged essential for this first publication of Mackintosh's writings in their entirety to present them intact. To have brought his written English into line with conventional usage would have required substantial editorial interference, diminishing the authenticity of the texts, and indeed depriving the reader of a rare sense of Mackintosh's personality.

Mackintosh's idiosyncratic errors are unexpected given the traditionally effective Scottish education he had received. However Professor T. A. Miles of the Dyslexia Unit, Bangor University has suggested that 'It is possible that Mackintosh suffered from what is now called "specific developmental dyslexia". This is an anomaly of development, almost certainly of physical origin, which affects reading, writing and other language skills. It is sometimes accompanied by high intelligence and creative power. Mackintosh's strange spelling errors suggest this, and it is perhaps relevant that he rarely committed himself to paper.'

The lectures were written to be heard, not read, and nuances of delivery and the ease of the spoken word, which would undoubtedly have transformed the material, are inevitably lost on the page. The fulsome preambles, characteristic of the period, an occasionally self-deprecating manner and recurring humour, reveal an assured platform manner which developed with experience. While the lecture scripts record what Mackintosh intended to say, there is of course no certainty that this is exactly what was delivered.

The papers are presented in chronological order, lettered A to G. Mackintosh's page-numbering often became confused and has been replaced with a sequential pagination, with insertions indicated as 26a, 26b, etc. In some places Mackintosh used broad dashes and wide spaces in a pronounced way as a form of punctuation, but no serious attempt has been made to indicate these in the transcription. Where sentence breaks are not punctuated extra space has been introduced to ease comprehension of the text.

# CHARLES RENNIE MACKINTOSH
# THE ARCHITECTURAL PAPERS

House at Corner of McLeod Street.
CRM May 1889

11. C. R. Mackintosh: Provand's Lordship, Glasgow (May 1889)
This drawing of the late seventeenth century rear wings of Provand's Lordship,
'the oldest house in Glasgow' dating from *c*. 1471, demonstrates Mackintosh's
early interest in the Scottish vernacular tradition.

FRANK ARNEIL WALKER

# Scottish Baronial Architecture

Anyone desirous of studying Scottish historical architecture must begin with MacGibbon and Ross. (Cruden)[1]

Nothing can be more dangerous than looking at prints of buildings, and trying to imitate bits of them. These architectural books are as bad as the scriptures in the hands of the Protestants. (Pugin)[2]

On the evening of Tuesday 10 February 1891, Charles Rennie Mackintosh presented a paper to the Glasgow Architectural Association which was, almost certainly, his first public contribution to architectural debate. He was twenty-two years old. His subject was 'Scotch Baronial Architecture',[3] a topic which he owned so 'dear to my heart and entwined among my inmost thoughts and affections' [A 1] as to make it difficult to disentangle sentiment and reason, yet one which, it was to emerge, he felt must command a measure of ideological commitment as well as archaeological interest. Whether he had been able to choose his title is not clear, though his evident enthusiasm would suggest that he had. It was, however, an opportunity not just to focus his thoughts onto a developmental understanding of indigenous architectural history but to construct, from this contextual basis, some kind of precocious polemic, even credo.

'Challenge' might be a better word than 'opportunity', for he had as yet built next to nothing.[4] As he leant over his drawing board at home or in the office, wondering how he might say what he wanted to say, presumption must have perched on his shoulder like some presbyterian demon. Yet it is, as Ruskin wrote, 'a marvellous thing – the Protestant mind'[5] and, if he could not be justified by works, then perhaps faith in the idea of a national architecture – a 'Scotch' architecture – could exorcise self-doubt. Perhaps ... but when the evening finally came and he rose to speak, even though his opening admission of 'feelings somewhat bordering on trepidation' [A 1] sounded like conventional modesty, he was probably still genuinely nervous.

He had, however, come prepared. In front of him lay an essay of thirty-six handwritten pages, together with a series of illustrations – pencil drawings, watercolour studies and photographs, several of which were 'the work of his own hands'.[6] While the manuscript enables us to read what Mackintosh wrote, it cannot tell us exactly what he said. Nor can we gain added insights from the illustrations since, with the exceptions of Rothesay and Bothwell Castles, we do not know which buildings mentioned in the text were highlighted by drawn or photographed exemplification. The survival of pre-1891 sketches made by Mackintosh at Glasgow, Elgin, Spynie and Rowallan[7] substantiates the likelihood that he illustrated the lecture with his drawings but, since his earliest sketchbooks are lost,[8] it is impossible to determine, first, whether he did or did not draw this or that building referred to in the lecture; secondly, whether he chose to illustrate this or that particular building on the occasion of his talk; and, thirdly, if he *did*, whether he used his own or someone else's drawing or watercolour or, indeed, photograph. Finally, and perhaps most regrettably, the issues raised in the discussion which took place immediately after the lecture must remain unrevealed.[9]

All this said by way of cautionary preamble, the text remains a valuable document. It tells us the direction in which the young architect's mind was turning. Of course, the integrity of his commitment to this line might be doubted and the text viewed either as immature or even opportunistically assumed to meet the obligations of the lecture's title were it not that Mackintosh's subsequent work is an entirely convincing homologation of these youthful ideas. Nonetheless it does not take the scholiast to detect that much of the content of these pages is not the original work of a twenty-two year old designer.

It was Robert Macleod who, in his 1968 study *Charles Rennie Mackintosh: Architect and Artist*, first recorded Mackintosh's tendency to plunder the literary work of others. Macleod's investigation of the 1893 lecture on 'Architecture' [F], revealed a 'rather too free use of Lethaby's phraseology'[10] drawn from his recently published *Architecture, Mysticism and Myth*.[11] He did not, however, advert to any similar dependence in the first of Mackintosh's literary efforts, and it was not until 1977 that Stewart Cruden drew attention to another substantial piece of plagiarising. Cruden does not go into detail but his assessment is damning: 'it is straight and unadulterated MacGibbon and Ross'.[12] Expressing the matter with something more akin to Macleod's generosity, it turns out that approximately two-thirds of Mackintosh's text is ... rather too derivative!

No publication has more comprehensively described, illustrated and classified *The Castellated and Domestic Architecture of Scotland*[13] than the monumental five-volume work by MacGibbon and Ross. It was and is the definitive source book on the subject. From the appearance of the first volume in 1887 it took five years for the entire work to be published; by the time of Mackintosh's talk in 1891 three volumes were available, more than enough to exemplify the structure and details of the four-period classification system which the authors had adopted in their sweeping review of Scottish architecture between the twelfth century and the eighteenth. Mackintosh was evidently familiar not just with the broad outlines of this work but with the intimate descriptions of the text. A close reading of his essay proves he had read volumes one and two (both published in 1887) with the most careful attention, since his text from pages 13 to 35 is no more than a re-presentation of MacGibbon and Ross's analysis, not as some reformulated and properly acknowledged précis but as a scissors-and-paste assemblage of textual theft.

Every hero has his Achilles heel. But while an antipathy towards quotation marks and, still more reprehensible, a failure to mention the names of
MacGibbon and Ross at any point in his written text reflect badly on the
young Mackintosh, it must be admitted that his familiarity with these
sources shows him remarkably *au fait* with the latest research. It may sully
the image to discover Mackintosh cribbing but, as Cruden pointed out, 'how
much greater would have been the disappointment had he youthfully dis-
dained MacGibbon and Ross?'[14] Moreover, such close knowledge of the most
recent publications prompts the inference that Mackintosh was also aware
of earlier commentators on the Baronial style and tradition, such as Stevenson, Kerr and, of course, Billings,[15] and would have drawn their work into
the matrix of his developing design intentions, as indeed his thinking was
already assimilating the wider philosophical views of Ruskin, Morris and
Lethaby. What matters, then, is not so much the critical academic gloss that
can be brought to bear on the form of Mackintosh's text as that more
permissive appraisal directed towards the significance of its content. Mackintosh is prepared to talk about 'Scotch Baronial Architecture'; the tenor of
his speech is enthusiastic; his later built work engrosses the same indigenous tradition: the pattern of commitment is consistent.[16] It is, therefore,
quite proper that he should prepare the background canvas for this pattern,
flying the shuttle of historical analysis across the centuries. There has to be
context for content.

How could it be expected that a twenty-two year old architect should
have acquired an exhaustive knowledge of the history of Scottish architecture, let alone been able to propose a reliable categorisation of its development? Sensibly enough, if a little ungraciously and dishonestly, Mackintosh
knew where to find all this and how to exploit it, so that when he began to
acquaint his audience with the evolutionary phases of what he referred to as
the 'national style' [A 4] he simply borrowed the systematic approach which
MacGibbon and Ross had proposed. Encyclopaedic as their review had been,
however, the ordering principle through which they attempted to bring
some clarity to the multiplicity of buildings studied was no more sophisti-
cated than simple chronology. For each of the four phases designated – First
Period, 1200-1300; Second Period, 1300-1400; Third Period, 1400-1542;
Fourth Period, 1542-1700 – morphological features were, of course,
identified. Indeed, it was doubtless these formal qualities which attracted
Mackintosh the designer more than archaeological niceties of dating or
attribution and which he referred to as 'the more prominent characteristics
of the style' [A 12].

These characteristics were readily enumerated. Plans developed first from
generally quadrilateral or sometimes circular enclosures reinforced by
square or round towers, regressed to a simpler tower-house model during
the war-torn fourteenth century, developed next an L-plan variant of the
latter, its staircase tower tucked in the angle, or alternatively restored the
courtyard plan of the former with its buildings set around the edge of the

barmkin, until in the final Fourth Period phase these two streams were augmented by more complex and more decorative Z-plan tower castles on the one hand, or more symetrically disposed open or courtyard ranges on the other. Parallel to this process, the formal elements and decorative aspects of the tradition evolved gradually from the plain parapetted walls of the earliest stone fortresses to the complexities of the Castles of Mar. Mackintosh's words describing this ebullient climactic architecture are, as in so many instances, exactly those of MacGibbon and Ross.

The walls are generally very plain, and the ornamentation is confined to the parapet and upper portions, where it often bursts out with extraordinary profusion and richness, as for instance Castle Fraser and Craigievar.

The roofs are high pitched broken up and adorned with numerous dormers and have picturesque chimneys and crow stepped gables. Corbelling, both plain and ornamental is one of the chief characteristics of the style. It is used on every possible occasion. The turrets, staircases, parapets etc. are all supported on corbels, and the towers are often changed from a circular base to a square upper part by means of large and elaborate corbels. [A 28 = M. & R. ii p. 3]

Nowhere, perhaps, is the evidence of this mature, distinctly Scottish architecture more compelling than in the early seventeenth century castles of Aberdeenshire, and in none is it more wonderfully realised than at Fyvie where 'we have all the distinguishing features of the style' [A 31].

Throughout his text Mackintosh employs this quintessentially Victorian word 'style'. At the outset he declares his objective is 'to give a general sketch of this *style* of Architec.' which had given Scotland its unique historical legacy of 'noble and artistic' building [A 4], while in his final sentence he speaks of contemporary evidence 'that this *style* is coming to life again' [A 36] (my italics). It is clear that he uses the word to entail both academic analysis and pragmatic programme; that is, he saw style as a living language of form with its own vocabulary, its syntax and semantic content, a language capable of sustaining the lithic poetics of Scottish culture from the past into the future. It was the passionate *parti pris* of a young designer knowledgeably and optimistically nationalistic.

Mackintosh's position is, then, fiercely committed. It is doubtful of course whether even respectable historical scholarship could so detach itself from predilection as to be wholly disinterested or catholic in its investigations and conclusions. Still less were practitioners objectively orientated. Many were, it is true, far from being single-mindedly committed, jumping from style to style with a sometimes fickle but frequently skilled facility. John Honeyman, Mackintosh's senior partner, was living proof that Victorian style was unquestionably, and in his case brilliantly, pluralist.[17] Nineteenth century architects were not, however, simply engaged in a crude 'battle of the styles', clashing violently under classical or mediaeval banners or skirmishing over some more exotic peripheral allegiances. Many were drawn into a deeper *Dilemma of Style*[18] which threatened a more critical inner conflict

12. Castle Fraser, Aberdeenshire – north elevation, drawn by R. W. Billings
'The walls are generally very plain, and the ornamentation is confined to the
parapet and upper portions, where it often bursts out with extraordinary
profusion and richness ...' MacGibbon and Ross, and Mackintosh [A 28].

between what Colin Rowe has called architectural *composition* and architectural *character*.[19]

For Rowe, a significant building is 'pre-eminently a structure organised
according to ... principles of architectural composition and infused with
symbolic content which is usually described as character'.[20] The principles
of composition are, in effect, the rules for combining the parts into a whole,
rules which, for most of the nineteenth century, were derived directly from
the styles of the past. Composition is thus the way of fitting bits together: it

13. Fyvie Castle, Aberdeenshire
Here 'in the south front we have all the distinguishing features of the style ...'
[A 31] which, despite its affinities with French work, was recognised by
MacGibbon and Ross, and thus Mackintosh, as 'most decidedly Scottish'.

THE GLASGOW SCHOOL OF ART.

SOUTH ELEVATION

14. C. R. Mackintosh: Glasgow School of Art – south elevation (1910)
Mackintosh's drawing shows a similar solid : void relationship and aggregation
of symmetries to those evident at Fyvie.

may be dependent upon physical structure, as is the case in Romanesque or High Gothic work, or upon putative structure, as in the Renaissance-Baroque system, but, above all, it affords a relational structure, a syntax of form. Character, on the other hand, describes the building's specific qualities of expression which may be 'either symbolic or functional'[21] or possibly, as Pugin would certainly have argued, both. Character proclaims association and meaning, purpose and value: it mediates semantic intent.

The dilemma for Victorian architects was to resolve this dialectic of composition and character in a stylistic synthesis responsive to the manifold technical, territorial and cultural transformations[22] of the times. Composition had to come to terms with the plans and sections needed by building types wholly without historical precedent – railway stations, factories, hotels, urban housing, etc. – and with new materials and methods whose structural and spatial potential greatly extended the compression-based limitations set by previous means. Character, however, had somehow to express the aspirational and functional qualities of nineteenth century society – easy enough perhaps when the task in hand was a church (though even here the spectrum stretched from stone-cut Puginian Gothic to the 'streaky bacon'[23] mediaevalist punk of Butterfield), but less immediately resolvable in the case of government ministries, town halls, warehouses, hospitals, department stores, etc. Eclectic reaction ran rife as history and geography were raped in an often perverted search for allusion and meaning.

For Mackintosh it was principally through character that the answer to the dilemma was to be approached. He was certainly not dismissive of practical planning requirements; we know from his later work just how creatively responsive he could be. Nor was he disdainful of new ways and means, for although he did later express the strongest misgivings over the 'rosetinted hallucinations' of some proponents of Crystal Palace architecture and rejected their technologically-grounded 'belief in the invention of a new style' [E 16], his Concert Hall design for the Glasgow International Exhibition of 1901, had it been built, would unquestionably have been an amazing structure for its day. But all this was a long way off. Now, at the beginning of his career, naive perhaps and certainly romantic, inasmuch as he would have shared Ruskin's careful use of that sacred word to '*characterize* an improbable or unaccustomed degree of beauty, sublimity or virtue' (my italics),[24] it was towards the claims of character rather than composition that his temperament inclined: 'The character of a style of art does not depend upon the mere material from which it has been fabricated, but upon the sentiments and conditions under which it has been developed.' [A 5]

It is in the presentation of this contextual thesis – which accounts for that unplagiarised part of the essay not taken up with the straightforwardly historical, in effect the first dozen or so pages and the last few sentences – that Mackintosh exposes his *own* philosophy. In an introductory passage of rather over-ripe prose, he starts by invoking the conviction of love over reason: the ties that bind us in filial affection exert their parallel pull on our cultural kinship, drawing us close to the ancient buildings of our own land – a mystery finally personified in the romantic image of the lonely architect compelled to wander the countryside 'not only under the balmy influences of summer, but along muddy roads and snowy path, and with glowing heart but shivering hand to sketch the humble cottage the more pretentious mantion or the mutilated though venerable castle with feelings of the most indescribable delight' [A 3]. The emotion is genuine enough but its expression, untempered by measured restraint and the 'instinctive affection' Mackintosh feels for the architecture of his native land, is allowed to curdle the literary flow. Phrases polished with an effusive sincerity bordering on the unctuous leave a cloying sheen of sentimentality on these early paragraphs, but by the turn of his third page Mackintosh is at least trying to muster more rational reasons why the style he admires so much merits study and appreciation.

For the moment, however, these reasons remain elusive. Having been told that Scottish architecture 'is marked out from that [of] other countries in the most signal and remarkable manner' [A 4], the architects of the Glasgow Architectural Association might have expected some substantiation of this assertion. Yet Mackintosh attempts no comparative formal analysis and, despite his quasi-functionalist evaluation of Scottish architecture's ability to combine the useful with the beautiful, he seems bent on building his case on the simple affirmation that Scottish architecture 'is the native architecture of our own country and that of our forefathers' [A 5], and that this, even allowing for an acknowledged affinity with the architecture of France, should be compelling enough to establish its special character. What makes Scottish architecture significant for Scottish architects is that it is the architecture of Scottish architects.

The argument is, of course, tautological. But then so too is the doctrine which sustains the nation's theological orientation, reformed religion's faith in justification by faith. Perhaps, in fact, there is something peculiarly Scottish in this philosophical preference for the transcendental over the empirical. If so, it has its dangers: cultural identity can, for example, be all too aggressively asserted in the arrogance of *Blut und Erkenntnis*, while there is nothing more notoriously susceptible to unloving intolerance than the self-righteous assurance of the elect. In neither case, however, have the risks eliminated the conviction. It is as if in each a necessary paradox lies at the heart of the matter, a paradox which in personal Christian terms expresses itself in the credo that we can only be loving because we are already loved, and which in the broader context of human affairs resides in an equivalent persuasion that if we are to play our part in the international arena of politics and the arts we must first acknowledge and espouse our own national culture.

It is to this positive tradition of romantic nationalism that Mackintosh subscribes, not to some xenophobic parochialism. It is true that his words might at times seem to propose an introspective narrowing of the perspective: 'If we investigate the architecture of Egypt or Assyria or of Persia, we find that it tells of races with whom we have no national or personal sympathy. If we go to the classic shores of Greece, though there we should be viewing the work of a race whose art and literature are, more than those of any other people, the property of the world, we never the less fail to find anything to connect them in any special sence with ourselves.' [A 7] But the intention here is not to denigrate but rather to draw architectural attention away from a protracted indiscriminate eclecticism and back to a creative engagement with native culture. As a strategy it was far from new. Well over a century had passed since Winckelmann first burst through the dam of classicism with his observation that 'as the circumstances of one people are not applicable to another, concepts of one culture are not valid for another'.[25] It was almost as long since Robert Adam, in his unprecedented but still classical castellar style, had begun to re-orientate architecture to the specific circumstances of the rugged Scots landscape.

It is this liberating legacy of romantic thought, freeing both individual and nation, which Mackintosh inherits. No surprise then that, just as his image of the lone sketcher wandering in all weathers from cottage to castle seems to conjure up a misty memory of those sublimely-dwarfed denizens of Caspar David Friedrich's melancholy landscapes, or his purpler prose to echo Wackenroder's more nationalistic *Effusions from the Heart of an Art-Loving Monk*,[26] so his ardent advocacy of Scottish architecture recalls Pugin's injunction that 'There is no need of visiting the distant shores of Greece and Egypt to make discoveries in art. England alone abounds in hidden and unknown antiquities of surpassing interest.'[27]

Well, not England alone, of course. Scots – like the English, Germans or French of Pugin's day or the Poles, Finns, Czechs, Hungarians, and others of Mackintosh's – could discover their own antiquities. Castles, mansions, or 'the very houses perhaps in which some of us live: the monuments of our own forefathers the works of men bearing our own name, whose armoral badges we are still proud to use: who spoke in its pristine form our own language; who sat in our own parliament were lords of still existing manors, founders of still surviving charities, men who fought the battles of which we are still proud, and laid the foundations of our liberties and of all those institutions which render the name of Scotland illustrious among the nations of the world. Surely the architecture which grew up among men so nearly allied to us has a preeminent claim upon our attention' [A 8].

As if to compensate for this further outburst of national fervour, Mackintosh suddenly lowers the temperature by recapitulating the reasons why this Scotch Baronial Architecture should command allegiance. But, just as before, these itemised claims prove no more than ill-defined variations on the theme of Scottishness and little is adduced to the argument beyond the familiar associations of national character implied in geographical, historical, geological, even biological affinities.

Finally, Mackintosh turns to 'intrinsic claims' [A 9]. The argument, if it can be called such, is at first no more convincing. Proposing that the national style possesses an inherent quality of abstract beauty, he defends the contention simply by assertion – even 'the most devout follower of classic or gothic antiquity could scarcely question the absolute beauty of many of our Castles' [A 9-10]. In the next paragraph, however, we learn that this beauty is not quite so inexplicably absolute as it had seemed. What distinguishes the Scottish idiom is its facility in 'decorating constructing, and in converting structural and useful features into elements of beauty'. All this is sound Puginian reasoning and a point of view which clearly adds the expression of function into the symbolic infusion of architectural character. In other words, beauty is to be determined not only as a matter of formal delight in which a 'purposiveness according to form'[28] is evaluated for its uniquely Scottish zest, but is also to be relatively measured by its degree of truth or purposive intention.

This done, the whole dilemma of style begins to find its resolution, for if it was the direct functional expression of architectural elements – gaunt cliffs of protective walling, windows, gables, chimneys, bartizans, parapet walks, etc. – which had produced the symbolically evocative character of Scottish architecture, so a similar expression 'meeting the conditions of purpose' [A 11], in whatever building type – cottage, mansion or castle – must have had corresponding compositional consquences. Now, for the first time, the syntax of Scotch Baronial Architecture begins to emerge. Mackintosh speaks of a versatile 'grouping of parts' and a readily varied 'external outline', both qualities resulting from an ability to respond to the contingent 'in which our style shapes itself to every accidental requirement', rather than conforming to the exclusive exigencies of formal rules [A 11-12]. He highlights the acceptance of symmetry where 'the conditions of the case' demand it but commends its frank rejection where there is no inner justification [A 12]. The character and composition of Scotch Baronial Architecture thus seem to induce a paradigm through which, paradoxically, the past can be escaped. Instead of a victory for revivalism or eclecticism in the battle of the styles, what Mackintosh is attempting to evolve is an almost ahistorical symbolism, grounded in functional inflection and, at the same time, capable of sustaining cultural meaning. He is, as it were, on the verge of solving the Victorian dilemma.

He did not stand alone on this threshold. Throughout *fin de siècle* Europe there were many designers – Wagner, Gaudí, Lechner, Jurkovič, Witkiewicz and Saarinen among them – ready to step forward into new territory. *Pour mieux sauter*, each cast a long lingering look back at the forms of his native landscape and, by way of contextual analogy, shot a sideways glance at what was happening in nineteenth century Britain. They saw an architecture both functional and symbolic: in one view they recognised their own indigenous vernacular, distant but distinct, and in the other, not always fully in focus, an English revivalism, Gothic, perhaps, but a Gothic increas-

15. Allardyce Castle, Forfarshire
An illustration from MacGibbon and Ross which both displays the architectural
elements of the Scottish tradition, and demonstrates the versatile manner 'in
which our style shapes itself to every accidental requirement' [A 12].

16. C. R. Mackintosh: The Hill House, Helensburgh (1902)
This view from the south-east illustrates Mackintosh's creative deployment of
the 'national style'.

ingly secularised and increasingly accommodated to 'modern conditions –
improved methods of lighting and ventilating, sanitary considerations, the
use of new materials',[29] new structural possibilities and new planning requirements. In England, these issues of function had become particularly
explicit. Since Pugin's early intuition of the functional in the liturgical, the
gospel of work had been more and more loudly proclaimed. Ruskin, Morris
and, later, Lethaby, all missionaries intent on the salvation of an errant
architecture, preached passionately about the redemptive significance of the
'well doing of what needs doing'.[30] Nowhere were the benefits of this com-
monsense philosophy plainer than in the characteristically unpretentious
English images of the mountaineer's cell in Cumbria, praised by both Wordsworth[31] and Ruskin,[32] and the Cotswold yeoman's cottage 'discovered' by
Morris and Webb. These humbler precedents, the legacy of survival rather
than revival, found new life in the work of Street, Gimson, Voysey and other
designers of the Arts and Crafts movement; Mackintosh was certainly not
unaffected.

In every culture such simple buildings were not without their symbolic
declaration of national identity. But bolder signs were needed. In England
the Gothic Revival had assumed a nationalist justification – as it did in
Germany and France – but it was Elizabethan architecture, suitably transitional in its formal organisation and unique in provenance, which best
caught the spirit of romantic nationalism. From the *cottages ornés* of Nash to
the vast rambling piles of Norman Shaw, its forms progressively enchanted
English designers, providing a better articulated language with which to
respond not only to the needs of Victorian residential living but to those
unprecedented demands set by a whole range of new building types. And
yet, however practical and functional, however much its 'picturesque
planning had suggested planning for comfort',[33] this Englishness remained
visually innocuous, no more than nostalgia. Victorian England required a
still more assertive formal language with which to flatter its imperial grandeur and commercial success. Perhaps in a confident and dominant society
the spirit of nationalism was in any case incapable of being the subversive
cultural force it threatened to be north of the border. Perhaps Elizabethan
architecture, for all its transitional and national qualities, still presented a
more decorative, more self-consciously arranged and thus less functionally
reactive composition than the cruder austerities of Scotland permitted. Perhaps even materials played their part: Tudor half-timbering, so evidently
mediaevalist, could scarcely be translated into modern structure whereas, as
James Salmon would point out,[34] the planar mass and corbelled shapes
of Scotch Baronial Architecture might readily lend themselves to fluid
realisation in reinforced concrete construction. At any rate, except in the
abstemious white-walled domestic vernacular of Voysey, to which both
Mackintosh and Salmon were sympathetic and susceptible, English architecture proferred no puritanical formal revelations.

17. Robert and James Adam: Cluny Castle, Aberdeenshire (c. 1793)
In this unexecuted design, as James Macaulay noted in *The Gothic Revival 1745-1845*, 'not only were all the traditional Scottish lineaments to be reproduced in the external architecture' but, later, 'even the characteristically Scottish Z-plan was to be duplicated'.

In Scotland the anglicisation of domestic architecture also occurred. From late Victorian times 'wretched Tudor'[35] entrenched itself in the suburbs to such an extent that its invidious dissemination can still be felt in the red-tiled pyramids of inter-war bungalurbia – a measure, perhaps, of the dependent unionism of the *nouveaux riches*. Many Scottish architects, including even Salmon and Lorimer, assimilated leaded casements, half-timbered gables, red bricks and red roofs to their stylistic experiments. No doubt the results had a beguiling charm. Mackintosh, however, largely eschewed the practice, though he was sufficiently attracted to Elizabethan architecture to prepare a sympathetic, if again derivative, lecture on the subject [D]. But for him it was always the Scottish tradition of building that held the key, a symbolic key, able to release architecture from its defensive keep of historicism out onto the open plains of the new century.

On page 13 of his text Mackintosh begins his structured description of the tradition. A chronological morphology emerges and with it the important observation that a tendency exists, during the later phases of the style, for certain forms to lose their initially functional justification while perhaps retaining some symbolic significance.[36] Thus respect is paid to the two

18. William Burn: Milton Lockhart, Lanarkshire – entrance front (*c.* 1829)
Burn's design shows the Scots-Jacobean beginnings for the Baronial revival of
the mid-century.

19. Ballikinrain, Balfron, Stirlingshire (1868)
The largest of David Bryce's Scottish Baronial mansions, in which his hard-
edged mastery of the style is everywhere apparent both in detail and in
compositional strategy.

principal aspects of Romantic criticism – the formative role of relative cultural context and the organic nature of artistic development. Consequent
issues are never explicitly addressed in the lecture. But two questions do
irresistibly arise. First, can contextual culture establish a creative dialectic
with the deeper international rhythms of economic, social and technological
change while still maintaining its specific identity; and, secondly, can the life
of contextual culture be cyclically renewed?

As to the first of these questions it is clear enough that Mackintosh believes Scottish architecture to have had both a national and an international validity, at least up until the time of the Union of the Crowns. The rot begins to set in, it seems, when an unreasonable striving after symmetry takes possession of designers' energies, a compositional delusion which has its complementary betrayal of character in efforts to make their buildings 'look like the Renassence work which they had seen in England' [A 35]. Mackintosh is here, as so often, Ruskin's man. Describing this later work of the seventeenth century as 'a mix up between Scottish Baronial & debased Elezibethan Italian Renaissence', he goes on (we are now on the last pages of the text) to record that 'since then we have had no such thing as a national style, sometimes we have been greek, sometimes Italian and again Gothic' [A 36]. No cyclical regeneration: no acknowledgement of Adam's romantic classicism; no sympathy for Burn's Jacobethan Scots; most surprising of all, perhaps, not a word for the ebullient Baronial of Billings and Bryce. No

20. C. R. Mackintosh: Scotland Street School, Glasgow (1904)
Features such as the stair towers were deliberately introduced to evoke
Scotland's architectural tradition and demonstrate symbolically its continuing
validity.

regeneration of Scottishness whatsoever? So it seems until the very last, and the most intriguing, words of the whole essay: 'whether the style can be developed . . . is a point which our forefathers left for us to decide  From some recent buildings which have been erected it is clearly evident that this style is coming to life again and I only hope that it will not be strangled in its infancy by indiscriminating and unsympathetic people who copy the an-

cient examples without trying to make the style conform to modern requirements' [A 36-36 verso].

Here, then, is the answer to that second question. The style *can* be revived.
Indeed, there is already some evidence of the cycle beginning again –
though what this might be, how recent are these 'recent buildings', gives
scope for fascinating speculation.[37] But here, in this final paragraph, a still
more revealing critical inference can be made, an inference not without
relevance for any further revolution in the 'revival cycle'.[38]

Mackintosh's intermittent stress on truth and honesty in buildings and
his warning about failing to pay due attention to 'modern requirements' is
not of itself particularly remarkable. What *is* significant is the manner in
which he expresses the design relationship between form and function. He
quite clearly identifies the priority of form; disparagingly, in his description
of those who merely copy the 'ancient examples', but approvingly in his
final implied belief that the way to proceed is 'to make the style *conform* to
modern requirements' (my italics). This is quite different from the Modernist
view that the form should be derived from the functional needs of activity,
environment, structure or construction. Mackintosh does not, of course,
deny that things must work; what he seems to say is that things must work
symbolically.[39]

Corroboration for this interpretation is not hard to find. Two years after
his first public lecture, in a paper on the more theoretically demanding topic
of 'Architecture', he quite explicitly states that 'we must have a symbolism
immediately comprehensible by the great majority of spectators' [F 16],
clearly an appeal in the Scottish context for a recognisably Scottish architecture, i.e. for 'a code of symbols accompanied by traditions which explained
them' [F 5].[40] But it is in his buildings that the most convincing proof is
to be found. There the use of certain encoded architectural elements is
deliberately evocative: forms like the cylindrical stair tower, the conical roof,
the skew gable and the eaves dormer appear not because they are the logical
responses to practical needs, but because they are Scotch; formal relationships like the predominance of solid over void, the direction of visual attention off-centre or the stuttering not quite coincident overlap of symmetries,
because they have a recurring presence in the tradition of Scottish building.[41] Those who imagine Mackintosh as a non-partisan genius who somehow manages to conjure up these echoes of a nations's past as chance by-
products from the operation of some disinterested principles of architectural
design, or, worse, who regard his Scottish allusions as an embarrassment,
parochial anachronisms staining the white cosmopolitan promise of the
International Style, know nothing of the creative power of cultural tradition
and next to nothing of how architects work.

NOTES

1. Stewart Cruden, 'Charles Rennie Mackintosh and Scotch Baronial Architecture', *C. R. Mackintosh Soc. Newsletter* 15 (1977) p. 6.

2. A. W. N. Pugin, quoted in J. Mordaunt Crook, *The Dilemma of Style* (London 1987) p. 47.

3. Although the title of this lecture is given by both Mackintosh's principal biographers as 'Scottish Baronial Architecture', following all four published reviews of Mackintosh's talk (see n. 6), the title appearing in Mackintosh's hand on his manuscript is 'Scotch Baronial Architecture'. Whether or not 'Scotch' was deliberately preferred by Mackintosh to 'Scottish' or 'Scots' is impossible to determine: since 'Scottish Baronial Architecture' predominates within the lecture text it seems unlikely that he was being fastidious. 'Scots' is generally considered correct usage though it is not perhaps without significance here that 'Scotch', which prevailed in Scotland from the late 18th into the 19th century, 'is still the regular vernacular form': see M. Robinson, ed., *The Concise Scots Dictionary* (Aberdeen 1985) p. 588.

Some comment may also be made on 'Baronial'. Strictly speaking its application to architecture implies reference to the buildings of the ruling landed class in mediaeval times; it was the baronage who administered justice from their fortified country seats. The 19th century Baronial Revival in architecture broadened usage to include not only the country houses of a now romantically inclined rural aristocracy anxious to espouse the architectural pretensions of the Scottish past, but also much of the urban building of Victorian Scotland and beyond, where similar aspirations were at work. In both historical contexts the distinction from humbler, vernacular building is usually to be inferred. Mackintosh does not make this distinction in his lecture text: the Scottish Baronial Style 'suits itself to every grade and every class of building to which it is applied. It is equally at home in the humble cottage as in the mighty Castle' [A 10]. He also eschews any direct reference to the Victorian Baronial Revival stemming from the plates of Billings and the mansions of David Bryce.

In his *House Architecture* (London 1880), the London-based Scots architect J. J. Stevenson spoke of 'Scotch architecture', 'the national Scotch style' and, indeed, 'Scotch "Baronial" architecture', though his consistent placing of the word 'Baronial' in inverted commas indicated some disparagement. Stevenson regarded some of the 'wonderful productions of modern Scotch "Baronial"' as 'all mustard with no beef' and 'not true expressions of national feeling', and while he is not an outright opponent of the 'old Scotch style', believing it to be 'well fitted for modern houses', he is clearly as uneasy about the exaggerated formalism of the Baronial Revival as he is about any exaggerated affirmation of Scottishness. From his English vantage point, he claimed that 'National peculiarities and differences have of late become softened down and assimilated by more frequent intercommunication with England and the influence of common culture. We should therefore expect that the architecture of the two countries should become assimilated . . .' Mackintosh undoubtedly assimilated English architectural influences into his *oeuvre*. Rarely, if ever, however, do these seem to subvert his sense of cultural priority: nor does he employ the words 'Scotch Baronial Architecture' in anything other than an enthusiastic and laudatory manner.

4. Thomas Howarth, *Charles Rennie Mackintosh and the Modern Movement* (2nd edn, London 1977) pp. 22-3, refers to the single commission for 'Redclyffe', 120-2 Balgrayhill Road, Springburn, Glasgow (1890), which pre-dates the lecture. It is interesting that he should find that this house's 'wall masses and chimney stacks recall unmistakably the Scottish vernacular'.

5. John Ruskin, *St Mark's Rest* viii § 88.

6. *Architect* 45 (1891) p. 113. Also *British Architect* 35 (1891) p. 152. At least four brief reports of the G.A.A. meeting appeared; all are similar and contain the same error describing the lecturer's five-period rather than four-period classification, clearly

the contribution of a single correspondent: *Architect* 45 (1891) p. 113; *British Architect* 35 (1891) pp. 151-2; *Builder* 60 (1891) p. 150; *Glasgow Herald* 12 Feb. 1891, p. 6.

7. Fourteen pre-1891 works are documented, including sketches of the Old College Glasgow (H.A.G.: see fig. 47); Glasgow Cathedral (H.A.G. and Mitchell Library Glasgow); Elgin Cathedral (H.A.G. and Aberdeen Art Gallery: see fig. 41); Spynie Palace (H.A.G.); and Rowallan Castle (H.A.G.).

8. Mary Newbery Sturrock, 'Remembering Charles Rennie Mackintosh', *Connoisseur* (Aug. 1973) p. 287.

9. Howarth (n. 4) p. 12, n. 1, drawing attention to a note in Mackintosh's hand on the back of the last page of the MS, 'very unkind of Mr Walton to ascribe all the artistic features to France', suggests that George Walton had 'raised a debatable point that was calculated to ruffle the temper of the lecturer – the real origin of many architectural features claimed as indigenous to Scotland'. The gist of this observation may be sound, though 'Mr Walton' is more likely to refer to Henry D. Walton, a vice president of the G.A.A. and a former lecturer. The names McGibbon and Anderson can also be made out in these jottings: see A n. 61. It is conceivable that David MacGibbon attended the lecture, or that his name arose in the discussion, but the reference is probably to the architect Alexander McGibbon. Both he and William J. Anderson served as presidents of the G.A.A. in the early 1890s.

10. Robert Macleod, *Charles Rennie Mackintosh: Architect and Artist* (2nd edn, London 1983) pp. 38-9.

11. W. R. Lethaby, *Architecture, Mysticism and Myth* (1891, repr. London 1974).

12. Cruden (n. 1) p. 5.

13. David MacGibbon and Thomas Ross, *The Castellated and Domestic Architecture of Scotland*, 5 vols (Edinburgh 1887-92).

14. Cruden (n. 1) p. 5.

15. For a brief review of the historiography of the Baronial Revival see Frank A. Walker, 'National Romanticism and the Architecture of the City', in G. Gordon, ed., *Perspectives of the Scottish City* (Aberdeen 1985) pp. 125-59.

16. Throughout Mackintosh's architectural career in Scotland there is built evidence of his acknowledgement of the national tradition and of his ability to transform and transcend it according to contemporary need without loss of allusion or identity. Beginning with 'Redclyffe' (1890), where immature and unexceptional features nevertheless seem to Howarth (n. 4 above) to 'recall unmistakably the Scottish vernacular', and ending with 'Cloak', Kilmacolm (1906-13), in quirky, even perverse, games with that same vernacular, Mackintosh made his allegiance clear. The Glasgow School of Art (1896-1909), Windyhill, Kilmacolm (1899-1901), The Hill House, Helensburgh (1902-3), and Scotland Street School, Glasgow (1904-6), perhaps his four finest works, all draw in significant measure upon their cultural context. Far from being deracinated, their revolutionary achievement is consciously rooted in national tradition.

17. See Brian Edwards, 'John Honeyman, Victorian Architect and Restorer and Partner of Charles Rennie Mackintosh', *C. R. Mackintosh Soc. Newsletter* 36 (1984) pp. 5-9, and T. J. Reilly, *The Works of John Honeyman, 1831-1914* (unpublished dissertation, U. Strathclyde 1965).

18. Crook (n. 2).

19. Colin Rowe, 'Character and Composition; or Some Vicissitudes of Architectural Vocabulary in the Nineteenth Century', in C. Rowe, *The Mathematics of the Ideal Villa and Other Essays* (Cambridge Mass. 1976) pp. 59-87.

20. Rowe (n. 19) p. 62.

21. Rowe (n. 19) p. 62.

22. See Kenneth Frampton, *Modern Architecture, a Critical History* (London 1980) pp. 8-40.

23. P. Thompson, *William Butterfield* (London 1971) p. 226.

24. John Ruskin, *Lectures on Architecture and Painting*, ch. 2.

25. J. J. Winckelmann, quoted in D. Irwin, ed., *Winckelmann – Writings on Art* (London 1972) p. 51.

26. See W. H. Wackenroder, quoted in E. G. Holt, ed., *From the Classicists to the Impressionists* (New York 1966) pp. 63-8.

27. A. W. N. Pugin, *Contrasts* (2nd edn, London 1841) p. 17.

28. I. Kant, quoted from 'The Critique of Judgment' (1790) in K. Aschenbrenner and A. Isenberg, eds, *Aesthetic Theories: Studies in the Philosophy of Art* (New Jersey 1965) p. 181.

29. Charles Eastlake, *A History of the Gothic Revival* (1872, rcpr. Leicester 1970) p. 315.

30. W. R. Lethaby, 'Art and Workmanship' (originally publ. in *The Imprint* 1913), in *Form in Civilisation* (2nd edn, London etc. 1957) p. 166.

31. See William Wordsworth, 'Lines written with a pencil upon a stone in the wall of the house (an out-house) on the island at Grasmere' (1800), in William Wordsworth and Samuel Taylor Coleridge, *The Lyrical Ballads, 1798-1805* (London 1926) pp. 242-3.

32. See John Ruskin, *The Poetry of Architecture; or The Architecture of the Nations of Europe considered in its Association with natural Scenery and national Character*, esp. ch. 4, 'The Mountain Cottage: Westmorland'.

33. Julius Posener, *From Schinkel to the Bauhaus* (London 1972) p. 19.

34. James Salmon, 'The Decoration of Steel and Reinforced Concrete Structures', *Builders' Journal and Architectural Engineer* 27 (1908) p. 271.

35. Nikolaus Pevsner, *The Englishness of English Art* (London 1956) p. 195.

36. Mackintosh, using MacGibbon and Ross, notes that the further back architectural elements of the tradition are traced 'the more real and necessary they are'. Although he does point out that the later examples of Scotch Baronial Architecture perpetuate old forms beyond strict functional justification, it is not clear whether this is to be regarded as entirely reprehensible. Certainly, he is unequivocal in saying that continued imitation results in forms 'losing their true purpose and significance'. But does this judgment entail more than *functional* significance? It seems more likely, given the evidence of Mackintosh's own work, that while formalist pastiche is to be condemned, the creative adaptation of recognisable forms and syntax may still hold a *symbolic* significance.

37. Just what Mackintosh may have had in mind when he averred that 'the style is coming to life again' is intriguing. One can only guess: probably not the Scots Renaissance Revival of Robert Rowand Anderson, but possibly the more vernacular essays of Hew Montgomerie Wardrop, e.g. at Tilliefour, Aberdeenshire (*c.* 1885); or Sydney Mitchell & Wilson's Well Court, Dean Village, Edinburgh (*c.* 1884); and certainly James MacLaren's extension to Stirling High School (1887-90), where a 'remotely Baronial' stair tower has been suggested as the forerunner of Mackintosh's Glasgow Herald tower of 1893: F. Sinclair, *Scotstyle* (Edinburgh 1984) p. 55.

38. See Charles McKean, *Local Roots and the Revival Cycle*, Alfred Blossom Lecture, Royal Society of Arts (1987).

39. Many instances of this conviction can be found in Mackintosh's work: one example may suffice. There is no compelling functional reason why the staircases in Scotland Street School, Glasgow (1904-6) should take the semi-cylindrical form they do; indeed, the arrangement of the stair plan – straight flights with perfectly orthodox rectangular landings – proposes no such external formal consequences. Howarth pictures Scotland Street alongside the office building of the factory designed by Walter Gropius for the Werkbund Exhibition at Köln (1914). The glazing of the staircase cylinders in each is an interesting coincidence, but the fact that Gropius' stair is helical and thus formally in tune with its cylindrical casing while Mackintosh's is not makes any simplistic functional inferences about the latter's design thinking somewhat spurious. Surely the conically capped stair towers at Scotland Street are deliberate evocations of a Scottish architectural tradition (Falkland, Tolquhon, Rowallan, etc.), the form adapted here to the problem of vertical circulation, while the literalist insertion of the turnpike stair is itself eschewed as

functionally unsuited to the to-and-fro bustle of a school. In short the architecture works at all levels and not least symbolically. Even the flat south elevation at Scotland Street, where allusion is necessarily confined to the almost graphic limitations of ornament, has its stylized thistle motif at the very centre of the façade.

40. These quotations, like much of the lecture, are from Lethaby (n. 11). For a full discussion of Mackintosh's use of Lethaby see David Walker's essay below.

41. For an outline presentation of this formal analysis see Frank A. Walker, 'Mackintosh and Art Nouveau Architecture', in C. J. Carter, ed., *Art, Design and the Quality of Life in Turn of the Century Scotland, 1890-1910*, Proceedings of Symposium, Duncan of Jordanstone College of Art (Dundee 1982) pp. 52-64.

CHARLES RENNIE MACKINTOSH

# A. *Scotch Baronial Architecture* (1891)

A 1     Scotch Baronial Architecture.

It is with feelings somewhat bordering on trepidation that I venture to
adress you on a subject which has never as far as I remember been more
than incidentally touched upon within those walls, a subject indeed dear
to my heart and entwined among my inmost thoughts and affections, but
one which for that very reason I feel it the more difficult to bring before
you through the medium of an essay. It may be at first sight imagined
that love of all the human feelings is best calculated to aid in describing
the beauties of its object, and in advocating its claims upon the admiration, but it is not so. We can hardly state our reasons why we love our
parents and our brothers. We know that it is a feeling that has grown
with our growth, and is part of our very existance yet it is probable that
an acquaintance who has never shared in these warmer sentiments,
might describe their characters and even their virtues more successfully
A 2     than our selves. If we seek to / investigate them, we find the research all
to cold and too methiodical to accord with the tone of our feelings, and
like the poet who wished to sing of the Atrides and of Cadmus, the cords
of our hearts responded only to love.[1]
    So it is with those who have harboured an early affection for the
Architecture of their native land. Strongly as I appreciate the intrinsic
beauty of the monuments of classic antiquity, and the merits of very
many works of the Revival I should doubt whether it were possible for
any unsophisticated youth before studying their Archi. as a science to
entertain towards its production in this country any feelings bordering on
real affection. He may see much in them to admire – much to lead him
to study the art which has produced them; – and in this study will
no doubt, often kindle those warmer feelings which ripen into love. But
this is a very different feeling from that deep and filial affection which
many a youth untaught in art but gifted by nature with a perception for
A 3     its beauties, has entertained from his tenderest / years towards the old
castle of his neighbourhood or that irrisistable attraction which compels
many of the members of this association to visit the various castles &
palaces in this country, not only under the balmy influences of summer,
but along muddy roads and snowy path, and with glowing heart but
shivering hand to sketch the humble cottage the more pretentious

1. An elegant allusion, perhaps borrowed, to the stance of certain Roman poets who,
professing inadequacy, rejected the serious and lofty genre of Homeric epic in favour of
'trifling' love poetry. See e.g. Propertius 1.7, 3.3; Horace *Odes* 1.6.

mantion or the mutilated though venerable castle with feelings of the most indescribable delight.

It is this instinctive affection which is so difficult to reason upon, and to which cold investigation seems so uncongenial: yet most pleasant is it in after life to find every new proof that our early feelings have not been misplaced; that those once callous, warm up when they are led to examine; that those who, strange to say, dislike the archi. of their forefathers, are now forced to admit some of its beauties: that the style once dispised has become gradually appreciated and its study become the favourite pastime of thousands.[2]

A 4    My object on the present occasion will be to give a general sketch of this style of Architec. untill it reaches its culminating point, stopping at the time when it reigned triumphant regoicing in the full attainment of the objects of its striving, and preceeding from strength to strength and from beauty to beauty. filling the counties of our country with creations at once noble and artistic, which surpassed any thing in the way of architecture which this country of ours had yet seen.

I will commence by considering or enumerating the various claims which this style has upon our study and appreciation.

The more carefully we examine into or investigate the subject, the stronger, and the more numerous do we find those claims to be. To a casual observer, the intrest we feel in the subject may appear to be the result of local prejudice or arbitrary choice, and our national style may seem to have no greater claim upon us than than the style of a hundred other periods or countries. The fact however is the reverse – that the style is marked out from that [of] other countries in the most signal and

A 5    remarkable manner. / I will briefly point out some of the circumstances which thus especially single it out.[3]

The character of a style of art does not depend upon the mere material from which it has been fabricated, but upon the sentiments and conditions under which it has been developed.

The genuine feeling about our architecture up till the point where we leave off will be evident to every one who has any discrimination, the special necessities of the times and positions being considered and though the difficulties and necessities imposed were very numerous the result of combining the useful with the beautiful is in most cases evident and satisfactory

The last of the historic claims of this arch. to which I will call your attention is, that it is the native architecture of our own country and that of our forefathers. Here again I must define my meaning for the sake of meeting a class of objectiors who delight to attach a false and exagerated

2. On the verso of A 1 is an earlier draft of A 3 with only minor textual variations.

3. Mackintosh here scored out 'In tracing the history of civilization we cannot fail to perceive'.

A 6    meaning to an expression I do not then mean that this style of /
architecture belongs to us in any different sence from that in which it
belongs to France or any other country I do not mean to revive the
claims of our country to its origination, nor to assert in its behalf any pre-
eminent share in its development   All I mean to urge is the simple fact
that, by whatever members of our family of nations it was shared, it was,
nevertheless the Arch. of our own country, just as much Scotch as we are
our selves – as Indigenous to our country as our wild flowers, our family
names our customs or our political constitution. In Scotland as in france
& england the same necessities (with (local variations) had grown up
with the new civilization. as it perfected its self it showed the same
tendences and the same yearnings. It is possible that france was more
rapid in developing the style[4] but in each the result had long been aimed
at: in each it was the natural consequence of what had already been
attained and was there fore not the property of one but the common
inheritance of both.  and each having attained it carried it on and

A 7    developed it in her own way, thus making it in every sence her own. / I
am however only urging this as a claim which our old arch has upon our
study

    If we investigate the architecture of Egypt or Assyria or of Persia, we
find that it tells of races with whom we have no national or personal
sympathy. If we go to the classic shores of Greece, though there we
should be viewing the work of a race whose art and literature are, more
than those of any other people, the property of the world, we never the
less fail to find anything to connect them in any special sence with
ourselves. If we transfer our researches from Greece to Rome – though
we now view the vestiges of that mighty empire whose world-wide sway
stretched its iron sceptre over our own land, and though we find among
them the germ of the architecture which forms the nuclus of all the
subsequent styles – they are still severed from us by so wide a gulf that
were it not for the modern revival of their style they would appear
perfectly alien to our race & climate. All these studies must be followed
up in distant lands, excepting only these few fragments of Roman work
scattered here and there in our own and neighbouring countries – the

A 8    evidence of universal empire, the / footprints and symbols of ancient
servitude.

    How different is the study of Scottish Baronial Arch. Its original
examples are at our own doors.  the very houses perhaps in which some
of us live: the monuments of our own forefathers the works of men
bearing our own name, whose armoral badges we are still proud to use:
who spoke in its pristine form our own language; who sat in our own
parliament were lords of still existing manors, founders of still surviving

---

4. Mackintosh here scored out 'carried on the perfecting [of the] architecture longer
than we did', and substituted 'was more rapid in developing the style'.

charities, men who fought the battles of which we are still proud, and laid the foundations of our liberties and of all those institutions which render the name of Scotland illustrious among the nations of the world. Surely the architecture which grew up among men so nearly allied to us has a preeminent claim upon our attention

I have thus traced out what appears to me to be the leading historical claims of the style and which I will recapitulate as being.

1st  That it is an architectural style of the modern. as distinguished from the ancient world.

A 9    2nd  That it is wholly or partially the architecture of this country alone, and is the only style which we can claim as being in whole or part our own.

3rd  That it is the last type of architectural treatment of buildings in this country that was national or that can be called a style, all the succeeding types being debased or simply wholesale importations of styles from other countries such as Roman & Greek.

4th  That it is thus, in a stronger sence than can be predicated of any other style Scottish Baronial Style

5th  and lastly, That it is pre-eminently the arch of our own forefathers and of our own land.

I will now proceed to direct your attention to some of the more prominent among its intrinsic claims.

Commencing then with abstract beauty  I will not treat this as a comparative but as a positive quality. Differences of taste & education lead us to form varied estimates of the relative merits of the several styles of

A 10    art, but the most devout follower of / classic or gothic antiquity could scarcely question the absolute beauty of many of our Castles

The next quality I will mention is the extraordinary facility of our style in decorating constructing, and in converting structural and useful features into elements of beauty.

The treatment of windows supplies an endless treasury of architecturel loviliness   The roof is usually high pitched adding dignity to the various edifacs of this period: while if need be its timbers are made to contribute liberally to the effect of the interior: And generally, whatever feature, whether homely or otherwise, which construction or utility demanded, was at once enlisted, and that with right goodwill and heartiness among the essential elements of the design.

In the same way it suits itself to every grade and every class of building to which it is applied   It is equally at home in the humble cottage as and in the mighty Castle. The manor-house farm & cottage, show equal

A 11    appropriateness of / treatment and evince the same power of meeting the conditions of purpose or material

Again many examples still remaining show how all the arts were united in one building.

In its normal form of stone arch it does not make all other materials confirm to the condition but treats them all according to its own demands  It is almost equally successful in its timber roof as in its stone construction and equally good at wood & stone carving. it treats plaster in a manner perfectly suited to the material conditions. it brings in painted decoration of a very primitive kind certainly but still they are there.

[5]the beautifuly simple pannelled ceilings, and in many other ways all the arts are brought in.

In variety of expression the Scottish style is very versatile being equally capable of the most stern and majestic severity, and the most exquisite and refined elegance as well as all the intermediate varieties. In beauty of external outline grouping of parts boldness freeness & variety of

A 12 conception / very few styles approach it. Time would fail me to tell of the wonderful manner in which our style shapes itself to every accidental requirement: grapples with every difficulty and converts it into a source of beauty disdains, on the one hand, all artificially effected symmetry, nor, on the other fears to submit to the most rigid uniformity (examples)[6] should the conditions of the case require being equally beautiful when no two parts are alike and also where scarcely any two are different; how it meets every emergency with the utmost frankness & honesty how it disdains all deception: thus contrasting itself, not with other genuine styles, for none really systematically admit of shams, but with the despicable trickiness which our modern architects have learned from their own plasterers & House painters

Having I fear at too great length, sketched out the claim of S.B.A. upon your study I will now proceed to point out the more prominent characteristics of the style from the earliest examples down to the end of the 16th Centy.

A 13 Beginning with the thirteenth century we will devide the style into four periods.

First Period embracing the whole of the 13th century.

Second Period 14th Century. Third Period 1400-1524 and Fourth Period from 1524 to end of 17th Century.

First Period. Up to the beginning of this period no Norman Keeps, indicating, like those in England and northern France, that the strong hand of that powerful race was laid upon the land had been erected in Scotland. The country was still independent and retained its own system of fortification  In the 13th Centy. the castles of Scotland were constructed after the extended system of the contemporary fortresses in France and England[7]

5. Mackintosh here scored out 'Plaster is enlisted to provide'.

6. This suggests that Mackintosh expanded on his written text.

7. As discussed in the introductory essay, much of Mackintosh's text, with minor changes and omissions, is plagiarised from David MacGibbon and Thomas Ross, *The Castellated and Domestic Architecture of Scotland* (Edinburgh 1887-92), hereafter 'M. & R.'

The general idea of these 13th Centy Scotch Castles is that of a large fortified Enclosure

The plan is usually quadrilateral, but more or less irregular to suit the site

The walls are generally of the plainest description and are strengthened with towers at the angles which serve to defend the curtains.

A 14     The ornament of this period when there is any / resembles that of the Ecclisiastical Arch. of the time, and in most cases similar to that of the corresponding date in England.[8]

In Bothwell and Rothesay Castles we have two of the very best examples of the 13th Centy. castles of Scotland. I have no doubt they are both quite familiar to all of you.

Fig 1. Architecturally, Rothesay Castle is one of our most interesting castles. We here see the great wall of enciente in its simplest form, defended by four round towers. This castle differs from most others in having the enclosing walls of a circular form instead of the usual quadrilateral but the ditch surround the wall & towers brings the whole to a square form.[9] See plan

Bothwell) Of our 13th Centy castles Bothwell is or was the finest, indeed it is probably the grandest ruin of its kind in scotland.[10]

This castle has the usual high enclosing walls strengthened with round & square towers and provided with a great round donjon dominating the whole.[11] These illus. will show the character of the work but of course it must be seen on the spot to be appreciated.

A 15     Caerlaverock Castle is another good type of this period. This castle is triangular on plan. With the close of the 13th Centy this system of fortification comes to a close.

The invasion of Edward I in 1296 and the disturbances of the 14th Centy. destroyed the prosperity of the country.

Thus we find a great gap between the style of the 13th Centy buildings and those which succeed them in the 14th Centy and we have to traverse a very long period ere we meet with castles of the size and elegance of those we have just been considering. The 13th Centy buildings of Scot-

---

The notes attempt to identify precisely these textual thefts; undoubtedly some sources have not been spotted – for this apologies. Mackintosh's use of M. & R. concentrated on the following: vol. i pp. 143-6, 'Introduction to the Second Period', and pp. 222-6, 'Introduction to the Third Period'; vol. ii pp. 1-20, 'Introduction to the Fourth Period', and pp. 567-75, 'Summary'. In addition Mackintosh must have made reference to the descriptions in M. & R. of those buildings he selected for discussion. All of his examples derive from M. & R.

    'Up to the beginning ... France and England.' M. & R. ii p. 567.

    8. 'The walls are generally [A 13] ... date in England.' M. & R. ii p. 567.

    9. 'Architecturally, Rothesay Castle ... a square form.' M. & R. i pp. 81-2.

    10. 'Bothwell ... scotland.' M. & R. i p. 93. The Glasgow Architectural Association visited Bothwell Castle shortly after Mackintosh's lecture, on 27 June 1891.

    11. 'This castle ... the whole.' M. & R. i p. 93.

land thus form a very distinctly marked period in the Architectural history of our country and constitute the first period of Scottish Baronial Architecture.[12]

Second Period.

During the 14th Centy the country was in a state of complete exhaustion consequent on the great struggle for National independence and was A 16    therefore not in a condition / to engage in extensive building operations,[13] or attempt to keep up with the rapid advance in military architecture which took place at that time in France and England. Besides, the policy of Bruce was opposed to the building of large Castles, as these were found liable to be taken by the enemy, and to afford him a secure footing in the country. Bruces policy was to destroy everything before an enemy of invasion, and leave only a barren country to occupy – a policy, the wisdom of which, in the relative positions of Scotland and England, was often proved subsequently by the starving out of the invaders.[14]

For the above reasons we find only few and small remains of castles or domestic buildings erected in the 14th Century, or at least till near the close of the Century[15]

Those we do find are in the form of a simple tower, similar to and evidently adapted from the "Norman Keep" formerly so prevelant in France and England, but now abandoned in these countries for over a century.

A 17    This type of habitation was found to suit the limited requirements and means of the time. Indeed, so admirably adopted was it to the circumstances of Scotland, combining as it did in the simplest and most economical manner security from without, with the accomodation considered adaquate within, that for nearly four centuries the norman Keep, with various modifications, continued to form the model on which the plans of the great majority of Scottish Castles were designed   A courtyard surrounded with a wall was attached to these Keeps, but the enclosing wall did not present the great size and extent of the 13th Centy castles.

The ornamental features of this period, which, as might be expected, are somewhat rare, were founded entirely on the defensive requirements such as, the corbel table of the parapet and bartizans, with its machicolations, corbels, embrasures &c. &c.[16]

12. 'The invasion of Edward I ... Scottish Baronial Architecture.' M. & R. i p. 143. In the last sentence Mackintosh has substituted 'Baronial' for 'castellated'.
13. 'During the 14th Centy ... building operations,' M. & R. i p. 143.
14. 'Besides, the policy of Bruce ... the invaders.' M. & R. i p. 143.
15. 'For the above reasons ... close of the Century', M. & R. i p. 143.
16. 'in the form of a simple tower [A 16] ... embrasures &c. &c.' M. & R. ii p. 568. Corbel: projecting stone or piece of timber supporting a superincumbent weight. Bartizan: a small turret projecting from the angle on the top of a tower or parapet. Machicolation: projecting parapet on the outside of castle towers or walls with openings in the floor through which missiles could be dropped on assailants. Embrasure: a small opening in the wall or parapet, usually splayed on the inside.

The dwellings of the peasantry were mere huts which were easily replaced after the storm of an invasion was past.

A 18    Castle Campbell is a typical example of the simple Keep. It was afterwards extended into a large Castle with buildings round a courtyard.[17]

The tower built castles just described are especially characteristic of the Scotch arch of the 14th Centy. In France and England the contemporary castles are of the grandest and most extensive description. such as Pierrefonds in France, and the immense Edwardian piles of Carnearvon & Conway in England.[18] The Keep plan was employed as we have seen not only in the smaller towers of the impoverished nobility, but even the royal palaces and castles (as Dundonald) were erected according to the same model.[19]

With the close of the 14th Cent a new style of castle building was introduced. we may therefore regard the end of this centy as completing the second period of S.B.A.[20]

A 19    Third Period. 15th Cent

During this period the Keep plan was still the ruling one. But the original simple form was now in some instances modified by the addition of a wing at one angle. Forming what is called the L plan. This was sometimes still further developed by the addition of a tower staircase in the angle. In the case of Borthwick, two wings were added both on the same side of the main Keep.

It is quite evident that these developments are the natural result of the increasing ease and refinement of the country.[21] This developing of the Keep plan is purely national and is not to be found in any other country. The great number of small chambers formed in the thickness of the walls which are so common in many of the Keeps of this date, are another feature peculiar to Scottish Cas's

At this period the Keep plan, even with the additional accomodation provided by means of the above modifications, was found by the more wealthy nobles to be too limited for their requirements and a new form of plan was now introduced

A 20    Third Period

This was the system of arranging the buildings round the wall of enciente so as to form a courtyard in the centre. Soon after its introduction this "courtyard plan" became the favourite arrangement of all the larger castles erected in this period, and many of the old keeps were converted into castles of this description by having additional buildings

17. 'was afterwards extended . . . round a courtyard.' M. & R. i p. 202.
18. 'The tower built castles . . . Conway in England.' M. & R. i p. 220.
19. 'The Keep plan . . . the same model.' M. & R. i pp. 220-1.
20. 'With the close . . . period of S.B.A.', M. & R. i p. 221. Mackintosh again has 'S.B.A.' for M. & R.'s 'Scotch Castellated Architecture': see n. 12.
21. 'During this period . . . refinement of the country.' M. & R. ii p. 568.

erected round the enclosing wall of the barmkin[22]  The ornament of this period, like that of the preceeding, is derived from the defensive features but these now begin to be applied in a more ornamental fashion, their pristine useful purpose being to a sertain extent departed from.[23]

A 21    The same general features are observable in the earlier and later examples of this period, but the details,[24] became gradually more refined as time advances. In the later bds of this period the defensive features are gradually reduced in importance although not altogether abandoned[25] In these later examples, especially linlithgow may be observed a gradual assimilation of the contemporary English style of Arch and in the early parts of the 16th cent there are distinct traces of the approaching advent of the renaissence, as at stirling & Falkland  This is very observable in the palace of Stirling built about 1500, where the classic ornament begins to be applied to the old forms and where grotesque imitations of cllassic sculpture are for the first time introduced[26]  The above style of castles with quadrangles marks a distinct period in the history of Scottish Arch. commencing with the 15th cent & ending about 1542.

A 22    It is distinguished from the preceeding period / in which we have seen there were no such castles   They[27] also distinguish it from the succeeding period for although there are numerous castles with quadrangles after the above date, we shall see as we proceed that they were marked by features which distinguish them from those of the third period

A considerable number of buildings of the second were converted into castles with quadrangles by additions made to old keeps in the form of buildings surrounding a courtyard such as Crichton, Craigmillar Castle Campbell &c.

The castles of this period have all a strong similarity of detail and are quite distinguishable from the succed & preceeding periods

Examples Craignethan Castle Lanarkshire simple Keep Avondale Cast Lanarkshire Keep with one or two wings   Keeps enlarged into castles surrounding a courtyard[28] Edzell Cas. Forfor Shire. Cas. Campbell Kilbirnie Cas. Ayrshire

22. 'The great number of small chambers [A 19] ... wall of the barmkin'. M. & R. ii pp. 568-9. Barmkin: outer fortification of a castle.

23. 'The ornament of this period ... departed from.' M. & R. ii p. 569. Mackintosh scored out the following paragraph: 'Towards the close of this period traces are found of the approach of Renaissance work, but the general tone of the designs whether on the keep plan or on the courtyard plan, is entirely Scottish, and its development from the earlier & simpler forms may be readily traced.'

24. Mackintosh here scored out 'whether ornamental or useful'.

25. 'the defensive features ... altogether abandoned', M. & R. i p. 223.

26. 'especially linlithgow ... first time introduced', M. & R. i p. 223. Mackintosh subsequently sketched at Stirling (1894) and the Palace at Falkland (c. 1900) (H.A.G.).

27. Here Mackintosh probably means 'castles with quadrangles', but 'they' could be a glancing acknowledgement of MacGibbon and Ross.

28. 'Keeps enlarged ... courtyard', M. & R. i p. xv.

A 23    Castles designed as buildings surrounding a Courtyard.[29] Doune Castle.
Perthshire  Spynie Cas. Elgin  Edinburgh Cas. Stirling Cas. Linlithgow
Falkland  Dunfermline Palace. Fife  Bishops Pallace  Kirkwall Orkney.[30]

A 24    Fourth Period. Not withstanding all these transformations in the
external appearance and ornamentation of our arch. the old plans were
firmly adhered to. As the country increased in welth and refinement
the desire for more stately and luxurious abodes was developed. This
naturally led to the more frequent use of the courtyard plan, by which
the accom. could be most conveniently increased to the desired extent
During the whole of the 4th period instances occur of buildings erected on
the simple Keep plan, or some of the modifications of it. The L plan,
introduced in the 3rd period is very often used. The Z plan is a development of the keep invented during this period  The persistence of the keep
plan from the time of its adoption, through all the other changes of time
and Circumstances, is very remarkable

The various modifications of the Keep plan, which the changes of the
time and the amelioration of manners had at different periods developed,
merely serve to emphasise the reluctance of the country to abandon the
old form.[31]

A 25    Fourth Period.

The chief causes of the transition from the third to the fourth period
were, first, the introduction of Renaissance art, which began to exercise a
very marked and decided influence towards the end of the sixteenth
century,[32] at first this was only observable in the details, the same
strength of will was still displayed in the grouping, later on when the
characteristic grouping was lost and renaissance art predominated, the
style was debased and can no longer be called Scot. Baronial or have a
place in this essay. The use of artillery which was developed during this
period had a very great effect in altering the forms of fortification used in
castles. Instead of building castles to resist a siege the owners now
contented themselves with a sufficient amount of fortifications to render
their dwellings safe against sudden attack. The result was that the
architecture at the end of the 16th Centy, was of an entirely different
order from that of the previous periods.[33]

A 26    Fortified castles were gradually superseeded by / ornamental country
houses, although built on the plans of the former period.

There being no need to build these houses on high and well chosen
ground for defensive purposes, the sites for new houses were now chosen

29. 'Castles designed ... Courtyard.' M. & R. i p. xv.

30. In 1889 Mackintosh had sketched Spynie Palace and Elgin Cathedral (fig. 41). He
did not visit Orkney till 1896; one sketch of Tankerness House, Kirkwall survives
(H.A.G.).

31. 'Not withstanding all these transformations ... the old form.' M. & R. ii pp. 570-1.

32. 'began to exercise ... sixteenth century', M. & R. ii p. 1.

33. 'Instead of building castles ... the previous periods.' M. & R. ii p. 2.

in low and sheltered spots near a river or some situation, chosen for its beautiful surroundings  Another event which had a powerful influence in developing the domestic arch of Scotland was the reformation. one of the results of that great movement was the secularisation of the church lands,[34] which mostly fell into the hands of the nobility of the country, and, thus enriched they immediately proceeded to use their riches in extending or erecting new mansions in keeping with their newly acquired wealth.

The close connection of England and Scotland during the reign of James VI led to the introduction of many of the features of the English Renaissence or Elizabethan style, from that country. It had also an

A 27     enlivening and civilizing effect on Scotland generally by / bringing it into contact with a richer and more polished people; and in this way many improvements were gradually imported from the south into the domestic arrangements[35] of this period.

During this period we find the same general characteristics in the design both of the plans and elevations as in the preceeding one. The two previous types of plan – the Keep and the courtyard, still continue to flourish together although in some instances they are considerably modified so as to suit the requirements of the time[36]

The ancient forms of military construction being no longer required for defensive purposes became gradually modified and transformed into ornamental features

In this respect Scot. Arch underwent a similar transformation to that of other European countries but the change took place not by the importation of designs from abroad, but by the action in Scotland of the same causes which had produced similar effects elsewhere

A 28     Among the leading external features of the castles and mansions of this period are the picturesque turrets corbelled out at every angle, covered with slated roofs. The walls are generally very plain, and the ornamentation is confined to the parapet and upper portions, where it often bursts out with extraordinary profusion and richness, as for instance Castle Fraser and Craigievar.[37]

The roofs are high pitched broken up and adorned with numerous dormers and have picturesque chimneys and crow stepped gables. Corbelling, both plain and ornamental is one of the chief characteristics of the style. It is used on every possible occasion. The turrets, staircases,

34. 'One of the results ... church lands,' M. & R. ii p. 2.

35. 'The close connection of England ... domestic arrangements', M. & R. ii pp. 2-3. Mackintosh has inserted 'English' before 'Renaissence'.

36. 'During this period ... requirements of the time', M. & R. ii p. 3. Mackintosh here scored out 'But although the plans and general forms are almost the same the external effect of these castles differs considerably from that of the previous periods'.

37. 'The walls are generally ... Craigievar.' M. & R. ii p. 3. Corbelling: the use of brick or masonry courses each built out beyond the one below to support turrets, parapets, etc.

parapets &c are all supported on corbels, and the towers are often
changed from a circular base to a square upper part by means of large
and elaborate corbels[38]

The combination of these features is oftern most successful, and the
appearance of every building of this style is so marked and characteristic
that it is scarcely possible not to recognise it at a glance as belonging to
this period.[39]

A 29     The examples of the fourth period can be best classified according to the
plans.

Beginning then with keep plans – which we still have in this period –
we have the following examples.

Amisfield Tower Dumfriesshire

The building affoards a fine and telling example of the love of corbelling
so prevelent in the 4th period and is probably the most striking example
of the adherence to the old Keep plan, while its external appearance is so
entirely altered by the multiplicity of the turrets and ornaments piled up
upon it as almost completely to conceal its origin.[40]

Coxton Tower Morayshire.

This is one of the most remarkable buildings of its class in Scotland.

The open angle turret at the South west angle[41] is a very uncommon
feature.

The roof is covered with stone flags, and also the angle turrets.

Bishops House Elgin

The arrangement of the plan of this House is peculiar  the north wing
A 30     is supposed to be an addition / which will account for this[42]

The most remarkable features of the exterior are the gabled crow-steps
on the gables, and the small oriel window in the upper floor of the east
front. These details show some indication of ecclesiastical influence[43]

Plans in the form of letter L.

Gilbertfield near Cambuslang. which you all know is of this plan

Auchans Castle Ayrshire is also of this type   The whole building is very
plain externally, but with its turrets and dormers forms a characteristic
and pleasing example of the Scottish mansion of the 17th Century.

The northern wing has been extended at a later time[44]

Plans in the form of Z.

Huntly Castle Aberdeenshire.

---

38. 'The roofs are high pitched ... elaborate corbels', M. & R. ii p. 3.

39. 'The combination of ... to this period.' M. & R. ii pp. 3-4.

40. 'The building affords ... conceal its origin.' M. & R. ii pp. 21-2.

41. 'This is one of the ... South west angle', M. & R. ii p. 23, with extensive omissions.

42. 'The arrangement of the plan ... account for this.' M. & R. ii p. 59, considerably
rephrased by Mackintosh.

43. 'The most remarkable features ... ecclesiastical influence', M. & R. ii p. 59. 'gabled
crow-steps on the gables': with a stepped profile.

44. 'The whole building ... at a later time', M. & R. ii p. 78.

In the upper part of this Castle we find a very uncommon feature in the three oriel windows. We have also fine examples of oriels at Pinkie & Maybole but strangely enough the finest oriels are to be found at the Earls Palace Kirkwall[45]

Earls Hall Fife shier is another Example of the Z plan.

A 31          Castles with courtyards

Cawdor Castle Nairnshire

There are a great many ancient & modern additions to this example which almost obliterate the original but the central Keep & some other parts are still to be found.

Fyfie Castle Aberdeenshire

This is one of the finest and most characteristic castles in the Scottish Style.

In the south front we have all the distinguishing features of the style.[46]

The staircase too is an admirable example of Scottish Work

Rowallan Castle Ayrshire.[47]

This example is different in many ways from the ones already given in this that there is not much corbelling used in the design

Argylls Lodging Stirlingshire. This is probably the finest specimen of an old town residence remaining in Scotland The building forms three sides of a square round an irregular courtyard.[48] There are some fine examples here of the enriched pediments of interlacing ornament so frequently seen in 17th Centy work.[49]

A 32          As the plans are evidently of native development so the ornamentation of the style may also be proved to be of direct descent from the earlier Scottish Arch. and to be developed from the features which were necessary in earlier times for defence. Hence we find that the further back we trace its component parts the more real and necessary they are. In the castles of the 15th Cent which we have considered every feature was useful In the 16th Cent also, however exaggerated some of the corbels and other features might be they are still distinguished from the later examples of the 17th Cent by their genuineness and utility. Thus, as we have seen in examining the plans, the position of the towers and turrets is arranged for the purpose of defence, and the buildings are provided with loopholes and angle turrets really intended for use. The corbelling although no doubt introduced mostly for effect is at least in a natural position[50] In contrast with this we find in the 17th Cent work that the

45. 'at Pinkie & Maybole ... Earls Palace Kirkwall', M. & R. ii p. 19. Mackintosh subsequently drew Maybole Castle, Ayrshire (1895) (H.A.G.).

46. 'In the south front ... features of the style.' M. & R. ii p. 354.

47. Mackintosh had sketched Rowallan Castle in 1889 (H.A.G.).

48. 'This is probably the finest ... irregular courtyard.' M. & R. ii p. 417.

49. 'There are some fine examples ... 17th Centy work.' Rephrased from M. & R. ii p. 420.

50. 'As the plans are evidently ... natural position', M. & R. ii p. 7.

old features are continued and imitated while their true purpose and
A 33  significance are / lost.

Thus the gargoyles which in the early work were used for carrying off
the water from the roof and were sometimes carved in imitation of small
cannons, are in the later work stuck on as ornaments in places where
they cannot be required.[51] (Castle Fraser & Craigievar)

The corbelling became even more fantastic than before, and is often
applied where it is not necessary.[52]

The insertion of numerous panels in the walls containing coats of arms
and inscriptions of mottos and texts of scripture are also characteristic of
late work.[53]

Among the strange revivals of old forms adopted at this time was the
re-introduction of groined vaulting instead of the plain barrel vaults
which had for centuries been almost universally employed in domestic
work.[54] The peculiarly picturesque effect of the buildings of this period
depends greatly on the large amount of corbelling employed together with
A 34  the free and / constant use of angle turrets[55]

Although pinnacles peaked roofs and angle turrets were common
everywhere about this time the latter are however a leading feature of
Scot Archi.[56]

The development of angle turrets from open bartizans is quite easily
traced in all its stages.

During the latter half of the 16th Cent the angle turret reigned sup-
reme, and gradually increased in size and importance till it reached its full
development at Castle Fraser, Earls Palace at Kirkwall &c.[57]

Amongst the other improvements in the planning of castes which took
place during this time was the enlargement of the principal staircase. In
the earlier Keeps the staircase was either a narrow flight in the thickness
of the wall or a narrow circular neuel staircase in the angle.[58] We now
find a tower provided large enough to admit a wide circular stair, another
form of stair may be seen at Newark Castle Portglasgow  this is a square
A 35  staircase / inside the building, which however only leads to the first floor
small circular stairs leading from this to the other floors. As time progressed there is a great advance towards modern arrangements and
comforts and a very marked tendency towards symmetry in the design of
the Elevation is gradually creeping in. We find many examples of this
kind. The door is placed as nearly as possible in the centre, and wings or

51. 'In contrast with this ... cannot be required.' M. & R. ii p. 7.
52. 'The corbelling ... not necessary.' M. & R. ii p. 7.
53. 'The insertion of ... late work.' M. & R. ii p. 9.
54. 'Among the strange revivals ... domestic work.' M. & R. ii p. 9.
55. 'The peculiarly picturesque ... angle turrets', M. & R. ii p. 10.
56. 'Although pinnacles ... Scot Archi.' M. & R. ii p. 10.
57. 'During the latter half ... Earls Palace at Kirkwall', M. & R. ii p. 11.
58. 'Amongst the other improvements ... in the angle.' M. & R. ii p. 17.

towers are placed so as to balance each other   But there is evidently a
difficulty experienced in reconciling the internal arrangements with the
external uniformity[59]   This period of decline although it teaches the
architect no artistic lesson directly emphazises the moral, that you should
not take a plan wholesale and try to fit on an elevation in another style
or as these old architects did they took a plan of their own and tried to
make the elevation look like the Renassence work which they had seen in
England.

A 36        In this they failed simply because they studied the two seperately, or
perhaps because they left the plan as it was and threw away all their
intellectul energy in trying to make a symmetrical elevation. This as the
result proves was the death blow to genuine S.B.A the subsequent work
of the 17th centy being a mix up between Scottish Baronial & debased
Elezibethan Italian Renaissence and since then we have had no such
thing as a national style, sometimes we have been greek, sometimes
Italian and again Gothic

It is evident from this sudden decline that as long as the S.B.A Architects were left to themselves they were all right but as soon as they saw
the contemporary english and other work they tried to imitate their work
and thus lost their individuality.[60]

It is a matter of regret that we dont find any class of buildings but
domestic in this style, whether the style can be developed beyond this or
not is a point which our forefathers left for us to decide

From some recent buildings which have been erected it is clearly
evident that this style is coming to life again and I only hope that it will
A 36 verso    not be strangled in its infancy by indiscriminating / and unsympathetic
people who copy the ancient examples without trying to make the style
conform to modern requirements.[61]

59. 'As time progressed ... external uniformity', M. & R. ii p. 18.
60. This paragraph was written on the verso of A 35.
61. The verso of A 36 is inscribed with semi-legible notes presumably made during the
discussion which followed the lecture (see p. 46, n. 9):
Cot. Rm.
Greek Arch. No pub building but for domestic buildings.
McGibbon rather sarcastic about
Asthetic reasons were any of the domestic buildings so asthetic as they were before
it it has no asthetic qualities [this line scored out].
very unkind of Mr Walton to ascribe all the artistic features to France.
[indecipherable] wall round court
unkind of Anderson not giving them any credit for
Heriot's Hospital is Elizabethan.

21. C. R. Mackintosh: Baptistry. Siena Cathedral (1891)

## PAMELA ROBERTSON

# *Mackintosh and Italy*

In 1883, a Travelling Studentship was established by the Trustees of the Alexander Thomson Memorial for prospective British architects, aged between eighteen and twenty-five, of 'approved moral character'. It was to be awarded for the 'furtherance of the study of Ancient Classic Architecture as practised prior to the commencement of the third century of the Christian era and with special reference to the principles illustrated in the works of the late Alexander Thomson'. The successful competitor received sixty pounds with which to fund a three-month sketching tour to pursue architectural study. Sketches, drawings and a manuscript memoir were to be submitted to the Thomson Trustees on completion of the tour.[1]

The first prizewinner, in 1888, was the young Glasgow architect W. J. Anderson.[2] In September 1890 the architectural press announced Charles Rennie Mackintosh winner of the second Studentship.[3] The 1890 competition brief had specified a public hall to accommodate 1000 persons, seated, with committee rooms; the design, appropriately in 'Greek' Thomson's memory, was to be in the Early Classic style, and for an isolated site. In addition each competitor was required to send in a study or studies of classic ornament or sculpture drawn from a building or cast.[4] Mackintosh's success was by no means unanimous. Five sets of drawings were submitted under mottoes in September,[5] the designers remaining anonymous until after adjudication. No decision was reached at the first meeting. A ballot at the adjourned meeting attended by eight Trustees gave Mackintosh's entry, 'Griffin', victory by one vote.[6] Even then two of the Trustees, W. F. Salmon

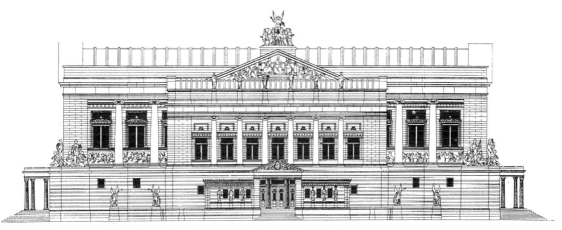

22. C. R. Mackintosh: Public Hall – elevation (1890)
Mackintosh's design combines Beaux Arts planning with appropriate Thomson Grecian details.

and Malcolm Stark, moved, unsuccessfully, that the runner-up be awarded the prize.

Mackintosh elected, as had Anderson, to beat the well-worn path to Italy. His training at Glasgow School of Art had well prepared him for such a trip. The importance of drawing and of the study of historic styles in the School's curriculum was clearly outlined in 1886 by the Chairman, Sir James Watson: 'As a Government School of Art our object is to give a thorough knowledge of drawing, designing, painting and modelling. In regard to drawing ... all our great industries, whether of shipbuilding or house-building, whether of engineering or machine-making, whether of pattern drawing or the higher art of painting, must first have their origin in drawing, and without this basis none of them can be established .... In regard to architectural and mechanical drawing I need scarcely mention their importance, the first comprising a knowledge of the various orders and classes of structures which have been erected in past ages down to the present ....'[7] At the School, Mackintosh's draughtmanship, including drawings from the cast and studies of historic ornament, won him a series of prizes. His knowledge, particularly of ancient art and architecture, apparent in the early competition designs, is clear from both the diary of the tour and the subsequent lecture manuscript. In the Uffizi, for instance, he saw 'the originals of many old and well known friends' [B 24 May]. Of ancient Rome he commented: 'It is intensely interesting to wander over those ruins and see for yourself all you have read about, & much that you have drawn to see exactly where this or that famous building ecclesiastical domestic or commercial was situated' [C 15]. These interests led him to many of the major archaeological and historical museum collections.

More recently, as an apprentice with the Glasgow practice of Honeyman & Keppie from 1889, Mackintosh would have become familiar with the Italianate designs of John Honeyman – and other Glasgow contemporaries – and the experiences of John Keppie, who had undertaken a sketching tour of Italy in 1886.

Mackintosh left Glasgow for London on 21 March, arriving in Italy, at Naples, on 5 April. A full itinerary over the next three months took him from Naples and Pompeii to Sicily, then north again to Amalfi, Rome, Tivoli, Orvieto, Siena, Florence, Pisa, Pistoia, Bologna, Ravenna, Ferrara, Venice, Padua, Vicenza, Verona, Mantua, Cremona, Brescia, Bergamo, Lecco, Lake Como, Milan and Pavia. From there he returned home via Paris, Brussels, Antwerp and London. The trip is relatively fully documented through correspondence with John Shields, Secretary of the Thomson Memorial Trust [Appendix 1], a diary [B], the memoir required by the competition [Appendix 2], and a lecture delivered in Glasgow the following year [C].[8]

The correspondence with Shields deals largely with Mackintosh's unsuccessful requests for money. The studentship regulations stipulated that the prize money was to be paid in two instalments – the first thirty pounds on departure, the second on satisfactory submission of the specified drawings

23. C. R. Mackintosh: An Antique Relief (*c.* 1886)
24. C. R. Mackintosh: Naples Museum (10 April 1891)
One of Mackintosh's first Italian sketches.

and memoir. The Trustees' refusal to provide the second instalment in advance prevented Mackintosh from extending his tour to nine months and visiting the south of France, an ambition not fulfilled until the end of his life. It also undoubtedly prompted the regular preoccupation in his diary with the cost of accommodation, fares and entry fees.

The diary, which begins with Mackintosh's arrival in Italy, contains brief notes recording virtually all of the places visited.[9] As the tour progresses, the entries become more perfunctory, until the final note announces his departure for Pavia on 7 July. Given his demanding itinerary and the sketching commitment of the Studentship, extensive descriptions in the diary were not a priority; nor indeed, as the scarcity of his writings in general attests, were they Mackintosh's natural inclination. Ancient Rome is described as a 'very interesting place' [B 20 April]. The breathtaking cascades at Tivoli are 'very nice' [B 30 April]. Occasionally however an architectural experience prompts a more fulsome description. Siena Cathedral, visited on 11 May, provoked five pages of voluble criticism. Although this is the most personal of the surviving manuscripts, it provides less insight than might be hoped into Mackintosh's professional or private life at this formative period. It is marked however by a refreshing lack of pomposity, an engaging humour, and Mackintosh's all-consuming enthusiasm for architecture.

The diary notes provided the basis for his lecture, 'A Tour in Italy', given on 6 September 1892 to the Glasgow Architectural Association and on 28 November of that year to the Architectural Section of the Philosophical

Society of Glasgow.[10] Subsequent reviews commented that 'the principal buildings' were 'noted and criticised in a very racy manner. The paper was illustrated by a large collection of admirable pencil and watercolour sketches and some good photographs.'[11] Despite his competence and his professional audience, Mackintosh had at the outset of the paper rejected a scholarly or technical analysis of Italian architecture in favour of 'a frank & spontaneous expression of the impression left on my mind after seeing each place' [c 2a], which certainly made easier work for him and his audience. The reviewer's comment suggests that a lively delivery enhanced the academic irreverence of some of Mackintosh's comments and the note of irony which occasionally tempers the effusions of the text. It was undoubtedly an entertaining performance. The lecture follows the chronology of the diary, making what Mackintosh described in his preamble as a 'judicious selection'. However the only major deletion was of the majority of the sites he visited in Rome, to allow for expanded accounts of 'Ancient Rome', Florence, Venice, Padua, Vicenza and Pavia. In the lecture manuscript his spelling is more accurate, and his style more polished, verging at times – as when he describes Florence or Padua, or particularly Venice – on a Ruskinian effusiveness.

Little revision is made to his original assessments though his comments on work in the south are adjusted with the benefit of his wider experience. Hence the sixteenth century tombs in S. Anna dei Lombardi and S. Domenico Maggiore, Naples, which impressed him initially as 'particularly good' [B 10 April], in Glasgow were described as being 'the best in Naples' but they 'do not come up to those in Florence and Venice so we will not drag them from their sweet oblivion' [c 5]. Similarly the seventeenth century Royal Palace, also in Naples, which was somewhat tentatively described in the diary as 'very grand and handsome but cant be put down as the best work' [B 12 April], met with harsher criticism in the lecture: 'as wild an exhibition of extravigant vulgarity as I ever wish to see' [c 6]. On a few occasions, his estimation is revised upwards. Most conspicuously the interior of Florence Cathedral with which he was 'disappointed' is subsequently poetically and extensively described in a passage whose polished style suggests it might have been borrowed to cover a conspicuous gap in his account.[12]

Regrettably neither the diary nor the lecture gives details of Mackintosh's return trip through northern Europe, which is recorded only in a few pencil jottings at the end of the surviving sketchbook.

The primary aim of the studentship was to enable study through drawing. Sadly only one sketchbook and a group of some thirty watercolours and as many drawings survive.[13] The sketchbook, containing seventy-six pages of Italian illustrations covers one third of the trip, i.e. the last month of the tour from Verona to Pavia. Obviously a substantial amount of material, comprising the majority of work from Pompeii to Padua, has been lost.

The sketchbook illustrations and the surviving drawings are 'notes' or 'jottings' – Mackintosh's terms for a visual shorthand executed in the time-

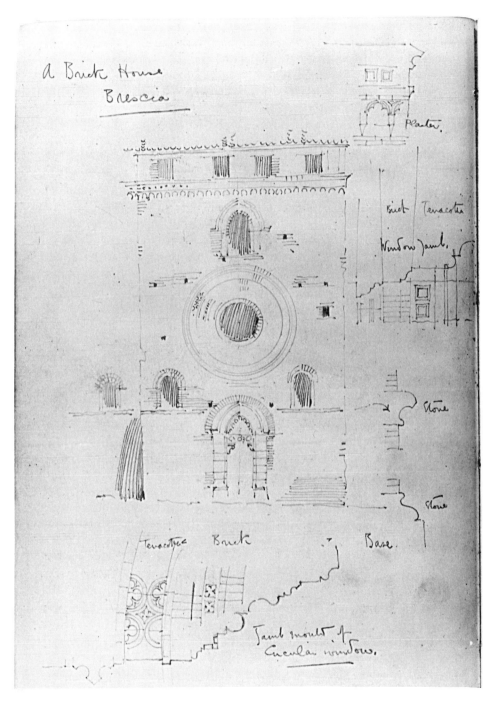

25. C. R. Mackintosh: A Brick House, Brescia (16 June 1891)
Mackintosh made several studies of vernacular Italian architecture, and
regularly recorded the use of brick, a material contrasting with Glasgow's native
sandstone.

saving medium of pencil. Details, rather than the main fabric often already familiar to him, tend to be swiftly but accurately recorded. The sketches are frequently annotated with details of medium and colour. While it is difficult to generalise on the basis of partial evidence, clearly the major monuments predominated, though more modest architecture such as brick houses in Cremona and Brescia also attracted him. This latter was an interest shared by other youthful contemporaries. Hoffman, for instance, on his Prix de Rome tour of 1895, was more struck with the simple vernacular of the Italian countryside than with the monuments of antiquity. In what he saw as its straightforward response to local needs and use of local materials, Mackintosh found confirmation of his developing vision of a valid modern architecture. Vernacular subject matter became the major preoccupation of his subsequent architectural sketching trips. Surprisingly, given his lifelong interest in the forms of nature, no drawings of plants or trees are known.

The watercolours comprise both pencil studies finished with wash and formal watercolour compositions. The latter category is uncommon in Mackintosh's oeuvre for it was only when released from professional demands for an extended period, either in Italy, or subsequently in Walberswick, or, at last, the south of France, that he had the opportunity to concentrate on landscape and architectural subjects. Though the majority of the studies were in pencil, his paints were a valued companion. The diary records his panic at the temporary loss of his colour box early in the tour: 'Got an awful fright. Fancy being with out colors. To dreadful to contemplate.' [B 23 April]

Together, these documents provide a valuable commentary on the tour. It was not a trouble-free trip: the early weeks in Naples, Pompeii and Sicily were marred by cold and rain, rough boat journeys, and inquisitive crowds distracting him as he sketched. Mackintosh was irritated by the erratic opening hours, had little patience with the Italians, and was appalled at the squalor he saw. Ancient Rome bore 'a very striking resemblance to some parts of the east end of Glasgow assuming about two thirds of the population to be dead of colera. It is as grimy, as filthy, as tumblesome as forlorn, and is as unpleasantly rendolent of old clothes, and old women who were washerwomen once upon a time, but who have long since fornsworn soap' [C 14]. These irritations however did not impede his energetic schedule which usually began at dawn and often took in several churches, architectural sites and museums in one day. Apart from the companionship of two fellow travellers, Paxton and Dods, from Siena to Verona, he travelled alone.

For the architecture of the ancient world, the prescribed area of study for Thomson scholars, Mackintosh displays a dutiful rather than enthusiastic interest. Of his two weeks in Rome, he devoted only four days to the study of the city's major ruins. In the lecture, after his irreverent comparison with Glasgow's slums, he flatters his audience into accepting his omission of any comment on the monuments, with the exception of the Pantheon: 'The

26. C. R. Mackintosh: Mosaics, S. Apollinare Nuovo, Ravenna (1891)

various ruins you are all familiar with ... so I will not detain you by describing the various Triumphal arches ... the well known temples', etc. etc. [c 15].

Mackintosh's preference, shared with Ruskin, was for Byzantine, Norman, Romanesque, Gothic and Early Renaissance architecture. The impact of these buildings on the Presbyterian Scot, nurtured on monochrome casts and prints, was considerable. Throughout the tour he was overwhelmed by

27. C. R. Mackintosh: Orvieto Cathedral (1891)
'Most beautiful cathedral especially the front. Built of white marble with bands of red, purble blue black brown yellow marble'. [B 5 May]

the sumptuousness of the ornament, in particular the mosaic decoration. At the twelfth century Capella Palatina of Palermo's Royal Palace, a jewel of Norman-Saracenic art, he was 'simply struck dumb with astonishment Here was something I have never seen, never even dreamt of. The interior is one mass of mosaics on a gold ground ...' [C 9]. As for the mosaics of

Monreale's twelfth century S. Maria la Nuova: 'golly what an interior. Fairly took away my breath' [B 14 April]. The Byzantine churches of Ravenna were 'like an osias in a desert' [C 28]. The most breathtaking however was St Mark's in Venice: 'This golden alcove of glory this inexhaustable treasure chamber, this stupendeous shrine glittering and trembling in its abundance of radiance fills you with unspeakable awe and veneration.' [C 44].

The young architect also responded to the effects achieved through the manipulation of colour and light. The façades of Orvieto Cathedral, the Duomo in Florence, and the Certosa di Pavia are noted for the polychromy of the marble. His sketches regularly record the colours of materials used. Mackintosh was particularly susceptible to the dramatic and atmospheric potential of light. Of Palladio's Basilica in Vicenza, for instance, he marvelled: 'The roof, one vast vault of timber casts a solemn gloom, which is not diminished by the wan light admitted through windows of pale blue glass. The size & shape of this colossal chamber, the arching of the roof, with enormous rafters stretching across it, and above all the watery gleams that glanced through the casement, possessed my fancy with ideas of Noah's Ark and almost persuaded me, I beheld that extraordinary vessel.' [C 48]. St Mark's, 'the most gorgeous but about the darkest church in Europe is glorified by the sun ....' [C 42].

Mackintosh was equally appreciative of individual details: well-heads, choir stalls, textiles, old manuscripts, admiring both their craftsmanship and the inventiveness of their conception. In Monreale Convent he marvelled that the one hundred and twelve capitals were nearly all different. The floor of Siena Cathedral, the relief panels in S. Antonio, Padua, and the windows at the Certosa di Pavia all impressed with their workmanship. Repeatedly he admired the Italian Renaissance woodworkers' skills – in the Certosa S. Martino, Naples, the Sistine Chapel, S. Zeno Maggiore, Verona, S. Maria Maggiore, Bergamo and the Certosa di Pavia. He betrays an unexpected sensitivity, given his later furniture designs, to the inherent character of wood when in Siena Cathedral he remarks of the stalls that 'They are undoubtedly good but like most Italian wood work they are very stony. Not designed like wood but stone' [B 11 May].

Occasionally early indications of his mature architectural designs surface. Of the Renaissance palaces in Florence he noted: 'The beautiful simplicity, the large masses of plain masonry & small windows, surmounted by tremendeous cornices beautifully designed, gives these palaces a simple but dignified grandeur' [C 26-7]. Siena Campanile, banded in black and white, is 'square & plain but very nice, not fussy & excited' [B 11 May]. The Pantheon in Rome impressed with 'the dignity with which it has been designed, the perfection with which it has been constructed, and the effectiveness of the mode of lighting' [C 15-16]. The massing and grouping of the palaces in Venice, the monuments of the Piazza S. Marco and the central monuments of Pisa were all admired.

29. C. R. Mackintosh: Wood Stalls, Certosa di Pavia (July 1891)

28 (*opposite*). C. R. Mackintosh: Cloisters, S. Maria la Nuova, Monreale (1891)
'Some most beautifully carved caps. There are some 112 all round and they are
all or nearly all different. Some of them wonderfully good'. [B 14 April]

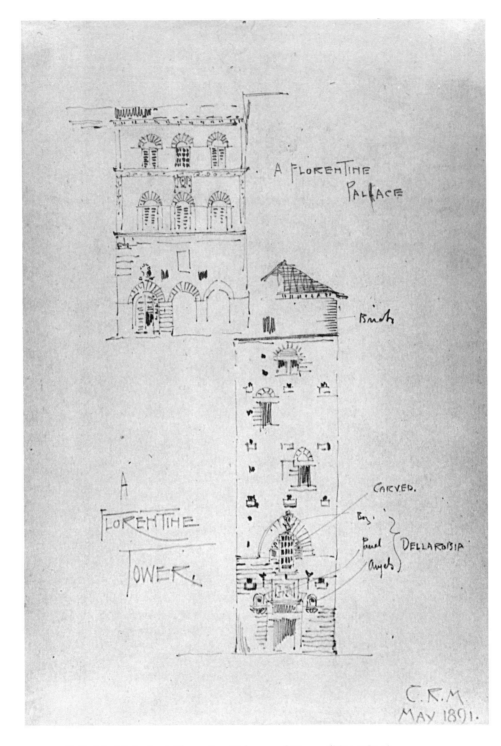

30. C. R. Mackintosh: A Florentine Palace and Tower (May 1891)

Mackintosh could be equally vehement in his condemnation, disliking the over-elaborate and ill-defined. Bergamo's Colleoni Chapel was 'renassince overloaded' [B 17 June]; the exterior of Milan's late Gothic Cathedral was 'certainly overdone being literally choked with carving & statuettes' [C 50]; S. Antonio in Padua appeared a 'confused pile of turrets and domes' [C 46]. Above all he decried fraud – of materials and technique, and of expectation between exterior and interior. Siena Cathedral, which is given the most detailed examination, fails on all counts with for instance its false windows

31. Siena Cathedral exterior

painted on the walls, and its façade 'one of those frauds so often seen in Italy, having evidently been considered quite independent & apart from the rest of the church' [c 17]. This recalls G. E. Street's earlier exasperation in Pavia: 'I begin really to wonder whether I shall see a west front before I leave Italy which is not a purely unnecessary and unprepossessing sham.'[14] Mackintosh may have been familiar with Street's published account of his 1853 Italian tour, a valuable guide for the architectural pilgrim with little time or money.

Mackintosh tended to have little sympathy with the restoration and renovation work he saw. The modern work at St Mark's was 'abominable' [B 2 June]; at Milan Cathedral, the parapet tower was 'all restoration very much inferior to old work' [B 28 June]; the old cathedral, Brescia, was 'not so bad but being frightfully restored' [B 16 June]. Mackintosh undoubtedly favoured a policy of judicious 'laissez-faire', a point of view published a few years later in *The British Architect*,[15] and anticipated in his comments on Rome: 'That the temples and palaces of the Forum & the Capitol should be delapidated & decrepit is in the nature of things ... The classical ruins are ruins and behave as such.' [c 14-15]. At the same time he could denounce unjustifiable neglect. Of Monreale he lamented 'there this beautiful work stands – unheeded and uncared for' [c 10].

With few exceptions, architecture later than the mid sixteenth century stirred little enthusiasm. Even within his preferred periods, there are notable exclusions: the elegant humanist architecture of Alberti in Florence and Mantua receives no comment, while Brunelleschi is mentioned only once, briefly, in the lecture. Mannerist architecture evoked no favourable response: Michelangelo's Porta Pia is dismissed as 'not much to look at' [B 24 April]; Giulio Romano's work is ignored in Mantua. Generally the grand effects of the Baroque did not impress. Maderno's majestic exterior for St Peter's, Rome, was, in line with much contemporary criticism, disparagingly treated: 'very very poor front' [B 21 April]. Bernini and Borromini are not mentioned. He saw no redeeming features in the neo-classical and the only contemporary work he admired was the recently-completed iron and glass arcades of the Galleria Umberto I in Naples (1887-90).

In much of what he looked at, particularly in north Italy, and in much of how he responded, Mackintosh was instinctively echoing Ruskinian teaching with its emphases on colour, light, texture, nature, craftsmanship and honesty. But Mackintosh's stylistic preferences were less dogmatic. Ruskin could not admire Palladio and Sansovino whose work unleashed 'a flood of folly and hypocrisy',[16] yet Mackintosh admired both, undoubtedly for the sheer academic brilliance with which they reinterpreted the principles and motifs of classical art and architecture. The Certosa di Pavia, which struck Mackintosh as 'most tastefully decorated' [c 52], for Ruskin presented 'meaningless ornamentation'.[17] S. Maria dei Miracoli, Venice, the 'most exquisite renaissance church' [B 4 June], was for Ruskin more 'a small museum of unmeaning, though refined sculpture, than a piece of architec-

32. C. R. Mackintosh: Blind Window, Certosa di Pavia (1891)

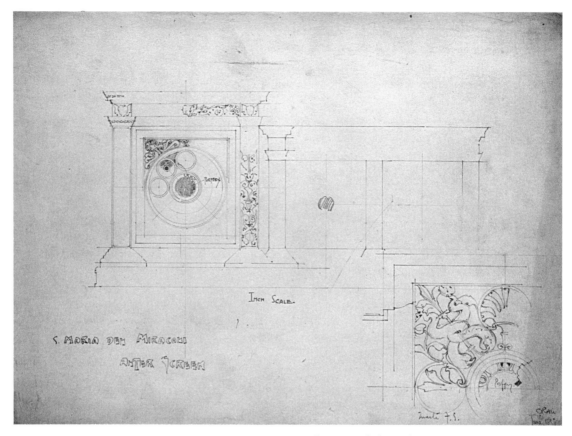

33. C. R. Mackintosh: Altar Screen, S. Maria dei Miracoli (1891)

ture'.[18] Occasionally Mackintosh could acknowledge the achievements of
the Baroque in Longhena's Salute in Venice or more particularly the late
classical Baroque of Fuga's façade for S. Maria Maggiore and Galilei's S.
Giovanni in Laterano, both in Rome. In the lecture, Mackintosh is in fact
careful to distance himself from a Ruskinian stance, avoiding the inclination
of those 'who's sympathies were touched by the beauties of the Italian
Gothic' to 'devote the paper entirely to its praises & exaltation' [c 1]. He
conspicuously passes no comment at all on the architecture of what for
Ruskin was 'the central building of the world',[19] the Ducal Palace, Venice.
Indeed Mackintosh exercises what with hindsight would seem uncharacter-
istic restraint, and, with one possible exception, refrains from making any
quotation from Ruskin's published work.[20]

In the other arts Mackintosh showed enthusiasm for sculpture both as
fine art and architectural ornament, seeking out the major collections of
antique art and admiring in particular the work of Michelangelo, Sansovino, Della Robbia and Donatello. While his competition designs show him
adept at embellishing his schemes with figurative sculpture, he rarely used

such ornament in his executed work, in contrast to the robust decoration favoured by many of his Glasgow contemporaries, notably J. J. Burnet. The major exception is the west façade of Glasgow School of Art which was to have included three large figure sculptures – interestingly all of Italians: Cellini, St Francis and Palladio. In painting his taste was equally narrow. He admired Michelangelo, Raphael and the Venetian School – particulary Tintoretto and Titian. In this he again reveals his early sympathy with Ruskin, though he ignores the work of the early masters, notably Giotto.

34. C. R. Mackintosh: Chimney Piece, Doge's Palace, Venice (June 1891)

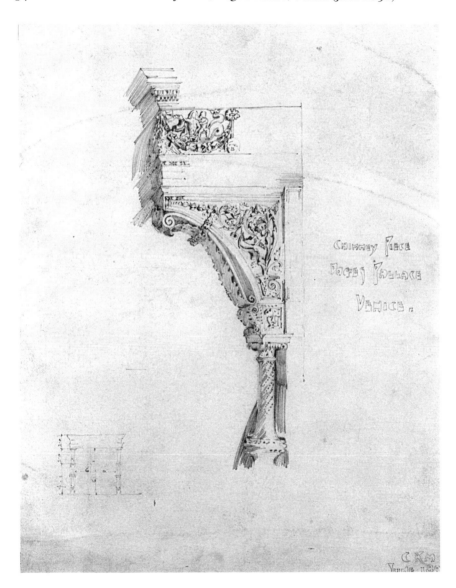

On his return, Mackintosh quickly put his newly-acquired knowledge to use. Despite his protestations in 'Scotch Baronial Architecture' against 'debased or simply wholesale importations of styles from other countries, such as Roman & Greek' [A 9], Mackintosh was prepared to tailor his designs to suit the requirements of competitions, or their juries. Prior to his departure, he had produced a limited portfolio of unexecuted architectural projects in varying styles including a Presbyterian Church with 'a Renaissance doorway and the whole somewhat American in style',[21] and a French Renaissance Museum of Art and Science. His first major project after his return from Italy was a scheme for a Chapter House for the 1892 Soane Medallion. No style was prescribed. Mackintosh not surprisingly, and with an eye to Aston Webb, one of the assessors, opted for Early Renaissance. Many of the

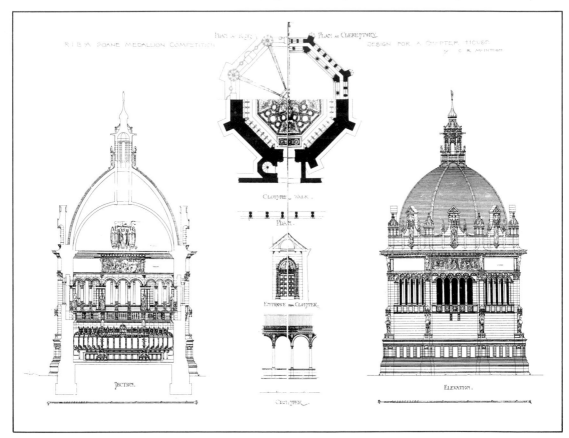

35. C. R. Mackintosh: Chapter House – section and elevation (1891)

major features of the scheme derived from Italian examples, notably its octagonal plan from S. Vitale, Ravenna, and S. Lorenzo, Milan; the dome from Florence Cathedral; wood stalls from S. Zeno Maggiore, Verona; and the candelabra from Annibale Fontana's work at the Certosa di Pavia. The

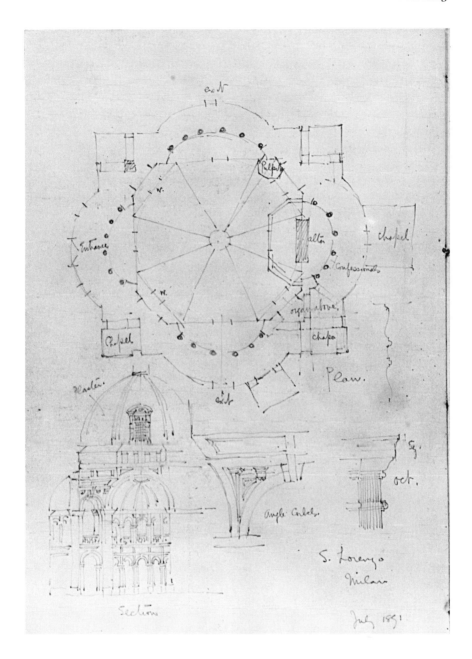

36. C. R. Mackintosh: S. Lorenzo, Milan (July 1891)
The octagonal plan was used in Mackintosh's design for a Chapter House.

scheme was richly embellished with figure sculpture, mosaic and fresco. Though unsuccessful in the Soane, the project won a gold medal at South Kensington later that year.[22] *The Building News* noted: 'The drawings treated exhibit considerable skill and taste, and the details are commendable.'[23] *The*

*British Architect* was also complimentary, describing it as 'a design showing considerable artistic powers with details well drawn', though the copying of the Pavia candlestick was picked up.[24] The sketchbooks were used again, though never as liberally, in the formative designs leading up to the Art School competition.[25] Classical details reappear only once thereafter in the playfully-conceived doorway of the Lady Artists' Club, Glasgow (1908).

The influence of Italy also appears occasionally in Mackintosh's interior designs. An arched doorway at S. Maria delle Grazie, Milan, inspired the 1893 hall at the Glasgow Art Club. Mackintosh's consistent admiration for Italian woodwork undoubtedly underlies the interior detailing at Craigie Hall, Glasgow, and his church interiors at Glasgow's Queen's Cross, Gourock and Bridge of Allan, with their extensive wood panelling. Classical motifs reappear for the last time in Mackintosh's interiors in the Art School Boardroom of 1906 with his fanciful adaptation of Ionic pilasters. The decoration of each, like the capitals at Monreale, is unique. Other features of this second phase of the Art School – the brick loggia and first floor corridor seating – must derive in part from Italian exemplars. Italian motifs are also used briefly in his graphic designs. Michelangelo's Delphic and Erythraean sibyls from the Sistine Ceiling, that 'most marvellous decoration' [B 2 May], appear in his 1892 Art School Club invitation card – and again on the façade of T. & R. Annan's Glasgow showroom (1906).

The drawings and watercolours themselves were put to good use over the following years. In October 1891 a selection was displayed at the Glasgow School of Art Club Annual Exhibition. *The Glasgow Herald* recorded 'A set of architectural sketches of Rome and Venice by Mr Charles McIntosh were an interesting feature of the exhibition.'[26] The 'Glasgow Boy' painter James Guthrie was reputedly so impressed with the work that he exclaimed to Fra Newbery, Director of the School, 'But hang it, Newbery, the man ought to be an artist.'[27] Two Venetian watercolours – *Palazzo Ca d' Oro* and *Venetian Palace* – were exhibited at the Glasgow Institute in 1892 and two of the Certosa di Pavia, *Central Doorway* and *Portion of Front*, at the Institute the following year.[28] Two drawings of fonts from Siena Cathedral were published in 1894 in the *Glasgow Architectural Association Sketchbook*.[29] A selection of drawings was also, unsuccessfully but to critical commendation, submitted for the Pugin Studentship in 1892. *The British Architect* commented: 'The pencil work of Mr Charles R McIntosh is broad and dignified in manner, both the selection of subjects and method of execution being good. The colour examples are daintly done.'[30] Aston Webb, Honorary Secretary of the R.I.B.A., judged Mackintosh's pencil drawings of Italian Renaissance work 'particularly admirable.... The coloured sketches of the Certosa of Pavia are also very delicate and full of feeling.'[31]

The student tour was the first in a series of contacts with Italy which continued over the next thirty years. In 1899 together with other Scottish designers and artists including Margaret and Frances Macdonald and Herbert MacNair, Mackintosh exhibited at the Venice Biennale.[32] Three years

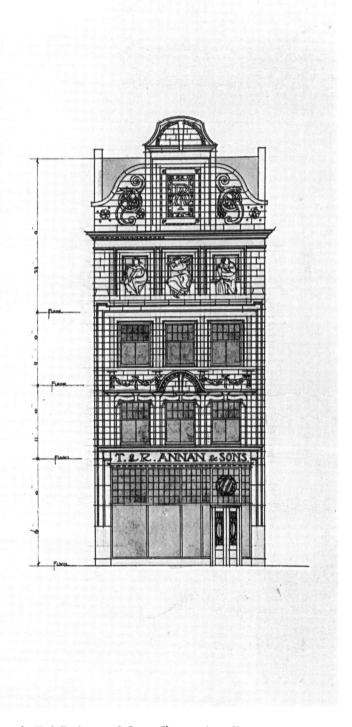

37. C. R. Mackintosh: T. & R. Annan & Sons, Glasgow (1906)

later to great critical acclaim he presented a major room setting, 'The Rose Boudoir', at Turin's International Exhibition of Modern Decorative Art.[33] Mackintosh attended the exhibition with Fra Newbery, but no record of this second trip survives. From Turin he may have travelled elsewhere in Italy. A postscript in a letter of 28 December 1925 to Newbery, intimating yet a further visit to Italy, records: 'I found Florence just as artificial in a stupid way as I did 25 years ago when I went as a small lad'[34] – a marked adjustment to his first impressions in 1891.

Mackintosh's contact with Italy in 1891 was of value in a number of significant ways. The Studentship constituted the twenty-two year old architect's first major professional success, widely reported in the architectural press. It provided his first experience of travel abroad and the opportunity, unique in his career, for extended and intensive study of architecture: this enabled him, fresh from his impassioned study of Scottish Baronial Architecture, to observe the evolution of another national architecture under different social, economic and environmental requirements. These observations provided valuable comparative material in his subsequent discussions of the nature of true architecture. From the tour he brought back a reference library of architectural sketches, and a portfolio of drawings and watercolours with which to develop his reputation as an artist. His contact with Italian art and architecture provided both aesthetic and critical stimulation at a formative period in his career, the impact of which is recorded both in his diary and the lecture manuscript.

NOTES

1. A full account of the establishment of the Studentship is given in the Alexander Thomson Memorial Minute Book (Coll. Glasgow Institute of Architects).

2. William James Anderson (1863/4-1900), an enthusiastic scholar of Italian art and architecture, published *Architectural Studies in Italy* (1890) and *The Architecture of the Renaissance in Italy* (1896). In 1894 as the newly-appointed Director of Architecture at the G.S.A. he initiated a lecture course on the Italian Renaissance. Anderson may have been responsible as President for Mackintosh's invitation to lecture on his Italian tour to the Glasgow Architectural Association: he had chaired Mackintosh's lecture on 'Scotch Baronial Architecture' [A] in 1891.

3. *Architect* 40 (1890) p. 183; *British Architect* 34 (1890) p. 223; *Building News* 59 (1890) p. 451; *Builder* 59 (1890) p. 253; *Building Industries* 1 (1890) p. 123.

4. None of Mackintosh's competition drawings, which became the property of the Trustees, survives. The Public Hall scheme was illustrated in *The British Architect* 34 (1890) pp. 386-7, 406-7; the designs were exhibited at Glasgow's Corporation Galleries from 4-20 September 1890, and the following year won a Silver Medal at South Kensington.

5. The entrants were Mackintosh; Ambrose Macdonald Poynter, London; Robert James Gildard, Glasgow; George Smith Hill, Glasgow; and John Daniel Swanston, Dollar. The Trustees comprised the President and Council of the Glasgow Institute of Architects, John Mossman, sculptor, Robert Blackie, publisher, and John Shields, the Secretary. See Minute Book (n. 1).

6. The Trustees present were John Gordon, James Chalmers, Alexander Petrie, William

Forrest Salmon, Alexander Skirving, Malcolm Stark, T. L. Watson and John Shields. The voting was as follows: Mackintosh 4, Poynter 3, Gildard 1. See Minute Book (n. 1).

The stringent conditions outlined in the Minute Book specified: 'The drawings are to consist of one or more plans, two elevations, two sections and a perspective drawing. The plan, elevations and sections to be drawn to a scale of $\frac{1}{2}$ inches to 10 feet, and to be outlined in ink, the sectional parts only being coloured, and the windows or other openings in elevations tinted in sepia or ink. The perspective drawing is to be finished in China ink, either with the pen or the brush. At least one sheet of details is required, which is to be drawn to a scale of 2 inches to a foot, and it may be finished in any manner in the option of the Competitor. Details showing carving or sculpture are desirable. The system of heating and ventilating might be illustrated.

Besides the foregoing drawings, each Competitor is required to send in a study or studies of classic ornament or sculpture, drawn from a building, or from a cast. These drawings are to be one-half real size, if the after mentioned size of paper permits of that scale, otherwise they are to be one-fourth real size, and, in either case, they may be finished in any manner in the option of the Competitor.

The drawings to be on sheets of paper 40 inches by 27 inches, and not less than eight sheets, or more than ten, are to be sent in.'

7. The proceedings of the A.G.M. held on 11 Jan. 1886 are recorded in the Annual Report for 1884-5.

8. The Thomson Memorial Archive (Coll. G.I.A.) contains: a statement dated 30 Aug. 1890 signed by Mackintosh certifying authorship of his competition drawings; Mackintosh's correspondence with John Shields and two receipts for the prize money [Appendix 1]; and Mackintosh's 7-page manuscript memoir [Appendix 2]. This material is on long-term deposit at the Hunterian Art Gallery.

9. The following are mentioned in the lecture but not in the diary: Palazzi Strozzi and Riccardi, Florence; S. Giorgio Maggiore, Venice; Il Salone and S. Justiana, Padua; Teatro Olimpico, Vicenza; the Brera Gallery, Milan; and details of Mackintosh's visit to Pavia. The correspondence with Shields reveals that Mackintosh visited Amalfi [Appendix 1, 14 June] and may have visited Genoa after Pavia [Appendix 1, 27 June].

10. The G.A.A. lecture was originally scheduled for 5 January 1892: *British Architect* 36 (1891) p. 100.

11. *Building News* 63 (1892) p. 351. 20 illustrations are referred to in the text, though Mackintosh's supporting material undoubtedly included more than this. Virtually identical accounts appeared in *The Glasgow Herald* 8 Sept. 1892, p. 6; *The Architect* 48 (1892) p. 172; *The British Architect* 38 (1892) p. 198; *The Builder* 63 (1892) p. 212. Mackintosh records buying photographs in Florence [B 25 May].

12. His source was not Ruskin for whom the interior had 'nothing whatever in it worth looking at': *Mornings in Florence*, iv § 69.

13. Sketchbook (Coll. G.S.A.). Annotations to the diary text [B] record the location of the surviving drawings and watercolours. Thomas Howarth, *C. R. Mackintosh and the Modern Movement* (2nd edn, London 1977) p. 11 lists a portfolio in the collection of the Royal Technical College, Glasgow, now Strathclyde University. No record of this exists.

14. G. E. Street, *Brick and Marble Architecture of the Middle Ages: Notes of a Tour in the North of Italy* (2nd edn, London 1874) p. 209.

15. *The British Architect* 46 (1895) pp. 326-7 gives Mackintosh's contribution to an ongoing discussion on the restoration of churches in Wareham, Dorset. The acceptance of conservative repair and alteration instead of restoration was a major objective of the Society for the Protection of Ancient Buildings, established 1877. Mackintosh's employer, John Honeyman, a keen mediaevalist, archaeologist and experienced restorer, had been a member from 1877-88.

16. John Ruskin, *The Stones of Venice*, i ch. 1, § 37.

17. Ruskin (n. 16) i ch. 1, § 35.

18. Ruskin (n. 16) iii Venetian Index s.v. 'Miracoli'.

19. Ruskin (n. 16) i ch. 1, § 34.

20. Mackintosh's description of Florence [c 20] possibly quotes from Ruskin. Alexander Thomson himself had had scant regard for Ruskin's writings: 'I know of no one who has done more to mislead the public mind in matters of Art than he.' *Art and Architecture* (1874) lecture 1, p. 6.

21. *Building News* 57 (1889) p. 135.

22. None of Mackintosh's drawings survives. The project is illustrated in *The British Architect* 37 (1892) pp. 180-1; a good survey of the Soane Medallion entries with comments by Aston Webb is given in *The Builder* 62 (1892) p. 82.

23. *Building News* 63 (1892) p. 131.

24. *British Architect* 38 (1892) p. 74.

25. For a useful discussion of Italian sources in Mackintosh's architectural designs see Maria Cristina Finucci, 'Il Viaggio in Italia di Charles Rennie Mackintosh', *Critica d'Arte* 51 (1986) pp. 55-64.

26. Howarth (n. 13) p. 11 notes that Mackintosh 'sent home a selection of these [Italian] drawings for inclusion in the Annual Exhibition of the School of Art Students' Club'. The Club exhibition was in fact held after Mackintosh's return at the end of October: *Glasgow Herald* 31 Oct. 1891, p. 6; 2 Nov. p. 6.

27. Cited by R. Eddington Smith, secretary of the Glasgow School of Art Club in a letter to *The Glasgow Evening Times* 17 Feb. 1933, p. 6.

28. *Palazzo Ca d'Oro* (778), *Venetian Palace* (796); *Central Doorway, Certosa di Pavia* (799), *Certosa di Pavia, Portion of Front* (800). None of these works survives.

29. *G.A.A. Sketchbooks* 4 (1894) pl. 121.

30. *British Architect* 37 (1892) p. 59.

31. *Builder* 62 (1892) p. 81.

32. Hugh Honour, 'Biennales of other days: a cautionary tale', *Apollo* 84 (1966) p. 28.

33. The exhibition was well covered in the Italian press. A good account of the Scottish section was published in *Arte Italiana Decorativa e Industriale* 11 (August 1902) pp. 61-8.

34. Coll. National Library of Scotland.

CHARLES RENNIE MACKINTOSH

## B. *Diary of a Tour in Italy* (1891)

B 5 April    Sunday April 5th 1891.

Arrived at Naples after having breakfast on board said good bye to all my friends on board the good ship Cuzco, got on the Tender along with Mr Mrs & Miss Swords.

Arrived on shore had to pass through the custom house where all my tobacco was seized. Wanted 10 francs duty which was more than I paid for it originally so I came away and left it. Drove to Hotel du Visuve arranged about a room, had a wash up & shave then started to see a bit of the town. Had not gone far when I met the fellows from the Cuzco going to Pompeii got on car and started with them. Got the train at 2.5 arrived at Torre Annunziata, drove to pompei which takes about 20 minuts. Entrance to pompeii free on Sunday. 2F other days.

Went to Museum first models of people very interesting, wine jars &c very nice /

Train from Torre Annunziata at 6.14 to Naples raining slightly when we arrived took cabs to grand arcade, most magnificent building, really good architecture.[1] From the arcade we went to an Italian resturant where we had dinner. We tried Maccaroni but could'nt manage to turn it round the fork in the most magnificent manner of the Italians after dinner we went to the fruit market where some of the boys bought oranges to take on board. Went down to the quay with the Cuzcoits and saw them off about 9 oclock. Went back to the Hotel had a smoke and went to bed about 10.30.

B 6 April    Monday. 6th April 1891.

Rose about 7.30 had breakfast in Hotel (bread butter & coffee) then took a walk to the public gardens which are very fine. Took car to Bank /[2] where I drew £10 got some tips about the town, next went to British Consul got permission to sketch in Museum, Pompiei, &c. Then started for Museum. Splendid collection of frescoes sculpture &c started to sketch but was turned out at four oclock.[3] Had dinner in hotel then went to Opera San Carlo with the Swords.[4] got home about 1 oclock & went to bed immediately

The footnotes provide brief information to identify sites visited and list documented sketches. 'Howarth' refers to Italian sketches in the collection of Dr Thomas Howarth; 'G.S.A.' to the other principal source, the one surviving sketchbook owned by Glasgow School of Art. Cross-references to the diary are provided in the notes to the lecture text [c].

   1. Recently-completed iron and glass arcades of Galleria Umberto I, 1887-90.
   2. Inscribed at top of page: 'British Consul at Naples Monte di Dio No 4'.
   3. 1 sketch of Egyptian pottery (Howarth).
   4. Teatro S. Carlo 1737, by G. Antonio, the largest opera house in Italy.

B 7 April     Tuesday 7th April 1891.

Rose at 7.30 had breakfast then started for pompei   arrived about 11 oclock did some sketching in museum   had some lunch went to Temple of Mercury started sketching.[5] Met Mr Nicoll of New York a young artist who has been in Italy for some months studying Art. Got train back at 6. stayed in the rest of the evening writing letters. /

B 8 April     Wednesday 8th April 1891.

Rose at seven oclock had breakfast at 8. Went to Posta Regia but got no letters  from Posta went to Piazza Trinità Maggiore where there is a very large & fairly good monument built of white marble with bronze figure of the Virgin at the top date 1748.[6] In this piazza is the church of Trinità Maggiore  not much outside but really magnificent inside  the decoration surpassed anything I had seen before.[7] Took a rough sketch of Doorway.[8]

Next went to the church of Santa Chiara[9] but found it shut  nothing to see in the exterior. Went round a lot more churches then came to the Duomo.[10] Front undergoing restoration & covered with scaffolding  wasnt particularly struck with inside  Next went to Porta Capuana about the best bit of work I have seen in Naples.[11] From there went to the church of S. Maria del Carmine  very good tower of which I took a sketch.[12] Inside of church very nice. Went home & wrote letters &c.

B 9 April     Thursday. 9th April 1891.

Rose at quarter to seven breakfast at 7.30 started for pompei  took a sketch of Porta Capuana while waiting for train, got train at 10.27.

Was going to do some water color but sun went down so had to be content with pencil.[13] Was more in the mood than I have been since I arrived. Saw Mr Nicholl. Got train back at 6.27 from pompei.

B 10 April    Friday 10 April 1891

Got up at 6.30 & found it raining very heavily. went back to bed till 7.30. breakfast at 8. Wrote letters to Herbert McNair & Geo. Murry[14] which took me till 9.30  started for / museum. Did some sketching and

5. 2 sheets of studies of architectural fragments and vases (Howarth).

6. Guglia dell' Immacolata, unusual baroque marble column 1747-50.

7. Trinità Maggiore 1584-1601, with embossed stone façade, a survival from a 15th C. palazzo. Interior 1603-31 enriched with coloured marbles and frescoes by Corenzio, Stanzione and Ribera.

8. 1 watercolour (Howarth).

9. S. Chiara 1310-28, by G. Primario.

10. Duomo originally 13th to 14th C., remodelled 1877-1905 by E. Alvino.

11. Porta Capuana, exterior decoration by G. da Maiano (1432-90).

12. S. Maria del Carmine rebuilt at end of 13th C.; interior decorated with polychrome marble. Campanile begun 15th C., completed 1631.

13. 2 sketches, of a table leg and an unidentified monument (Howarth).

14. J. Herbert MacNair (1868-1955), in 1891 Mackintosh's fellow apprentice at Honeyman & Keppie. George Murry may have been another apprentice.

measureing.[15] was turned out at 4 oclock  went to some churches. The tombs in S. Anna dei Lombardi and S. Domenico Maggiore particularly good.[16] Some churches are open from 10 till 12 & some from 3 till 5  find it a great nuisance going to a church & finding it shut.

Still raining so went back to Hotel and laid down measurements taken at museum.

B 11 April  Saturday 11th April 1891

Rose at 6.30 intending to go to Paestum but found it still raining so reluctantly posponed my departure. Spent forenoon in Museum. Cleared up about 12 oclock  went to Certosa S. Martino.[17] One of the most interesting places in Naples.

Very fine wood panelling in Conversation Hall and Chapter House. Splendid frescoes / in Choir of church  splendid wooden stalls in Choir and Sacristy.

The inlay work of the latter is the finest I have ever seen. Most beautiful design and workmanship, Wood work in Choir of the lay brethern is very good.

All these rooms are very richly decorated with frescoes, and together form a very interesting sight. Very beautiful baluster round high alter in church. Very nice well in Cloister[18]

View from Belvedere really magnificent  Can see the whole of naples from one end to the other. Most beautiful sight seen from this point

Very fine collection of glass & porcelain in Museum. Collection of Arms & shield in courtyard.

Next saw Castle S. Elmo. not much to see.[19] Very much disgusted to find out just at this point that I had somehow lost seat of my stool. Awful bother. /

B 12 April  Sunday 12th. Found it still raining so determined to start for Sicily. Had a stroll around then went for Ticket. Rather expensive trip  On way to Hotel went in to see Royal Palace[20]  Everything very grand and handsome but cant be put down as the best work  Some very fine tapestry and pictures. Grand staircase best part of interior. Went to Hotel had lunch and then started for boat. Started at 5 oclock after being fleeced on every hand by these beggerly Italians  All italians on board. Great many soldiers and sailors who all slept in a bundle on deck.

The "Leoni" in which we went was the most miserable of miserable boats.

15. 1 sketch (Howarth): see fig. 24.
16. S. Anna dei Lombardi founded 1411; S. Domenico Maggiore, Gothic 1289-1324, much altered. Both contain fine Renaissance sculpture and monuments.
17. Certosa S. Martino founded 14th C., transformed in late 16th and early 17th C., frescoes by Cavalier d'Arpino (1568-1640).
18. 1 sketch (Howarth).
19. Castel S. Elmo 1329-43, altered in 16th C. by P. L. Scriva of Valencia.
20. Royal Palace 1600-2. Grand staircase 1651.

Dinner was served soon after we started. most disgraceful repast. could'nt look at it  had to leave the table. Every one left the table but two  <u>They</u> were Italians. They seem to be able to eat anything. By this time the boat was rolling and tossing about in the most / reckless manner possible. It wasnt awfully rough but the boat was about as bad as could be. Just like a Clyde tug boat  Thought I had got my sea legs on the "Cuzco" but found out my mistake, for before we had been out 2 hours I was as sick (in company with most of the passengers) as a dog, and remained that way for about an hour. I then managed to crawl to the cabin (tumbling over prostrate soldiers and sailors? by the way) and then somehow got into my bunk. Felt more comfortable then but spent a most miserable night. I quite dread the return journey. Got up about 7 in the morning found the sea comparatively calm and still the "Leoni" was in great distress  must have been drunk. Arrived in Palermo about 9.15

B 13 April  Monday 13th April. Went to Hotel Trinacria  rather expensive. Started for British /[21] Consul. No difficulty about sketching. Nobody has any objections as a rule.

When I left Consuls office it was just pouring of rain, went as quickly as possible to the Cathedral.[22] Went inside immediately and was most disgusted with the effect. All most miserable classic not like the outside Had a walk around, rather nice holy water basins. Went out still raining very bad. While taking refuge in the porch happened to see a small hotel right opposite. Good idea. Will see what they take. Went over and found it very respectable. All included 6F per day. Closed on the spot. Started sketch of cathedral porch from door of Hotel.[23] Very cold had to stop sketching  went to Royal Palace. Piazzo Vittorio. Chapel most magnificent.[24] Decorated with mosaic. Almost fainted on the spot with the magnificence of the interior of this chapel.

Next went to see some of Palermo  Much /[25] charmed with the town. Good things turning up everywhere. Very much finer town than Naples. Some really charming bits to be seen. From Royal Palace went to S. Giovanni degli Eremiti an old romanesque church much ruined.[26] Church of La Martorana very good norman work in Front.[27] Next went to Church of S Francesco. fine old norman tower splendid bit.[28] church closed didnt

21. Inscribed at top of page: 'Best Hotel in Palermo Hotel de France Piazza Marina'.
22. Cathedral founded 1185; the exterior dates from 12th to 15th C. Dome 1781-1801 by F. Fuga who altered the interiors, which are predominantly Baroque and Neo-Classical. 1 sketch of east turrets (Howarth).
23. Probably the south porch, the main entrance, Catalan Gothic of 1453.
24. Capella Palatina 1132-40 with 12th C. mosaics.
25. Inscribed at top of page: 'British Consul Via Stabina'.
26. S. Giovanni degli Eremiti 1322-48.
27. La Martorana founded *c.* 1140.
28. S. Francesco d' Assisi 13th C.

see interior. Not very much to be seen in Palermo Museo.[29] Now getting dark so went back to Hotel where I stayed the rest of the evening after dinner.

B 14 April  Tuesday 14th April.

Most abominable still raining and very cold. went from Hotel Trinacria to Hotel Rebecchino. Via Vittorio Emmanuele. Started to sketch cathedral from window Had to stop it was no good  no light & shade  Started for Monreale go by car in half an hour then half an hours walk up / a steep & rugged mountain path. Got up at last. Church not much outside but golly what an interior.[30] Fairly took away my breath. most magnificently decorated in mosaics. This church quite surpassed anything I had yet seen.

Next went to the convent. The cloister of which is very good. Some most beautifully carved caps. There are some 112 all round and they are all or nearly all different. Some of them wonderfully good  Some parts of the convent very good romanesque. Magnificent view of valley from garden. Raining in torrents  had to abandon all work was so dark and cold. Got home about 5 oclock  Had dinner then went for walk in town  Came on rain again had to go home. Went to bed about 9 oclock /

B 15 April  Wednesday 15th April

Rose at I dont know what time to find it still dull. Came on rain before I was dressed. Had breakfast about 9. Went to sketch Campanile Maratano.[31] Gathered such a croud. About 50 people looking at me as if I was a wild beast. Got very angry  then thought I would try the effect of laughing. Laughed at the crowd. The just looked at me as if I was mad. Standing right round me couldnt see Campanile so had to stop  Took up my board & went away. Came back in 5 minutes, found the remnants of the croud still there went home and finished sketch in hotel.

Finished sketch of Front doorway in afternoon. Very fine doorway but very difficult to sketch. After dinner had Italian lesson from Emile son of Hotel proprietor. —

B 16 April  Thursday 16th April.

At Monreala all day.

Sunshine and shower time about most miserably cold, when the sun isnt out.

Had Lunch at Monreala  got some of the nicest bread I ever tasted. Most extraordinary people  they all carry umbrellas no matter what their occupation cab drivers and stone breakers alike.

29. Described in the lecture as 'a fine collection' [c 9].
30. S. Maria la Nuova 1172-6. Mosaics completed 1182. Convent and cloisters 12th C. 1 sketch of fountain in cloister (Howarth). 1 watercolour of cloister (Coll. Wilma Paterson): see fig. 29. 1 sketch of clerestory (Christie's London 16 March 1982, lot 268).
31. 1 watercolour (Howarth).

B 17 April    Friday. 17th April
              Up early. much better day but still cloudy. Finished sketches of
              Cathedrel  Started for Museo about 3 found it closed. Only open from
              11–3 admission 1fr. free on Sundays.
                  Martorana admission 1Fr.
                  Sketch of Cathedral tower.
                  Italian lesson in evening from Eimile – Got very warm in afternoon. /

B 18 April    Saturday. 18th April
              Up early. Splendid day. Went to do some sketching at porch of cath-
              edral but had to stop owing to croud looking on. Set of loafing black-
              guards. seem to have nothing to do but loaf about. Went to Museo. Had
              lunch then got ready to start for Naples. Got on Board about 4.30. Most
              charming day. Splendid view of town from Boat. Great many passangers.
              No english all German & Italian. One Italian boy Tomaso Martino could
              speak some French & some English  had a talk with him. Managed to sit
              out dinner. Went to bed immediately spent a most miserable night  boat
              as if it was drunk. All the people round about sick  most disgusting noises.
              Rose at 6.30. Got into Naples about 8 oclock /[32] Drove to Station left
              luggage went for breakfast got ticket got into train and started for Rome
              at 10 minutes to 9.
                  Country rather nice. After we were out from Naples passed a great
              many vine fields miles & mils corn planted on ground  trees growing
              about 10 feet to 15 feet apart in long avenues and vines growing up and
              from tree to tree. leaves just coming out. Vine fields got tiresome. Not
              much to see till we came on a bit. Towns or villages all nestling in a most
              extraordinary manner half way up the mountain side.
                  Cassino very nice place. Convent on top of very hill. Snow on tops of all
              the mountain. Train disgustingly slow. Got to Rome / about 8. oclock
              Went to Hotel d' Europe had dinner & went to bed immediately. Quite
              tired out.

B 20 April    Monday. 20 April.
              Rose about 8. Had breakfast then went for a turn in Rome.
                  Went along Corso to Piazza Popolo not much to see.[33] Went to bankers
              drew £10  then to British Consuls then to Post Office where I only got
              three newspapers, expected some letters. Next went to director of arts for
              permissions. Took car to Ancient Rome. Very interesting place. more of it
              again. Called on Mr Summers out of town. went from Hotel d' Europe to
              Pension Michael. 7 F per day, very nice hotel & very nice people

        32. Inscribed across top of following two pages: 'British Consul. Mr. Franz, Piazza San
    Claudio Via Maggetto'.
        33. Piazza del Popolo 1814, by G. Valadier, with Baroque S. Maria dei Miracoli and S.
    Maria in Montesanto by Bernini and Fontana 1675-8, and Porta del Popolo 1561 after
    Michelangelo, remodelled 1655 by Bernini.

B 21 April　Tuesday, 21st Started early for St Peters. Very very poor front. Interior much better but the great attraction it seems to me / to lie in the vastness of the fabric. It is very difficult to keep in mind when looking at it the scale, untill you see perhaps some people at the other end and then you can form an opinion of its extent & vastness. Met the Lords in S Peters. still staying in Rome. Next went round the outside of S Peters to the Vatican Museum entrance 1 F. Very fine collection of antiquities & art treasures. Egyptian mummies & Vases very fine. Architectural collection most charming & interesting stole some notes. Statuary very very good. Was most charmed with Raphaels frescoes most exquisite compositions and painting coloring something grand. In picture collection liked Titian best. Saw the Original Transfiguration. Very fine picture Didnt get half through. Go again. Closes at 3. awful fraud.

B 22 April　Wednesday. 22nd April. Started for Pantheon. Saw "Dogana di Terra" by the way.[34] new ch. with facade of old columns 8 in number very much broken up. St Andrews. Ch. good tombs.[35] Pantheon. The exterior is very vast but much of the effect must be lost owing to the marble being gone. Facade very imposing. Interiors most beautiful. Very large vault. Marble decoration said to be modern very good. Next went to Campo di Fiore square where they sell fruit vegetabls & flowers. Great noise. Took sketch of window from Palazzo Cancelleria.[36] Very fine palace but in very narrow street. couldnt get a sketch. Got into shop to sketch window. Went home for lunch.

　　Made colored sketch of Arch of Titus[37] in afternoon. Then Colloseum. Then the House of Nero where there are some very nice fresco decorations.

B 23 April　Thursday. Good gracious whats that. Most terrific noise then the house starts shaking and all around are females screaming. Got out of bed, windows rattling and breaking on all sides. The shaking lasted for about 2 minutes. Heard after it was a magazine explosion 3 mils away. Had breakfast then went to Arch of Constantine.[38] Took sketch but sun going down I started to go home for lunch. Just my luck left color box in bus. After waiting about 1 hour and a half got bus again and also box. Gave conductor 4 francs. Was mighty glad to get them back Got an awful fright. Fancy being with out colors. To dreadful to contemplate. Went to Post office got letter from Geo Murry & one from Herbert and a paper

34. Dogana di Terra, formerly a custom-house, by 1890 the Borsa (Exchange), not a church. The façade incorporates eleven Corinthian columns from a temple dedicated to Hadrian by Antoninus Pius, once thought to be a Temple of Neptune.

35. Probably S. Andrea delle Valle, 1591, by Fr. Grimaldi and Giac. della Porta.

36. Pal. Cancelleria begun 1486 with Florentine influences. Mackintosh was obviously interested in such designs in Rome and Florence. 1 sketch of a doorway of the Pal. di Venezia, begun 1455, completed 16th C. (Howarth).

37. Arch of Titus A.D. 81.

38. Arch of Constantine A.D. 315.

from Father. Sauntered home about four. Couldnt / do much. Laid down some measurements  This explosion will make the glazier leap with joy. Half the windows in the town are broken. Streets just covered with glass. Most extraordinary occurrence. Must read about it,

B 24 April    Friday. 24th April.

Not a very bright morning. Started for S.M. Maggiore. Went to Porta Pia by the way. Said to be designed by M Angelo. not much to look at.[39] Chiesa M. Maggiore very good both outside and in.[40] Some good monuments  Sketch campanile, which is different from rest of ch. Came on wet. Went into small ch opposite S. Prassede.[41] Very old and very good inside. Mosaic work in chancel. Very funny old doorway to chapel some good tombs. Was turned out at 12. Discovered a very nice old ch on way home  S. Pedenziana.[42] Didnt go inside. Wet all afternoon but went to Trinita di / Monte where there isnt much to see.[43] Medici Villa closed. open tomorrow. S. M. Del Popolo, at Porta Popolo.[44] very nice ch. outside. Just full of good monumental work inside. Especially in Sacristy. 3 very fine old tombs.

B 25 April    Saturday 25 April.

Forenoon sketching in S. Prassede. Saw Porta Pinciana on way home.[45]

Afternoon Museo Lateranese, very good[46]  S. Giovanni in Laterno  was very much pleased with this ch.  quite as good as St Peters not so large of course. very good front. Old cloister attached  could'nt bribe keeper to let me sketch.[47]

Sacristy (seperate entrance very interesting  Next went to S. Croce in Gerusalem not much to see there.[48] very poor. S. Martino. undergoing alterations  couldnt see much but seemed to be rather a good thing.[49] /

39. Porta Pia 1561, Michelangelo's last work; exterior face 1868, by Vespignani.

40. S. Maria Maggiore founded 4th C.; 12th and 13th C. additions. Main façade 1743, by F. Fuga. Campanile, loftiest in Rome, mainly 14th C.

41. S. Prassede, built 822, with later restorations. Doorway to 9th C. Chapel of S. Zeno incorporates antique columns, architectural fragments and sculpture with 9th C. mosaic busts. 1 sketch of a doorway (Howarth).

42. S. Pudenziana, one of the oldest churches in Rome, rebuilt 384-99 and subsequently.

43. Trinità dei Monti begun 1493, fronted by magnificent Spanish Steps, 1721-5.

44. S. Maria del Popolo begun 1099, rebuilt 1227 and 1472-7. Early Renaissance façade. Mackintosh ignores Raphael's Chigi Chapel.

45. Porta Pinciana, a fortified gateway of *c*. 403.

46. 1 sketch of exterior (Howarth).

47. S. Giovanni in Laterano founded 4th C., rebuilt 1646-9 by Borromini. Principal front by A. Galilei (1734-6). Cloister 1215-32, a magnificent example of Cosmatesque art by I. and P. Vassalletto.

48. S. Croce in Gerusalemme modernised 1743-4.

49. S. Martino ai Monti founded 4th C., rebuilt 500 and 1650; incorporates remains of Roman baths.

B 26 April Sunday, 26 April.

Saw two or three unimportant churches then went to Presbyterian church where Professor Blackie from Edinburgh was preaching. enjoyed service immensely. Wrote letters to Maggie, Billy and Mr Keppie in afternoon.[50]

B 27 April Monday. 27 Splendid morning. Went to S Passede and finished sketch of monument then went to S Pietro.[51] saw M. Angeloe's "Moses" most beautiful piece of work  Saw chains with which Peter was bound when in prison

Went home for lunch then went and sketched Arch of Constantine dont know whether it is a success or not. Had a stroll through ruins of "forum" before going for dinner

B 28 April Tuesday 28 April

Went to M Angelos Moses again. then S Adriano, nothing to see[52] /

Next Marmorata prison. most interesting spot just overflowing with exciting and awful tradition.[53] Capella dell'Incarnazione interesting traditionally but not architecturally[54]  S. Araceli on Capitol Hill much finer  Some good tombs & pictures. Steps leading up to it very interesting.[55] Capitoline Museum very good. Saw the famous Dying Gladiator  the fawn  Venus  the Centors  boy with goose and lots of other good old statuary.[56] Some good ornament.

In afternoon S. Angeli, very large ch by M. Angelo.[57]

S. Lorenzo – (Campo Santa) very fine thing most beautiful Corinthian columns, and above a frieze & cornice made up of various scraps from ancient temples. Very fine ornament.[58]

B 29 April Wednesday 29th April.

At S. Lorenzo all day sketching. /

50. John Stuart Blackie (1809-95), Professor of Greek at Edinburgh, was a fellow Glaswegian and a well-known character. 'Maggie' may refer to Mackintosh's sister Margaret, or possibly his future wife Margaret Macdonald, who had entered the Glasgow School of Art in 1890, though Mackintosh is not known to have abbreviated her name. If the latter, their friendship began some years earlier than generally believed. 'Billy' may be his brother William. John Keppie (1862-1945): partner in Honeyman & Keppie.

51. S. Pietro in Vincoli founded 442, restored under Sixtus IV by M. del Caprina.

52. S. Adriano, Roman Senate House converted in 638.

53. Probably S. Pietro in Carcere, later the Mamertine Prison where St Peter was confined.

54. Capella dell' Incarnazione possibly Capella del Crocifisso, in same church as the Mamertine Prison.

55. S. Maria in Aracoeli dates from 7th C., exterior rebuilt 13th C.; staircase 1348.

56. Antique sculpture: Dying Gaul, Satyr Resting, Capitoline Venus, Young and Old Centaurs, Boy with Goose.

57. S. Maria degli Angeli, adapted by Michelangelo 1563-6, altered by Vanvitelli 1749.

58. Probably S. Lorenzo in Miranda, 11th C., incorporating a Temple of Antoninus Pius and Faustina.

B 30 April     Thursday 30  at Museo Diocletian Bath, and Tivoli. 16 miles from Rome
by Steam Car. not much of intrest in the country over which you go.
Tivoli situated on very top of a hill which is covered with olive trees. The
town itself is very nice  old temples of Vesta & Sybil. in ruins. Cascades
very nice.

B 1 May        Friday, 1st  May day demonstrations in town  every thing shut. got into
St Peters spent forenoon there. Went for drive on Pincian Hill in afternoon. Dreadfully warm  worst I have yet felt. positively can't do anything.
as limp as a herring.

B 2 May        Saturday 2nd  at the Vatican. Spent all fore noon in Sistene Chapel. most
marvellous decoration by M. Angelo. was very much impressed with the
last Judgement. most beautifully composed picture, very much time worn
which is a pity. /

B 3 May        Sunday, 3  St M. Sopra Minerva, only gothic church in Rome.[59] S. Agnes.
small ch.[60] S. Lorenzo in Domasco very good architecture.[61] Scotch
Church  writing letters in afternoon.

B 4 May        Monday. 4. At Vatican, Sistine Chap. Picture Gallery, then Borgese Palace
Picture Gallery, fine collection, saw four most exellent little old Italien
pictures, of marble. Quite the style. Left for Orvieto at 3. got there at 5.30.
Went to Hotel Aquila Bianca  Most beautiful cathedral especially the
front.[62] Built of white marble with bands of red, purble blue black brown
yellow marble, beautiful twisted columns. Bronze evangelists, and just
covered with gold mosaic bands  mosaic pictures in front said to be
modern restorations. Chapel in interior beautifully painted[63] / Otherwise
not much in inside

B 5-9 May      Tuesday. 5  Wed. 6  Thursday 7  Friday 8  Sat 9  All at Orvieto Sketching.[64] Weather very bad. two thunderstorms, one hail storm, and some
rain every day.

B 10 May       Sunday 10th. Left for Siena at 12.54  still raining. Cleared up on the way.
Thought I was never coming to Siena. Saw the famous Campanile about
2 hours before we got to the Station. Railway goes right round the base of
the hill then backs into a siding and starts the other way. Got to Siena
about 6.30 drove to Pensione Chiuserilla 5F. Went down to dinner and

59. S. Maria sopra Minerva, rebuilt 1280 by Fra Sisto and Fra Ristoro; restored 1847.
60. S. Agnese in Agone, ancient church reconstructed in 16th C. by Rainaldi with a
Borromini façade, 1653-7.
61. S. Lorenzo in Damaso 15th C., restored 1868-82.
62. Orvieto Cathedral 1290 to early 17th C., façade early 14th C. by L. Maitani.
63. Capella Nuova, contains frescoes by Fra Angelico and Signorelli.
64. 3 sketches of Cathedral (Howarth). 1 watercolour of Cathedral (H.A.G.): see fig. 27.
1 sketch of pinnacle (Christie's London 16 March 1982, lot 266).

found Paxton and a fellow Dods sitting there. It turned out rather lucky for me as I found out.[65] /

Monday 11th. Went for permission to sketch in Cathedral & Pal. Pubblico,[66] found it rather slow work as the lazy Italians did'nt turn up till near 12. Sketching in Cathedral in afternoon.[67] The whole church didnt strike me as being very fine architecturally. On the exterior to begin with the front is a <u>fraud</u> as it gives no indication of the interior Then when you examine the design you find that it is almost "<u>not there</u>" Then you begin to see that were it not for the fine material the whole thing would be very poor as a composition There are many nice bits of detail, and there are very many bad, clumsy, & vulgar things. Which when found out detract very considerably from the effect or impression the ediface makes on you at first sight. So much for the front. Then the sides, well / they take the cake. There are no windows in the aisles so this part is plain and might look well so, but it wasnt good enough for the Sienese No they must have windows, so they painted windows along the wall: designed & painted in the Gothic style. Very beautiful? examples, and it is a pity that the rain is wearing some parts of them away.

The Campanile, is more successful I think.[68] Square & plain but very nice, not fussy & excited like the front. The principal of getting better as you ascend is very plainly exemplified here. Starting solid, in the second or third division there is one opening or window and in each successive story the number increases by one till you have 6 at the top. The finish or roof of this tower and also / the finish of the front turrets is very far from satisfactory, being brought to a point in the most clumsy and unseemly manner conceivably.

At the back of the church may be seen some of the worst work one could conceive, most clumsy. In the interior I found little bits of detail far more attractive than the whole church. I couldnt raise any enthusiasm over the interior It is built in bands like the exterior but above a certain height the bands are only painted. Of course this is not apparent and has therefore no effect on the ordinary individual. There is a very brilliant and beautiful example of glass in the front rose window seen in the afternoon the effect is very beautiful.[69] Very rich and / warm bright colours are used. principally red, purple green & blue.

The floor, of inlaid marble is really magnificent, and makes one sorry that it is a floor.[70] It is partly covered up but drawings of all the parts can

65. Paxton and Dods accompanied him until 12 June.
66. 1 sketch of Pal. Pubblico window (Howarth). This sketch also includes an exterior view of Pal. Pollini, 1537, by B. Peruzzi, an architect not mentioned by Mackintosh but particularly admired by the previous Thomson Student, W. J. Anderson.
67. Cathedral begun 1196, completed late 14th C.
68. Campanile 1313.
69. Late 14th C. rose window, depicting the Last Supper.
70. Floor late 14th to mid 16th C., series of 56 designs.

be seen in the Opera del Duomo. Some of these are most exquisitely designed illustrating the bible, especially the one of Moses striking the rock  There are some fragments of the ancient scraffeti work in the Opera which will make your hair stand on end. Figures drawn with shadow only. white or cream or ivory marble ground and shadows a pale & sympathetic green plaster or cement. I was greatly delighted with them and am sorry I didnt have time to make a sketch /

The interior of the front door is very clumsy and almost ugly, grand massive carving on circular columns  The next thing seen on entering is two white marble fonts.[71] Both late in date but very nice detail  Then you come to a very nice alter Renaissence. Very refined, to much so in fact, some of the parts having the effect of cast plaster.[72]

Small tomb by M. Angelo with Sybil & 2 angels which are right enough but the tomb is a caution in M. Angelo's usual style.

Then you come to the entrance to the library which is a very beautiful piece of renaissence detail. Very richly carved and jamb of door inlaid with panels of different coloured marbles. Some of the carving is most beautiful and / very nicely executed.[73]

The entrance to the Babtistry of the trancept is also very nice. Then the wooden stalls are really very good  one half are late gothic with just a feeling of classic about them and the other pure renaissence[74]  They are undoubtedly good but like most Italian wood work they are very stony. Not designed like wood but stone. The colour of the wood is most lovely, a very rich walnut. The carved panels all over are very interesting and very good design. Well worth careful study.

The little boys on the arms of the stalls are most interesting and very beautifully modelled, all in different poses. The old reading desk is also very fine.

The printing in the old bibles will / repay very careful study, as they are all hand done on velum, and the printing & coloring of the Initial letters are both very good.

Some very nice marble & a very good cloth in high alter.

I could not see anything beautiful either inter or externally about the dome. Very badly designed

The font in the baptistry is well worth going to see, as it contains some very beautiful brass panels by Lorenzo Ghiberti & Donatella.[75]

71. Fonts 1462, by A. Federighi. 2 drawings of fonts were published in the *G.A.A. Sketchbook* 4 (1894) pl. 21.

72. Altar 1506, by B. Peruzzi, with sculpture by G. di Stefano, 1488, and Fr. di G. Martini, 1499.

73. Libreria Piccolomini founded 1495, decorated by Pinturicchio. 1 watercolour of doorway (British Museum).

74. Intarsia choir stalls by Fr. del Tonghio and others, 1362-97, G. da Verona, 1503, and Riccio and school, 1567-70.

75. Baptistry font 1417-30, depicting Life of St John the Baptist. 1 watercolour (Coll. Wilma Paterson): see fig. 21.

The gothic pulpit with renaissence stair in the Cath is also a very good bit of work.[76]

Some of the Palaces, especially Publico are very interesting. Chapel in connection with Publico, some wood stalls. Iron screene &c[77] Some very good iron torch bearers. /

Not much more to see in Siena

12-19 May    Tues 12  Wed 13  Thursday 14  Friday 15  Sat 16  Sunday 17  Monday 18  Tuesday 19  All at Siena sketching at Cathedral[78] left for Florence. got there at 7 oclock

Florence Pensione Laurent  Via del Presto 11. £4.50-5[79]

B 20 May    Wednesday 20  Morning went to Piazza Signora & Pal. Vecchio, early gothic with bad tower, crib from Siena. Logia dei Lenzi very good & very large.[80] Rape of Sabins stupid thing.[81]

Duomo, very elaborate marble work liked view from [it] with dome & chapel best. Front modern,[82] Giottos tower very good.[83] Much dependent on effect for / colour of marble. Interior a fraud. Babtistry not much. Donatella door exquisite.[84] Interior simple & neat. Was disappointed with Florence Cathedral

Church of S. Croce. Chancel end very good nice glass in windows. Splendid tombs. Exterior poor. Pulpit good  Cloister not much. Chapel with Della Robbian friezes &c.[85]

S. Maria Novella. Exquisite glass window in chancel. lovely colours.[86]

S. Lorenzo. Medici Pew, good. Library. benches & windows very good. Cloister poor [87]

S. Marco not much to See.[88]

76. Pulpit 1265-8, by N. Pisano.

77. Pal. Pubblico 1297-1310. 1 watercolour (Private Coll.). Capella del Consiglio with stalls 1415-28, by D. di Nicola and iron screen 1434, attrib. to I. della Quercia.

78. 1 sketch of pulpit capitals and stall panels, 1 sketch of pedestal and 1 sheet of unidentified studies of ironwork (Howarth).

79. Mackintosh absent-mindedly notes the hotel charges as pounds sterling rather than francs.

80. Loggia dei Lanzi 1376-82, by B. di Cione and S. Talenti.

81. Giambologna *The Rape of the Sabines*, 1583. See E 38.

82. Duomo with Gothic-style façade 1871-87 by E. de Fabris. No comment on Brunelleschi's cupola, though brief mention in lecture [c 26].

83. Campanile 1334-59.

84. Baptistry remodelled 11th to 13th C., doors by A. Pisano and Ghiberti, not Donatello.

85. S. Croce begun 1294, consecrated 1443. Tombs include Michelangelo's. Pulpit 1472-6, by B. da Maiano. Two cloisters by Arnolfo and Brunelleschi. Pazzi Chapel 1429 to 1470s, by Brunelleschi with Della Robbia friezes.

86. S. Maria Novella 1246 to 14th C., most important Gothic church in Tuscany. Glass probably that in Capella di Filippo Strozzi by F. Lippi. No mention of Alberti's façade.

87. S. Lorenzo: Mackintosh ignores Brunelleschi's designs of 1425-46. Biblioteca Laurenziana begun by Michelangelo c. 1524. Cloister 1457-62, by Manetti.

88. S. Marco founded 1299; rebuilt 1442, and 1588 by Giambologna.

B 21 May     Thursday, 21  Sketching at S. Croche.[89]

B 22 May     Friday 22nd  S. Croche in morning.
             Museo di S. Marco. nothing to sketch worth seeing, went to S Miniato
             good way out but worth going. Beautifully decorated roof. Fine / mosaic
             floor, and beautiful marbel screene.[90]

B 23 May     Saturday. 23rd  S. Badia. 3 good tombs[91] Museo National, goot armour
             architectural fragments Donatella friezes & tils.[92] Pal. Vecchio beautiful
             quadrangle.[93]

B 24 May     Sunday. 24. Pal Uffitzi & Pitti. both especially Uffitzi crammed full of good
             pictures & statuary.
             Saw the originals of many old and well known friends.
             Was much impressed with the Perugino School, & the gothic painting
             in long gallery,
             Some charming work by Rapheal M Angelo Titian &c &c. liked Titian
             best of all. Flora exquisite  Some very fine Statuary.

B 25 May     Monday, 25th. Taking water color sketch of Pitti Bridge. Jottings / in
             various parts of the Town and then to Museo National. Buying Photo-
             grafs in afternoon.[94]

B 26 May     Tuesday 26.
             Up at 4.30 Sketch of Bridge
             left at 9.30 for Pisa.
             Arrived at 11. Cathedral leaning tower & Babtistry form a very interest-
             ing group  was very much disgusted with exterior of Cathedral.[95] Arcades
             are good enough but. here it is all arcade and no design. The Babtistry is
             better,[96] and the effect of the arcades on the town is very effective owing
             to the rows of shadows produced. But altogether the exteriors are very
             irritating  want some place to rest the eye. The interior is indifferently
             good. Best thing is the wood stalls which are very good indeed. Some nice
             glass.
             Some other very nice churches.
             Left at 8.20 for Pistoya arrived at 11.30

89. 1 watercolour of tomb of Carlo Marsuppini (Howarth).
90. S. Miniato founded 1013. Open timber roof with polychrome decoration. Pavement
contains early 13th C. intarsia panels. 1 watercolour of roof (Howarth).
91. S. Badia probably Badia Fiorentina founded 978, rebuilt 1284-1310, radically
altered 1627-31 by M. Segaloni. 1 sketch of carved angel (Howarth).
92. 1 watercolour of Della Robbia frieze (Howarth).
93. Quadrangle 1453, by Michelozzo.
94. In the lecture Mackintosh refers to photographs of the Sistine Chapel ceiling [c 13].
95. Cathedral restored 1602-16.
96. Baptistry founded 1152, remodelled by N. and G. Pisano 1260-84, and completed
14th C.

B 27 May    Wednesday 27th. Went round Pistoya
Cathedral & Baptistry fairly good. Nothing else up to much except frieze
on exteriors of Pal [left blank] by Della Robia.[97] Left at 3.30 for Bologna.
arrived at 5.15. saw round some of town then had dinner  Some good
work in S. Pietra.[98] Good screene, outside front unfinished very early
renaissence  sides gothic, brick.
Very nice little brick ch. S – [left blank] the inevitable leaning tower, Via
Cavour Via & Piaz Vict Emmanuel & Garibald are to be seen here.
Plenty of good bad & indifferent caps in loggias of Bologna.[99]
Left at 7.30 for Ravenna

B 28 May    Thursday 28th  Went round Ravenna / Very delightful Place.
S. Appolinare nuove, & classe are of course the jems  Some ripping
mosaic work in both.[100] Both brick churches & very uninteresting
outside  S. Vitale is also a good church octogan plan.[101] quite a distinctive
form. fine marble floor. Some mosaic in side chapel.
S. Giov Evangelistia very interesting, very nice tower.[102] little bricks on
roof very effective. Duomo very poor  Baptistry very fine. Good
mosaics[103] Altogether a very picturesque town & well worth visiting.[104]

29-31 May    Friday, Sat, Sunday 29, 30, 31 all sketching at Ravenna, Baptistry, S
Apollinare in nuovo, classe & S Vitale[105]

B 1 June    Monday 1st June. Left at 9.30 for Ferrara. got there at 10.50,
Some very beautiful frescoe decoration / in Castello by, Dosso Dossi.[106]
one picture by Titian.
Cathedral front very good. interior modern.[107] Side very poor, Campa
nile about as ugly as they make em.[108] Frescoes in Pal Schifanzo worth
seeing.[109] Some nice bits through the town. but they are very few, and far
between.
Left at 5.30 for Venice arrived at 12 – .

97. Probably Ospedale del Ceppo, founded 13th to 14th C.; façade decorated with work
by G. della Robbia.
98. S. Petronio founded 1390. Fine example of Gothic brickwork.
99. 1 sketch of capitals (Howarth).
100. S. Apollinare Nuovo and S. Apollinare in Classe 6th C.
101. S. Vitale 6th C.; the octagonal plan was also admired in S. Lorenzo, Milan.
102. S. Giovanni Evangelista 5th C., with tower from 10th to 14th C.
103. Duomo founded early 5th C. but severely damaged in 1733 and rebuilt. Baptistry
converted from a Roman bath house in 5th C. Interior contains Roman and Byzantine
mosaics. 1 sketch Baptistry mosaics (Christie's London 16 March 1982, lot 267).
104. Mackintosh probably attended the Glasgow Architectural Association lecture by
W. Leiper, 'Ravenna and some other Italian cities', held on 23 Sept. 1890 at the G.S.A.,
and open to its students.
105. 2 watercolours of mosaics (H.A.G.): see fig. 26.
106. Castello Estense 14th to 16th C.
107. Cathedral 12th to 13th C., interior remodelled 1712-18.
108. Campanile 1412-1514.
109. Pal. di Schifanoia begun 1385, enlarged in 15th C. Salone dei Mesi contains

B 2 June    Tuesday. 2nd June. Sailed up grand canal to get an idea of the place was quite charmed with the delightful colouring & grouping of the various pallaces, a few of the pallaces are very good, in the gothic (venetian) the Cardorre is the best,[110] but they are all founded on the same type, and that type is taken from the Dojes Pallace. Some of the Renaissence / work is very good.

In afternoon went to Piazza & Church of S Marco. The exterior – well its S Marco. The interior is a caution  its simply superb as a piece of mosaic architecture. the gold ground has a magnificent effect.

The modern work is abominable. Floor very good.

B 3 June    Wed. 3rd June. S. Salute, good effect outside.[111] Fine Titian in interior.

S. Rocco, fine decoration by Tintoretto  Annunciation by Titian very fine. Academy Belle Arts, worth seeing. Went for Bathe at Ledo in afternoon.[112]

B 4 June    Thursday 4. S. Miracoli, most exquisite renaissence church. most beautiful carving, most complete little ch. in venice or anywhere else[113]

S. Giov e Paoli. some very fine tombs both gothic & classic.[114] /

Dojes Pallace.[115] good chimney pieces in Museo.[116] Courtyard very good splendid bronze well heads.[117] Giant stair good.[118]

B 5 June    Friday 5  Murano & Torcello, both very interesting old churches.[119]

B 6 June    Saturday 6  sketching.

B 7 June    Sunday. 7th do

B 8 June    Monday 8th  do  at S Miracoli[120]

B 9 June    Tuesday 9th  do.

---

frescoes by Fr. del Cossa, E. de' Roberti and others. 1 sketch of courtyard in unidentified Ferrarese palace, possibly here (Howarth).

110. Ca' d' Oro 1425-40. 1 untraced watercolour was exhibited at the 1933 Mackintosh Memorial Exhibition (164).

111. S. Maria della Salute 1631-81, by B. Longhena.

112. 1 watercolour (H.A.G.).

113. S. Maria dei Miracoli 1481-9, by P. Lombardo.

114. S. Giovanni e Paoli, Gothic brick, begun 1246, completed 1430. Burial place of twenty-five Doges.

115. Doge's Palace *c.* 1340-1450.

116. 1 sketch of chimney piece (Howarth): see fig. 34.

117. Two well heads by A. Alberghetti 1559, and N. dei Conti 1556. 1 sketch of a well head (Howarth).

118. Sala dei Giganti 1484-1501, by A. Rizzi with statues 1566 by Sansovino.

119. Probably Murano: S. Maria and S. Donato *c.* 1140; Torcello: S. Fosca early 12th C., and S. Maria dell' Assunta, founded 639, rebuilt 1008.

120. 4 sketches, of chancel, carved pilasters, altar screen (fig. 33) and pulpit (Howarth). 1 sketch of Campanile, St Mark's Square (Howarth).

| | |
|---|---|
| B 10 June | Wed 10th left for Padua. |

Wandered all over the town but found very little of interest except S Lorenzo and S Antonio.[121] Went on to Vicenza better than Padua. Good place to study Paladdios work  all the churches very poor. Municcipio by Paladdio very good.[122] Left at night for Verona

| | |
|---|---|
| B 11 June | Thursday 10th.[123] On the tramp again spent all forenoon looking / |

through churches and at Pallacs  S. Anistasia very good.[124] Duomo some good work, S Maria & organo & S Giov in Parva [?] all good[125]

landed at S Zeno, very beautiful example of Italian gothic brick & stone work, some of it very early, wood stals very good,

very simple & nice interior choir raised with chapel below.[126]

| | |
|---|---|
| B 12 June | Friday 12th  Sketching at Verona[127]  J Paxton & R. Dods left for Munich. |
| B 13 June | Saturday. 13th  at Verona |
| B 14 June | Sunday 14th  Up at 5, sketching door of Cathedral |

left at 10 for Mantova.

went all over the town and then all the churches but found nothing of interest,[128] went on to Cremona / Cremona Albergo Capello, 2F for room  arrived at 6 oclock had a look round before dinner. Cathedral disappointing[129]

| | |
|---|---|
| B 15 June | Monday 15. started early on the tramp ransacked the whole town. |

Nothing in the place worth seeing but the Cathedral. Forced myself to do some sketching.[130] at 3 oclock found myself with nothing to do, and utterly tired out with tramping about. Left for brescia at 6.20. arrivd at Brescia at 8.35. Alb. Capello. 2F for R. Baptistry at Cremona very good.

| | |
|---|---|
| B 16 June | Tuesday 16. Brescia.[131] Duomo poor also old cathedral not so bad but |

being frightfully restored[132]

121. S. Lorenzo unidentified. S. Antonio 1232 to 14th C. No mention of Giotto's Scrovegni Chapel, recently restored in 1887.

122. Loggia del Capitaniato 1571.

123. In fact Thursday 11 June.

124. S. Anastasia, Gothic brick, 1290-1323, 1428-81.

125. S. Maria in Organo founded 7th C., remodelled late 15th C.; probably either S. Giovanni in Fonte or S. Giovanni in Valle, both 12th C.

126. S. Zeno 12th to 14th C.

127. G.S.A. sketchbook begins in Verona: 17 pages including S. Zeno, Pal. Ragione, S. Anastasia and S. Maria in Organo.

128. No mention of work by Alberti, Mantegna or Giulio Romano. 1 page of unidentified details (G.S.A.).

129. Cathedral 12th C. with later additions.

130. 1 study of capitals (Howarth). 6 pages including Baptistry, Duomo, S. Michele and Cathedral (G.S.A.). 1 sketch of arcade over Cathedral porch (H.A.G.).

131. 5 pages including Castle, Broletto and Brick House (fig. 25) (G.S.A.).

132. Duomo 1604 by G. B. Lantana; Duomo Vecchio early 12th C.

S. Carmine in Via Vic Em. Very rich piece of Renassence work.[133] Left
at 5 50 for Bergamo
   arrived at 7.35.
   Hotel Capella d'Oro. /

B 17 June    Wednesday 17th June. Bergamo.[134] Nothing of importance. S. Maggiore
some good Intersia work in stalls  exterior early & crude. interior re-
novated.[135] Capella Chap. renassince overloaded. poor design.[136]
   Library in square very good gothic. Good renaissence in street right
down from Cath.

B 18 June    Thursday 18  morning left for Lecco nothing there. Went up L. Como to
Colici then down to Cadenabbia very nice place[137] Hotel Belle Ile. 7F

B 19-25 June    Friday 19  Cadenebbia  Sat 20  Sunday 21–22–23–24 25 Cad.

B 26 June    Friday 26  Left Cadenabbia for Como at 2.15.[138] Como Cathedral very
good. Two side doors very suggestive  Trancepts & chancel very good
renaissence work.[139] S. Fedele is / very good whats left. interior restored in
very bad classic.[140]
   Basillica S. abbondio outside town very charming old church. some old
frescoes in interior but not up to much.[141]

B 27 June    Saturday 27th  left Como at 12 for Milan arrived about 6– wrote letters
&c.

B 28 June    Sunday. 28th. Went to Cathedral and was surprised at the splendour of
the edifice.[142] The old bits are rather good especially the side aile
windows. Parapet tower all restoration very much inferior to old work.
The interior is disappointing. the effect is not bad but there is a want of
the grand solemnity associated with large gothic Cathedrals. The columns
have no caps[143] / nitches with figures taking their place. The said nitches
being rather nice. All the windows are filled with very very poor <u>painted</u>

133. S. Maria del Carmine 14th C. with 15th C. portal.
134. 5 pages including Quartiere S. Agostino, Biblioteca and S. Maria Maggiore (G.S.A.).
135. S. Maria Maggiore 1137 by Maestro Fredo. Intarsia work in choir stalls 1522-5. Baroque interior.
136. Colleoni Chapel 1476.
137. 2 pages of views of boats (G.S.A.). Mackintosh must have taken a well-earned rest at Cadenabbia.
138. 6 pages including Cathedral, Broletto, S. Abbondio and S. Fedele (G.S.A.).
139. S. Maria Maggiore, mainly late 14th C. Side doors carved by T. and I. Rodari of Maroggia c. 1500.
140. S. Fedele 12th C.
141. S. Abbondio 11th C. 1 sketch (Howarth): see fig. 38.
142. Cathedral begun c. 1386. 2 watercolours, of St. Jerome and a buttress (Howarth). 3 pages of interior details (G.S.A.).
143. Inscribed at bottom of this page: 'fine view from tower'.

glass. The painted tracery on the vaulted ceiling detracts very considerably from the internal effect. The chancel with light behind has a good
effect but the work itself is very inferior. Passed through grand Arcade.
Very much inferior to the new arcade at Naples. Went to Brera and got
into an exhibition of modern art. Mostly very weak. Venetian artists being
the best. Some very good sculptures much better than the paintings

The Churches of Milan are being mostly late of a very inferior / quality.
The most interesting is S. Ambrogio a quaint old thing in stone brick and
plaster.[144]

S. Eustorgio is also nice.[145]

S. Lorenzo interesting plan[146]

S. Maria del Grezie is also worth seeing. has a very good renaissance
porch. but the renaissance work on the exterior of the dome & trancepts
is to speak mildly comical[147]

The ospedale Maggiore is a very good brick & Terracotta building.[148]

The picture gallery contains some very good examples. of which Gio
Bellini & Francesco, Maioni Dosso Dossi are best represented although
there are examples of. Paolo Veronese (not very strong) Perugino Giotto,
Tintoretto (very fine) Gentile Bellini Titian (not very good) Ambrogio
Borgognone Vicenza Foppa, Salvatore Rosa very like / Titian) & Gulio
Campi.[149]

The archelogical museum contains some (for a small collection) very
good things. Two doors & a renaissance monument being specially
good.[150]

The Museo Poldi Pozzoli No 10 Via Maioni contains a most valuable
collection of art.[151] Some most exquisite tapestries, one Persian Carpet
being most exquisite colour.[152] The pictures are the finest for a small
collection I ever saw  Francesco is very strong here. Mostly all of that
school. Then there are china sets  Armoury (most excellent) pottery silver
ware fans. Ivory stuffs &c altogether a most interesting collection especially the pictures.

B 7 July     Tuesday. 7th July left for Pavia.

144. S. Ambrogio 379-86 and 11th C. 3 pages (G.S.A.).

145. S. Eustorgio 11th C., rebuilt 12th to 13th C., façade reconstructed 1863-5.
3 pages (G.S.A.).

146. S. Lorenzo founded 4th C., rebuilt 1103 and 1574-88 retaining original octagonal plan. 1 page (G.S.A.): see fig. 36.

147. S. Maria delle Grazie 1466-90. No mention of rebuilding by Bramante 1492-9, or
of Leonardo's *Last Supper*. 1 page (G.S.A.).

148. Ospedale Maggiore 1456, by A. A. Filarete. 1 page (G.S.A.).

149. Vincenzo Foppa (*c.* 1427-1515); Giulio Campi (*c.* 1502-72).

150. 2 pages including studies of entrance door (G.S.A.).

151. Museo Poldi Pezzoli, newly opened in 1881.

152. 2 watercolours from the border of a 16th C. Persian carpet, Kashan (inv. 424)
(H.A.G.).

38. C. R. Mackintosh: S. Abbondio, Como (June 1891)
The twin tower arrangement was later used in Mackintosh's 1892 scheme for
Glasgow Art Gallery (fig. 57).

CHARLES RENNIE MACKINTOSH

# c. *A Tour in Italy* (1892)

c 1    A Tour in Italy.

I have no doubt almost every one here would have a different way of writing an essay on such a subject. Some there are who would enter into the task of treating the whole thing from an historical point of view, and give us a long list of dates and facts which I doubt not would interest a few while to others it would be very dry & tiresome, some who's sympathies were touched by the beauties of the Italian Gothic would devote the paper entirely to its praise & exaltation, and en equally loud & lengthy denunciation of all things Classic, and there are others who would reverse this and reserve all their condemnatory vigour for the Gothic and all things pertaining thereto. Others there are again who would devote the time allowed for those papers to a very interesting (sometimes) desort-

c 2    ation on their travels, taking up an unbiased position, / and neither praising up one side or the other, would simply give you a description of the various places & things of interest and leave each member to form his own Conclusions. In justification of my remarks, and to fortify myself against the possibility of arousing within you feelings of anger or disap-

c 2a    pointment I will classify my essay under the later category /[1] in so far as a due appreciation & admiration goes – but differing in this way that I will not even try to give any matter of fact detailed description of any building or object, but will rather endeavour to give a frank & spontaneous expression of the impression left on my mind after seeing each place  For the rest I would refer you to the sketches of the various places, which I trust & believe will give you a far greater degree of benefit than any

c 2b    verbal description no matter how ably done. / I would also like to advise you not to expect to be told about every thing there is to see, all I can do, is to make a careful & I hope judicious representative selection. I will endeavour to do this and give you each one as I found it myself, whether the discovery was always made under the most favourable auspices you shall be the judges.

c 3    To any one of you [who] is or who may be hereafter / contemplating a tour in Italy I would advise you to go there as I did by sea, as it sets you up splendidly for the hard work before you and Im sure you'll not regret doing so especially if the weather & other conditions are as conducive to enjoyment as when I went.

    1. Mackintosh here scored out 'I will now endeavour – with your kind attention – to describe in as frank and spontaneous a was as possible to describe my tour.' and inserted 'in so far ... ably done.'

I left Glasgow in February and after spending some days in London, sailed for Naples where I arrived on the 5th of March.[2] The weather during the whole voyage was of the most charming description. I shall never forget wakeing up one morning and seeing Naples through the Port hole of our cabin. I have no doubt that to most of you this famous aspect of Naples is known to exist, but to realize the grandeur of it you must see it.

c 4     The morning of our arrival was perfect in every respect, the ship lay at anchor about a mile from the shore, which / gave us a fine expanse of blue Italian sea, and beyond that was naples, rising up in a grand mass from the edge of the watter and terminating in the grand old Certosa of S. Martino, just bathed, literally steeped up to the neck in glorious sunshine.

I afterwards came to the conclusion that Naples was best seen from a distance; when you land all the beauty of the vision vanishes like a dream: a more noisy, filthy place Im sure you could'nt find anywhere The streets are narrow, the people lazy & filthy, in fact every thing about seems to do its very levelest to make the place disagreeable and increase the pestilential smell which pervades the whole town. But we will leave that smell and take ourselves to whatever places of interest there are.

c 5     First among these is the Museum / where there is a magnificent collection of frescoes & sculptures from Pompei In fact there is more of Pompei here than there is at the excavations of the town itself.

There is also a very fine collection of Architectural Fragments, glass, Pottery & Pictures in one of the rooms of which, there is a beautiful bronze tabernacle  See ill.

There are very few churches of interest in Naples, the best being Trinita Maggiore, which is richly decorated within (see ill of door) S. Chiara, & S. Maria del Carmine (see tower). The Duomo being under repair and covered with scaffolding I was unable to see much of it but what I did see I unhessitatingly pronounced as bad. The tomes in S. Anna dei Lombardi & S. Domenico Maggiore, although the best in Naples do not come up to those in Florence & Venice so we will not drag them from their sweet

c 6     oblivion. / Two of the gates of Naples Porta Capuana & Porta [left blank][3] see ill – are very good.

One thing in Naples which is a constant incentive to bad language is that some of the churches are open from 10 – 12 & others from 3 – 5 to find out <u>which is open</u> when is the puzzle  None of the Neopolitan Palaces are of any note. I went through the Royal Palace and found the interior to be as wild an exhibition of extravigant vulgarity as I ever wish to see.

Far different from this is the Certosa S. Martino which is really a place of great interest. Situated above the town the view from some balconies of

2. In fact 5 April. Naples: see B 5-12 April.
3. Possibly Porta Alphons (1454-67).

this building is really grand. The church, Chapter House &c are finished in a most elaborate manner  every inch is covered with beautiful marbles frescoes, wood carving, intersia, mosaic & tiles, and some of them are

c 7    really good. / They have here a splendid collection of glass & porcelain ware, and in the courtyard is a good well (see ill) and a fine series of Heraldic Arms.

Castello di S Elmo should also be visited at this point.

Naples forms a spendid centre to travel from; Pompei which is quite one of the most interesting & instructive places in Italy,[4] Salerno, Sorrento, Paestum with its famous Greek Temples, Amalfi with its Duomo & Capri can all be got at easily from naples.

Sicily. We left Naples at five in the evening  The good ship "Leone" in which we went didn't seem at all comfortable on such a stormy night as it turned out to be, and kept rolling & tossing about in the most reckless manner possible  I thought I had got my sea legs on the way out to Naples but I soon found out my mistake, for before we had been out two

c 8    hours I was, in company / with most of the passengers very bad  after lying groaning for some time I tried to walk round the ship, but found myself tumbling over prostrate soldiers and sailors? who lay in large numbers upon the fore deck for all the world dead, and Im sure many of them wished they were in that happy state where there is no sea sickness.

We arrived at Palermo about 9 in the morning & Im sure we were all thankful to get on shore.[5]

If any of you ever go to Palermo <u>dont</u> stay at Albergo Rubecchino, Via Vittorio Emmanuel Numero une dieci.

The Cathedral at Palermo is very interesting externally (see ill)  the dome has been renewed, and the interior with the exception of two holy water basins and some other fittings has been done up in the same abominable style.

At this point of my tour snow fell on two or three occasions, which

c 9    rather interfered with / the work I had to do.

The Chapel in the Royal Palace (see ill) is the finest thing here, and when first I got inside I was simply struck dumb with astonishment  Here was something I have never seen, never even dreamt of. The interior is one mass of mosaics on a gold ground, and being the first example of this kind I had seen I was very much fetched.

I was greatly delighted with Palermo which is just full of good & interesting features  The churches of S. Giovanni Eremiti, La Martorana &

c 10   S Francesco, being all goot. There is also a fine collection in the museum. / I next went to monreale.[6] The tram car takes you out to within half an hours walk up a steep and rugged mountain path. This fine old Monas-

4. Pompeii: see B 5, 7 and 9 April.
5. Palermo: see B 13-18 April.
6. Monreale: see B 14 and 16 April.

tery of Monreale gave me quite as much pleasure & delight as anything I saw in Italy, every bit – the exterior which is very old with its plain square tower and beautiful bronze doors, the interior which like the Capello Palazzo Reale is covered with mosaic representing sacred history, the cloisters the garden everything in fact is fine. But there this beautiful work stands – unheeded and uncared for – left to the tender mercies of two or three custodians, while the people who dwell around it – who ought to be influenced by its incomparable beauty, seem to devote all their small affections on their umbrella, – cab-drivers donkey drivers –

C 11     stone breakers – policemen &c. all carry their umbrellas / in a most exemplary & constant manner if not for the Shower – then for the Sunshine  After spending a week in Sicily I returned to Naples and from there on to Rome  The country by the way is very interesting for a bit but after passing 30 or 40 miles of vine fields one begins to wish for some diversity.

Of Rome and Roman architecture you all know more or less, usually more I would say.[7]

To enumerate all the churches of Rome would be absurd  there are some 360 of them and some in fact most of them have some features of interest  Of course there is St Peters — I would'nt like to give expression to my opinion of St Peters, the exterior you all know – the interior well it is vast – vast – I try to get away from the word vast but it won't work – I

C 12     know there is lots of beautiful marble real and imitation, lots — / lots of silver and bronze, lots of jewels & precious stones, lots of fine frescoes & an abundance of gold paint, but the whole of this vast structure, all this conglomeration of marble, plaster stone gold silver bronze & paint did not give me a fraction of the pleasure I derived from any one of the mosaics at Monreale.

In st Peters it is difficult to realize the vastness of the place, untill you see some people at the other end, and then indeed you come to the conclusion that man is small and St Peters is large.

The other churches that should be mentioned are St Pauls which St Peters not excepted is the finest in Rome,[8] St Lorenzo, the interior of which is built of fragments of ancient Temples &c & S. Aracili on the Capitoline Hill.

The vatican museum. (see ill)

The collection of art treasures here is really wonderful comprising,

C 13     Antique Architectural / Fragments, Sculpture, Painting, Pottery, and Glass, everything you can imagine in large quantities, and of the very finest quality. To start and enumerate any of these wonders would lead into such a lengthy description, which, no matter how long, would in no way exhaust this vast collection, that I think it is perhaps best to refrain

7. Rome: see B 19 April-4 May.

8. S. Paoli fuori le Mura, 19th C. reconstruction of an ancient basilica founded by Constantine.

altogether, and[9] (see ill) of M. Angclo's I may mention however the paintings on thc cciling of the Sistine Chapel by Mick Angelo and the Last Judgement which are perhaps the finest examples of pictorial art ever produced. There are also a grcat many frescose[10] in some of the other appartments by Raphael but they are very much inferior to M Angclo's. The screen & Pulpit in the chapel are most beautiful, and for delicacy of workmanship cannot be surpassed.

Besides the Vatican, there are The Capitoline & Latern Museums & the Villa Borgese which are all good.

c 14     I show various palaces from Rome which are all more or less interesting according to taste. And now we must push on to Antient / Rome and by the way I may add that the road from the Capitol to the Colosseum taking in the forum Romanum & the Campo Vaccin, bears a very striking resemblance to some parts of the east end of Glasgow assuming about two thirds of the population to be dead of colera.

It is as grimy, as filthy, as tumblesome as forlorn, and is as unpleasantly rendolent of old clothes, and old women who were washerwomen once upon a time, but who have long since fornsworn soap, either for their own or for others use. That the temples and palaces of the Forum & the Capitol should be delapidated & decrepit is in the nature of things and offers no protext for grumbling I do not feel inclined to echo the opinion of the intelligent American tourist who describes Rome "As a nice place, but the public buildings much out of repair" The tumbledown structures

c 15     I object to are the modern ones. The classical ruins are / ruins and behave as such. The delapidated domestic edifices are not picturesque and their discrepitude is not veneiable.

The various ruins you are all familiar with, you have all, at some date more or less remote drawn the various orders of Roman Architecture, so I will not detain you by describing the various Triumphal arches (see ill) the well known temples of Vespa Saturn, Venus & Roma, the famous Colosseum, the Basilica of Constantine, or the world renowned baths of Caracalla or Diocletian.

It is intensely interesting to wander over those ruins and see for yourself all you have read about, & much that you have drawn to see exactly where this or that famous building ecclesiastical domestic or commercial was situated There is one old building in Rome more impressive than any other, not only because of its better state of preservation but because of the dignity with which it has been designed, the

c 16     perfection / with which it has bccn constructed, and the effectiveness of

9. Mackintosh here scored out 'I will content myself with showing you what photos I have [(see ill] of M. Angelo's] frcscoes in thc Sistine Chapel' and inserted 'I may mention . . . ever produced.'

10. A separate page contains an earlier draft covering Monreale to the Vatican: 'I next went to Monreale [c 10] . . . there are also a great many frescose'. In the final version Mackintosh added his comments on the neglect of the Monreale monuments.

the mode of lighting. You cant conceive the grandeur of the old Pantheon when first you enter, it is so vast and grand.

But we must now start for Florence. on the way you come to Chusi, and you can either go by orvieto & Siena or by Perugia and Assisi. I went to Orvieto and found it a most interesting [town] away up on the top of a hill, with a most gorgeous cathedral leterally covered with gold, but which though grand and imposing presides over nothing but idleness, dirt and misery.[11] (see ill)

Siena is another most interesting place,[12] besides the Cathedral there are numerous church & Palaces, and the pictures by Sodoma which are here very abundant are not the least attraction in this town. The Cathedral situated on the highest point of the town, is a fine example of the

C 17    beauties and peculiarities of Italian / Gothic. The front, one of those frauds so often seen in Italy, having evidently been considered quite independent & apart from the rest of the church, is of marble worked into innumerable arches, pinnacles, ornaments and statues, many of which are so bad and clumsy, that they detract very considerably from the effect. Then the side, there are no windows in the aisles, so that was plain and might have looked well enough so, but it was'nt good enough for the Sienese, so they had windows put there, very beautiful examples of Italian Gothic, & I was indeed sorry to see that the rain was washing them quite away. The calm repose (see ill) of the Campanile is in very striking contrast to all the excitement and fuss of the front, starting solid at the base in the first story you have one window, and there is a gradual increas at the rate of one

C 18    opening per / story untill at the top where there are six. The finish of this tower as well as that of the front pinnacles is very clumsy Internally this church is of black & white marble in alternate bands for a certain height up, after which the bands are only painted, which is very bad.

Above the clerestory a cornice runs right round the church filled with busts of all the popes, in terra cotta, and above this the roof is blue with gold stars. The pavement of this church demands special attention being covered with marble inlays representing bible subjects – Moses striking the Rock, The Slaughter of the Innocents &c &c. In the Opera del duomo are some antique fragments of Scrafetto work which was once on the pavement. The shades of the figures are beautifully drawn on the ivory white marble & filled in with a most beautiful green cement. I was

C 19    very / greatly delighted with them and was only sorry that I had not time to make a sketch To return to the church, near the high altar stands the pulpit, supported on granite pillars rising from the backs of Lions which serve as pedestals

The wooden stalls and reading desk, in the choir are very elaborately carved & panelled see ill. The little boys on the arms being specially fine. From the church you enter through a beautiful Renaissence Screen, the

11. Orvieto: see B 4-10 May.
12. Siena: see B 10-19 May.

library which is filled with Missals exquisitely illuminated. The frescoes on the walls of this appartment are after designs by Raphael.

In the rear of the church and beneath the choir is the ancient Battisterio, with a beautiful font (see ill) with bronze sculptures by Lorenzo Ghiberti, Donatello, and Jacopo della Quercia.

Iron torch bearers  see ill.

Florence. Upon turning a long curve on the Railway we discover

c 20    Florence surrounded / by gardens and villas, rising one above the other, the sun which seems to shine with a peculiar charm upon this place, was doing its best when we arrived. Florence ranks with rome & Venice as one of the most attractive towns in Italy  An amazing profusion of art treasures, such as no other locality posesses within so narrow limits, reminisinces of a history which has influenced the whole of europe perpetuated by numerous and imposing monuments & lastly the delightful environs of the city, combine to make it one of the most interesting and attractive towns in the world.[13]

"Like the waterlily rising on the mirror of the lake, so rests on this lovely ground the still more lovely Florence  From the bold airy tower of the Palace to Brunelleschis wondrous dome of the Cathedral, from the old house of the Spini to the Pitti Palace the most imposing the world has

c 21    ever seen — / from the garden of the Francescan Convent, to the environs of the Casini, all is full of incomparable grace. Each street of Florence contains a world of art: the walls of the city are the calyx, containing the fairest flowers of the human mind: and this is but the richest jem in the diadem with which the Italian people have adorned the earth[14]  The first things we saw at Florence were the Piazza Signoria, with the Palazzo Vecchio & the Loggia which is full of statuary.

Then we went to the Uffitzi & Pitti Pallaces with their extraordinary collection  I felt on first entering this world of refinement as if I could have taken up my abode in it for ever but, confused with its multitude of objects, I knew not on which first to bend my attention, and ran child-

c 22    ishly by the endless array of sculptures, like / a butterfly in a garden, that skims before it fixes over ten thousand flowers. Having taken my course down one side of the galleries about a quarter of a mile long, I turned the angle and discovered another long perspective, equally stored with masterpieces in Bronze & Marble  A minute brought me to the extremity of this range vast though it was, then flying down a third adorned in the same delightful manner. I paused – under the bust of Jubiter Olympius. opposite appeared the features of Minerva breathing divinity and on the other side Cybele the mother of the gods – and [I] began to reflect a little more maturely upon the company in which I found myself.

13. Florence: see B 19-26 May.

14. A separate page contains an earlier draft from 'reminiscences of a history [c 20] ... adorned the earth'. In this the quotation beginning 'Like the waterlily ...' is terminated at 'adorned the earth'. The source is so far unidentified but may be Ruskin.

After a time the transport of enthusiasm begins to subside, and one begins to feel able to pass from chamber to chamber & from Cabinet to

c 23     Cabinet without falling into errors of rapture and / admiration. You go slowly through the large rooms containing the portraits of painters, good bad & indifferent from Raphael to Leotard then into a museum of bronzes, which would afford amusment & instruction for years.

When I had rather alarmed than satisfied my curiosity by rapidly running over a multitude of candelbrum, urns & other sacred utensils, we entered a small luminous apartment surrounded with cases richly decorated and filled with the most exquisite models of workmanship in bronze & various other metals. Among these now neglected images, are preserved a vast number of talismen, cabalistic amulets & other grotesque relics of ancient creduality.

c 24     We now pass through room after room containing miles of pictures by Dutch French, German, Flemish, British and Italian painters. We next reach the octagonal tribuna, containing a magnificent and almost unparalled collection of masterpieces of antient sculpture & modern painting  Need I say I was spell bound the moment I set my feet within it and saw full before me The Venus di Medici's, the warm ivory hue of the original marble is a beauty no copy has ever imitated, and the softness of the limbs exceeded the livliest idea I had formed to myself of their perfections.

The day was far gone before I could snatch myself from this Tribuna

On the way home I looked into the cathedral, an enormous fabric inlaid with the richest marbles and covered with panels and carving on

c 25     the / exterior, while the interior is plain & simple  The nave is vast & solemn, the dome amazingly spacious with the high altar as a center enclosed by a circular arcade some 200 feet in diameter  There is something imposing about the decoration as it suggests the idea of sancity into which none but the holy ought to penetrate. However profane I might feel myself I took the liberty of entering and sat down in a niche. Not a ray of light enters this sacred enclosure but through the medium of narrow windows high up in the dome and richly painted  A sort of yellow green tint predominates which which gives additional solemnity to the altar and paleness to the votary before it. I was concious of the effect and obtained at least the colour of sancity. Having remained some time in this

c 26     pious hue I left the church and went into / the Battesterio, a most admirable octagonal structure, where are the three famous bronze doors, one by Andrae Pisano & two by Lorenzo Ghiberti  The floor is very early and has the signs of the zodiac beautifully worked in marble panels.

Looking here at the Batesterio & the Cathedral one is very much struck by the changes which came over the architecture of Italy, in the Battisterio you have an early example of renaissance built in 1128 the cathedral in gothic 1294 and Brunellescos famous & masterly dome built in 1420 designed once more in the classic renaissence, here all in one

place you have three distinct & opposite styles of Architecture all built
within a period of 300 years. In domestic structures Florence has its own
peculiar style of which[15] the Strozzi & Ricardi are the best.[16] The beautiful

c 27  simplicity, the large masses of / plain masonry & small windows, surmounted by tremendeous cornices beautifully designed, gives these
palaces a simple but dignified grandeur. The walls are adorned at a height
of five feet from the ground with beautiful iron & bronze rings to which in
the middle ages horses were attached by the bridle while the Cavaliero
transacted buisness with the nobles within.

The good churches of Florence are very numerous including St Croche,
La Badia which both contain beautiful tombs, St Miniato,[17] the decoration
of the roof & choir, the pavement, and the alter & alter screen all being
exceedingly beautiful  St Maria Novella which has exquisite glass
windows in chancel, St Lorenzo where there is the Medici Pew and many
others.

The Medici Chapel by M Angelo is also most beautiful & imposing. In
the museo Mational there are many beautiful architectural Fragments
and a great number of Della Robian sculptures. The Ponte Vecchio is also
an interesting sight in Florence. We now leave florence & go to Pisa

c 28  where there is the Cathedral Battistero leaning tower, Campo /[18] Santa
& Various churches & Palaces[19] – then Pistoya The Battistero & Palazzo
Publico being good then Bologna.[20] I have very little to say of Bologna as
we only stayed an afternoon there but what we did see was not calculated to keep us any longer. From Bol we went to Ravenna which came to
us like an osias in a desert[21] – the mosaics in St Appolinaris Nuovo & S
Appolinaris In Classe – S Vitale – the Battisterio, & St Giovanni Evangelista being superb.

Ferrara. with its interesting cathedral some beautiful decoration in the
Castello by dosso Dossi & some small things scattered through the town.[22]
And now we come to Venice which to see properly you should not go to
by rail but should get at [from] some of of the towns on the mainland
such as Mestra Secondo or Fasina.[23] embarking our luggage at the last
mentioned place we stepped into the gondola whose gliding & graceful

c 29  motion was most welcome after the jolting of the train / As soon as we get

15. Three separate pages contain an earlier draft for c 22-6: 'After a time the transport
of enthusiasm ... own peculiar style of which'. In the final version Mackintosh added the
preceding sentence: 'Looking here at the Batesterio ...'

16. Pal. Strozzi 1489; Pal. Medici Riccardi 1440-60. 1 sketch of a Florentine palace and
tower (Coll. C. R. Mackintosh Society, Glasgow): see fig. 30.

17. Mackintosh here scored out 'should on no account be mist'.

18. Inscribed at top of c 28: 'Lucca Cathedral see ill'.

19. Pisa: see B 26 May.

20. Pistoia: see B 27 May. Bologna: see B 27 May.

21. Ravenna: see B 27 May-1 June.

22. Ferrara: see B 1 June.

23. Venice: see B 1-10 June.

out of the canal an expanse of sea opened to our view, the Domes & towers of Venice rising from its bosom. We pass Murano, St Michele, St Giorgio in Alga and several other islands detached from the grand cluster. Still gliding forward we every moment pass some well known church or pallace in the city, suffused with the rays of the setting sun, and reflected with all their glory of colour, on the surface of the water. I have no terms to describe the effect of the ensemble looking up that part of the grand canal terminated by the Rialto. The first sight of this scene simply takes ones breath away. All attempts at a verbal rendering of this effect, would be so tame & presumptious that I will not attempt it. I can only assure you that not even in your happiest & most imaginitive moments can you realize in the slightest degree what Venice is like at any time, and more

c 30    especially at night under the magic influence of the setting sun. / We established ourselves at Pensione Anglais which is situated on the Grand Canal  As night approached another paradisical treat was given us.

Innumerable lights began to appear on the canal, every boat had its lantern, and the gondolas moving rapidly along, were followed by tracks of light which played and danced upon the waters.

I was gazing in rapturous delight at those dancing fires, when the sounds of music were wafted along the canal towards us, as they grew louder and louder a barge, illuminated with numerous lights of various hues, filled with musicians issued from the Rialto, and stopping under one of the palaces, began a serranade which stilled every clamour & sus-pended all conversation in the galleries and porticos: till, rowing slowly away it was heard no more. The gondoliers catching the air, imitated its cadances, and were answered by others at a distance, whose voices,

c 31    echoed on the palaces / on either side acquired a plaintive and interesting tone. I retired to rest full of the sound and long after I was asleep the melody seemed to vibrate in my ear. And thus ended my first experiences of Venice.

In the morning I visited St Maria della Salute, erected by the Senate in performance of a vow to the Holy Virgin who begged off a terrible pest-ilence in 1630.

The great bronze doors opened while I was standing on the steps leading to it, and discovered the interior of the dome where I expiated in solitude, no mortal appearing except an old priest who trimmed the lamps and muttered something presumably a prayer, before the high altar, still rapt in shadow. The sunbeams were just striking the windows of the dome as I was wafted in a gondola to the spacious platform in front of St Giorgio Maggiore, one of the most celebrated works by Palladio – When I

c 32    had examined this church I had time to look around me and view at / my leisure the vast range of Pallaces & churches, of domes & towers opening on every side and extending out of sight  The Doges Palace and the tall columes with the Winged Lion of St Marks and St Theodore on a croco-dile at the entrance to the piazzetta form, together with the arcades of the public library, the lofty and beautiful campanile, and the domes of the Ducal Church, one of the most striking groups of buildings that art can boast of.

To behold at one glance those stately fabrics, so illustrius in the records of former ages, before which, in the flourishing times of the republic, so many valiant chiefs and princes had landed, loaded with oriental spoils was a spectacle I had long and ardently desired. I thought of the days of Frederic Barbarossa, when looking up the piazza, along which he marched in solemn procession to cast himself at the feet of Alexander the Third, and pay a tardy homage to St Peters successor. Here was no longer

c 33  those splendid / fleets that attended his progress, one solitary ship anchored opposite the palace of the Doges surrounded by a crowd of gondolas was all I beheld.

c 34  We will now enter St Giorgio Maggiore[24] / After admiring the masterly construction of the roof and the lightness of its arches my eyes naturally directed themselves to the pavement of white & ruddy marble polished and reflecting like a mirror the columns which rise from it. Over this I walked to a door which admitted me to the principal cloister which is surrounded by Ionic Columns. The refectory opens from this, where the chef d'ae'ouvre of Paolo Veronese, representing the Marriage of Cana in Galilee is seen.

c 35  I moved out of the church and entering the gondola was landed at the steps of the Redontore a simple & elegant structure.[25]

We next landed at the steps in front of the ducal palace and after fighting for about 10 minutes with the gondoliers about the fare I directed my steps towards the great church of St Marco. I looked a moment at the four stately coursers of Bronze & gold that adorn the cheif portal, and then took in at a glance the whole extent of the piazza with its towers & standards.

A more noble assemblage was never exhibited by Architecture.

Having enjoyed the general perspective of the piazza I began to enter into particulars and examine the bronze pedestals (see ill) of the three standards before the great church, designed by Sansovino in the true

c 36  spirit of the antique and covered with relievos at once bold & elegant.[26] / It is also to this celebrated architect we are indebted for the stately facade of the Procuratie Nuove which forms one side of the piazza, and presents an – uninterrupted series of arches & marble Columns exquisitely wrought.[27]

On the opposite side is another arcade which though much inferior to Sansovino's impresses veneration & completes the whole in a very fitting manner.[28]

24. S. Giorgio Maggiore founded 1566, by Palladio.
25. Il Redentore 1577-92, by Palladio.
26. Pedestals 1505, in fact by A. Leopardi.
27. Procuratie Nuove 1580-c. 1640, by Sansovino.
28. Procuratie Vecchie by M. Coducci, reconstructed 1512.

The Campanile rising distinct from the pavement is of immense dimensions & in spite of some trivial defects in design is a most awe inspiring structure.[29]

A beautiful building called the Loggetta which though far from diminished is in a manner lost at the foot of the Campanile.[30] Two beautiful bronze gates by Sansovino adorn the entrance to this chamber which once served as a waiting room for the procurators, whose office it was during the Sessions of the great Council, to command the guards. The

C 37   bronze Statues of Peace, / Apollo, Mercury & Pallas, and the various reliefs are also by Sansovino.

Crossing the ample space between this graceful ediface & the Ducal Palace I passed through a labyrinth of pillars and entered the principal court. Two beautiful well heads of bronze (see ill) diversify the area. In front is a flight of steps which lead to the entrance which is guarded by colossal statues of Mars & Neptune which give to the stair the appellation of Scale dei Giganti  this I ascended not without respect, and, leaning against the beautiful balustrade, formed like the rest of the building of the rarest marbles, – contemplated the tutelary divinities. My admiration was shortly interrupted by one of the custodians, who told me the gates were upon the point of being closed, so hurrying down the steps I left a million

C 38   delicate sculptures unexplored, for every pilaster, every panel / and every entablature is carved in the most delicate manner, and enriched with panels of porphery, verde antique and other precious marbles.

The various portals, the strange projections in short the striking irregularities of those stately piles delighted me beyond idea; and I was sorry to be forced to abandon them so soon especially as the twilight, which bats and owls love not better than I do, enlarged every portico, lengthened every collonade, added a certain misticism, and increased the dimensions of the whole just as the imagination desired.

This faculty would certainly have had full scope, had I been allowed to remain an hour longer. The moon would then have gleamed upon the gigantic forms of Mars & Neptune, and discovered the statues of ancient

C 39   heroes emerging from the gloom of their niches. / combination of objects such regal senery transported me beyond myself. The custodian thought me distracted.

This fit of enthusiasm was hardly subsided when I passed the gate of the palace into the great square which received a faint gleam from the restuarants, just beginning to be lighted up and to become the resort of pleasure and dissipation. Numbers were walking in parties upon the pavement, some sought the convenient gloom of the porticos with their favourites, others were earnestly engaged in conversation, and filled the gaily illuminated appartments, where they resorted to drinking coffee &c

29. Campanile 888-1511.
30. Loggetta 1537-49, by Sansovino.

&c, with laughter & merriment. A thoughtless giddy transport prevailed, for at this hour anything like restraint seems perfectly out of the question,

c 40 and, however solemn a magistrate or senator / may appear in the day time, at night he lays up wig & roll & gravity, to sleep together, runs intriguing about in his gondola, takes the reigning sultana under his wing, and so rambles half over the town which grows gayer and gayer as the day declines. The novelty of the Scene afforded me no small share of amusement as I wandered from group to group, and from place to place.

The excessive heat at Venice in summer makes one glad to mingle with the throng and go out to the Island of Ledo where there is a grand Cascino & where the evening festivities of Piazza S. Marco, are equalled in variety & charm if not excelled by day.[31]

Next morning directing my course immediately to the ducal palace, I entered the great court, ascended the giant stair and examined, those

c 41 things I had left unseen the night before. Then taking / directions from a guide I wandered through inumerable corridors into the state apartment which Tintoret & Paolo Veronese have covered with the triumphs of their country.

There are many interesting things to see here (see ill) including the dungeons & the various modes of torture practised in earlier times,

The bridge of sighs which connects the highest part of the prison to the secret galleries of the palace, from whence criminals were conducted over the arch to a cruel and mysterious death. I shuddered while passing and believe it is not without cause, this structure is named Ponte dei Sospiri.

We now find ourselves outside again; about sunset the cheerful view from Fondamenti Nuovi, a vast quay or terrace of white marble, which commands the whole series of islands from S. Michele to Torcello, That

c 42 rise and glitter o'er the / ambient tide, is very refreshing.

I like this odd town of Venice, and find, every day, some new church or palace of interest & beauty.

The great church of St Marco with its immense variety of marbles the mazes of delicate sculptures & the cupola glittering with gold mosaic is a never ending source of delight. A run up the Campanile and a leisurely survey of Venice beneath, with its azure blue sea, its great stretch of flat red tiled roofs, broken and diversified by innumerable towes, domes & cupolas no one should miss, for besides being interesting in itself, it gives you a remarkably good insight into the geography of the town.

We now enter the[32] Basilica of St Marks the most gorgeous but about the darkest church in Europe [which] is glorified by the sun. The contrast

c 43 is the more / striking, as the rest of the church is so dark and like a gloomy wilderness, through which you might wander long enough before

---

31. Mackintosh's text has 'XX' at the beginning and end of this sentence suggesting it was either to be omitted or inserted elsewhere during the lecture.

32. Mackintosh scored out 'There is a certain time in the afternoon when a certain part of the' and substituted 'We now enter the'.

you discovered that all around you were columns of porphery of malachite and verde antique, panels glowing with gold & jems & pavements dazzling in mosaics.

Lost in unbrageous dimness are the sumptuous Battisterio, the jewel crouded chapel of the Madonna di' Mascoli, the two fanciful pale[33] that flank the high altar, nay even the famous Icone Bisantina, and the stately Baldacchino have but a faint and uncertain glimmer. At this moment the sun in the west sends a gigantic ray of light through the central window, which just tips the heads of the Evangelist statues on the rood loft, touches the topmost members of the altar screen, and ends in the semi

c 44    circular recess behind the altar. / The great recess is all at once in a blaze; looking out of the darkness you might fancy the high altar to be on fire.

Understand that this apsis is wholly covered with golden mosaic, and that in the centre is a colossal figure of the redeemer. This golden alcove of glory this inexhaustable treasure chamber, this stupendeous shrine glittering and trembling in its abundance of radiance fills you with unspeakable awe and veneration. (see ill)

The great door of St Marks leading to the vestibule where the story of the Creation and the Fall, and of the Deluge is told with such quaint simplicity is always open. see (ill)

There is much more in Venice which is delightful, but which Im afraid must be overlooked on this occasion, but I may mention the Academia

c 45    della Belle Arti where are the works / of Gentile Bellini, Boccaccino da Cremona, Rocco Marconi, Bonifazio, Tintoretto, and Titian are all well represented.[34]

The Scuola di S Rocco containing the council halls of the brotherhood possesses a magnificent facade, and handsome old staircase and hall. The interior is painted by Tintoretto & Titian. The bronze doors in front of the high altar in the great Hall are by Gius. Filiberti. (see ill)[35]

The Palazzo Contarini, Palazzo Foscari  Pal Pisani, Pal Spinelli, Pal Grimani, Cà d'Oro, (see ill) are all interesting. (see ill)[36]

The most interesting churches beyond those already mentioned are S. Zaccaria, St Salvatore, St Maria Gloriosa dei Frari, St Maria del Carmine, S. Giovanni e Paolo, St Maria dei Miracoli, & S Giorgio dei Greci, (see

c 46    ill)[37] / Torcello & Murano should both be visited from Venice as there are

33. Pale: altarpieces. It is not known which paintings flanked the high altar in 1891: possibly Paolo Veneziano's cover of 1385 for the Pala d'Oro, and the present high altar-piece, a largely unstudied Venetian work of *c.* 1400. More probably Mackintosh is inaccurately referring to the two marble tabernacles *c.* 1385 by P. P. and J. dalle Masegne.

34. Boccaccino da Cremona (*c.* 1467-1524); Rocco Marconi (fl. 1504, d. 1529).

35. Giuseppe Filiberti (1733-75).

36. Mackintosh deleted from the list Pal. Pesaro and Pal. Calergi. 1 untraced water-colour *Venetian Palace*, exhibited G.I.F.A. 1892 (796).

37. S. Zaccaria 1444-1515: 1 sketch of altarpiece (Coll. C. R. Mackintosh Society, Glasgow). S. Salvatore rebuilt in 16th C., Baroque façade 1663. S. Maria Gloriosa dei

very interesting churches of an early date with some fine mosaics at
each.[38]

We left Venice for Padua on Wednesday 10th June

The first object which arouses interest is a confused pile of turrets and
domes (see ill) which are dedicated to the blessed St Antony. On entering,
the nave is full of women & children kneeling by baskets of vegetables
and other provisions, which by good St Anthonys interposition they
hoped to sell advantageously during the day. Beyond these nearer the
choir and in a gloomier part of the ediface, knelt a row of rueful peni-
tents, smiting their breasts and lifting their eyes to heaven. Further on, in
front of the dark recess in which the sacred relics are deposited, a few
c 47     desperately melancholy sinners lay prostrate. / A lofty altar decked decked
with the most lavish magnificence supports the shrine.[39] Those who are
profoundly touched with its sancity may approach and walking round
may look into the various corners & crevices.

But supposing a traveller ever so heretical I would advise him by no
means to neglect this pilgrimage, since every part of the recess he visits is
decorated with exquisite sculptures. Sansovino and other renowned artists
have vied with each other in carving the alto relieivos of the arcade,
which for design & execution cannot be surpassed. (see ill).[40]

The above record will give you some idea of the circumstances under
which ecclisiastical architecture is studied in Italy. This is no exceptional
case, but may be taken as true generally.

The next interesting structure is the great Hall of the town a most
c 48     spacious / place, designed by the great Palladio (see ill)[41] timber casts a
solemn gloom, which is not diminished by the wan light admitted
through windows of pale blue glass. The size & shape of this colossal
chamber, the arching of the roof, with enormous rafters stretching across
it, and above all the watery gleams that glanced through the casement,
possessed my fancy with ideas of Noah's Ark, and almost persuaded me, I
beheld that extraordinary vessel.

St Justiana is the only other ediface that calls for mention in Padua.[42]
Vicenza.[43]

The first morning being dull & wet we went to Palladios Theatre[44]

It is impossible to see this building without feelings of sincere admir-

Frari Gothic brick c. 1250-c. 1443. S. Maria del Carmelo 16th C. façade. S. Giorgio dei
Greci 1539, cupola 1571.

38. Torcello and Murano: see B 5 June.

39. Altar 1445-50, by Donatello and assistants.

40. Chapel of S. Antonio with nine reliefs of the miracles, including two by Sansovino.

41. Mackintosh must here be confusing Padua's Pal. della Ragione, commonly called Il
Salone (from 1219, rebuilt 1306 by Fr. G. degli Eremitani), with Palladio's Basilica in
Vicenza, 1549-1614.

42. S. Giustina 1502, by Il Riccio.

43. Vicenza: see B 10 June.

44. Teatro Olimpico 1580, Palladio's last work.

ation or conceive a structure more truly classical, or to point out a

c 49    single / ornament which has not the best antique authority. I am not in
the least surprised that the citizens of Vicenza enthusiastically gave into
this great architects plan & sacrifised large sums to erect so beautiful a
model.

There are various palaces in Vicenza by Palladio which are of great
interest but none of the churches are of any value.

Verona.[45] The Amphitheatre here is perhaps the most entire monument
of Roman days. There are various churches & palaces here which are
more or less good, especially S Anastasia, The Duomo  S. Maria in Organo
& S Zeno Maggiore which is a most interesting church with beautiful
entrance doors & some exquisite wooden stalls in the choir  The Gothic
tombs of the Scale family are also worth seeing.[46]

c 50    We now visit Mantua, Cremona, Brescia, / Bergamo and Como on the
way to Milan.[47]

At the latter place [i.e. Como] the Cathedral and the Churches of S
Fedele and the Basilica of S Abbondio are very goot.

Milan  In Milan there is a lot that is worth seeing and a great lot that
isnt.[48] First there is the Cathedral which has many good points but the
exterior is certainly overdone being literally choked with carving &
statuettes  In the interior the nave piers have no definite caps a series of
panels & niches performing that office (see ill)  There is a beautiful bronze
candelabra in the transept which is evidently very well known.[49] All the
windows in this Cathedral are filled with most abominable glass. There is
also a beautiful fan vaulted ceiling, which might be mistaken for the real

c 51    original had some of the plaster not fallen down, / thus laying bare the
deception

The Brera contains works by all the principal Italian Painters[50]  The
principal churches in Milan are S. Ambrogio, S. Eustorgio, S Lorenzo & St
Maria del Grazia  near this is the Last supper.

The Museo Poldi Pozzorli Numero deici Via Maroni contains for its size
the finest collection of art treasures I saw anywhere.

The only places we have now to visit are Pavia where there is the
beautiful old church, certainly the best of its kind in Italy, of S Michale,
and the Certosa which is distant from Pavia about 5 miles.[51]

45. Verona: see B 10-14 June.

46. Tombs of the Scaligers.

47. See B 14-27 June.

48. Milan: see B 27 June-7 July.

49. Trivulzio Candlestick bronze, French or German, 13th or 14th C.

50. Mackintosh here scored out his cumbersome list: 'There are some very good paint-
ings in the Brera by Giov. Bellini Gentile Bellini Francesco, Maioni, Dosso Dossi, Paolo
Veronese, Perugino, Giotto, Tintoretto, Titian, Ambrogio Borgognone, Vicenza Foppa,
Sabastina Rosa & Gulio Campi'.

51. S. Michele consecrated 1155. Certosa di Pavia, Carthusian monastery founded
1396, completed 1452; church 1472 with 16th C. façade. Mackintosh's admiration for

C 52

The facade of this ediface, by Ambrogio Borgognone, an example of the richest / Renaissence style, is entirely covered with marble of different colours, and most tastefully decorated. at the base are medallions of Roman Emperors, and above them scenes from sacred history, beyont them are the magnificent windows, which for beauty & delicacy of workmanship cannot be equalled anywhere.

The interior which has a very gorgeous effect was also decorated by Borgognone  Every chapel contains valuable pictures & other objects of Interest and are seperated from the nave, as is the transepts & choir, by beautiful iron & brass screens.[52] The choir stalls are covered with intersia which is perhaps the best in italy.[53] A beautiful door to the right of the choir leads to the Lavatorio where there is an exquisite marble fountain, which perpetuates the memory of the architect of this noble pile.[54] The

C 53

cloisters which are got at through / another beautiful door, are surrounded by marble colums and charming decorations, in terra cotta

This was our last place in Italy so we returned to Milan, & came home by Paris, Brussles, Antwerp & London, and thus ended a tour, and I only hope that all those present who have not yet been will some day sooner or later have the pleasure and privalege of undertaking a similar tour.

the rich sculptured and polychrome decoration of the exterior is unexpected. 17 sketches (Howarth): see fig. 29; 6 pp. (G.S.A.); 1 watercolour (G.S.A.): see fig. 32. The building was not by A. Borgognone but the work successively of C. and A. Mantegazza, G. A. Amadeo and C. Lombardo.

52. Baroque of 17th to 18th C.

53. Choir stalls 1498.

54. Door 1447-1522, by G. A. Amadeo; lavabo early 16th C., by A. Maffiolo of Carrara. 1 sketch of a fountain (G.S.A).

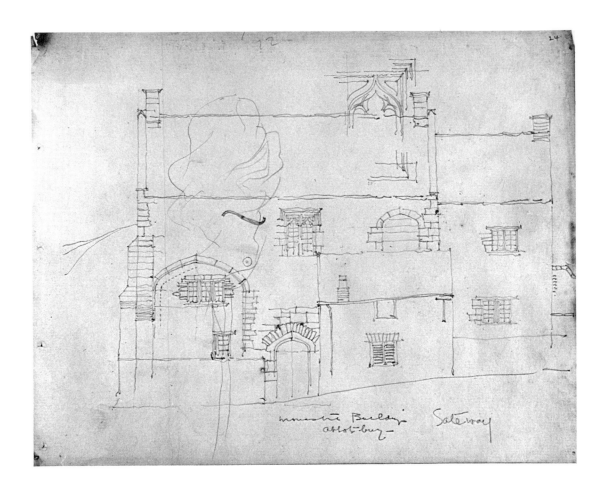

39. C. R. Mackintosh: Monastic Buildings, Abbotsbury, Dorset (1895)
Abbey House, a haphazard growth of Mackintosh's 'Transitional period'.
The drawing is overlaid with a detail of earlier window tracery.

JAMES MACAULAY

# Elizabethan Architecture

It is curious and perhaps at first disturbing that, when there was such a degree of interest in the architecture of his native land, Mackintosh should compile a paper on Elizabethan architecture. Unfortunately, the paper contains no clue as to the nature of the audience or the date of composition although from the internal evidence of Mackintosh's printed sources the year 1892 might be a possibility.[1]

The paper presents a chronological survey of Elizabethan architecture, concluding with brief comments on garden design, monumental sculpture and interior design. Just as Mackintosh had relied on MacGibbon and Ross in his exposition of 'Scotch Baronial Architecture' [A], so here too he made copious use of other printed sources, this time acknowledged, if only in part. There are direct quotations from William Harrison's *Description of England*, a primary source compiled in the last quarter of the sixteenth century and reissued in 1889; James Dallaway's *A Series of Discourses upon Architecture in England*, published in 1833; and, most particularly, James Fergusson's *History of the Modern Styles of Architecture*, the third edition of which was published in 1891 and was, presumably, the edition used by Mackintosh. The opening section of Fergusson's second volume covers the reigns of Queen Elizabeth and King James, a period which he categorised as transitional, as did Mackintosh. To condense his argument Mackintosh ignored Fergusson's treatise on English collegiate architecture but otherwise quoted at length from Fergusson's text, changing a word here and there and in one instance, when referring to Heriot's Hospital, Edinburgh, substituting 'Elizabethan' for 'Jacobean', presumably to reinforce his own hypothesis.

Mackintosh's opening sentence begins 'At a period so famed in the history of our country . . .' – which smacks of those who refer to England when they mean Great Britain, a trap into which Mackintosh also falls later in his paper. Or was there a deeper significance? Was Mackintosh's opening sentence an indication, albeit subliminal, that nationalistic Elizabethan glories had become ingrained in Scotland's architectural consciousness?

In the early decades of the nineteenth century the Gothic revival became infused with Tudor and Elizabethan motifs. At Fonthill Abbey, Wiltshire, which was commenced in 1795 by James Wyatt and would become the largest and most celebrated product of the Gothic revival in Regency England, the private apartments were garbed in quasi-Tudor with square-headed windows, drip moulds and a double height window bay.[2] Such a domestic scale, when allied to a convenient plan, could generate the 'utility and comfort' which Mackintosh considered in his opening remarks as being of benefit to his own generation.

The problems encountered by architects when adhering too rigidly to the Gothic canon had been shown up by William Atkinson, a former pupil of James Wyatt, at Rossie Priory, Perthshire (1810) where a gable hall was set athwart the main elevation which was closed by a pair of spire-capped towers. Such an assemblage of Gothic parts, without regard to their original functions, only served to reveal that 'the difficulties of matching medieval liturgical requirements to the somewhat looser living habits of the Regency were too much'.[3] It is not surprising, therefore, that at Abbotsford Sir Walter Scott attempted a compromise. Himself knowledgeable about the architecture of his own country, Scott had preferred the initial elevations by Edward Blore in 1816 'as being less Gothic and more in the old fashioned Scotch stile [sic] which delighted in notch'd Gable ends and all manners of bartizans'.[4] Scott wished neither to build a castle nor a priory but an 'old English hall such as a squire of yore dwelt in' which alone could provide 'a variety of snugg accommodation', which Scott most sought. Scott's equivocal description of his creation was a 'Scottish manor-house', which he recognised as being 'a picturesque, appropriate, and entirely new line of architecture';[5] and, indeed, Abbotsford, with its pictorial silhouette of crow-stepped gables, towers and turrets, was the precursor of Scots-Baronialism.

That it was not taken up immediately was because Tudor architecture, once introduced into Scotland by William Wilkins at Dalmeny House, West Lothian (1815), in the capable hands of William Burn became the style for the next generation for a country-house. That was paradoxical in Scotland. Yet, when Sir John Forbes of Craigievar was considering building a new house in 1829, a friend recommended 'the Manor Style. It admits of being added to – it is neat and light and airy within and it affords a good opportunity ... for your paying respect to your Ancestors by erecting [?] what may seem to have been of their day. You are not a proud man nor vain of your familie's [sic] antiquity ... and in this feeling I would put up a house with an elevation that I would think more than twice about, were I a new man.'[6] There was the later consideration by Robert Kerr that 'notwithstanding all the facilities which we possess in inexpensive decoration' Tudor architecture provided a requisite comfort and convenience without pretentiousness.[7]

Mackintosh could have seen several of Burn's Tudor mansions. While staying on the Ayrshire coast with John Keppie (the partner of John Honeyman after 1888) he made numerous sketching expeditions into the rolling countryside of south Ayrshire where he could have viewed Blairquhan (1820). Then there was Garscube House (1827) on the western edge of Glasgow's limits. Both displayed mullioned and transomed windows, crested parapets and a central lantern tower, illuminating a saloon, set over symmetrical façades. Internally, plaster was used both for decorative and pseudo-structural effects. Yet, as Pugin would write, 'as for plaster, when used for any other purpose than coating walls, it is a mere modern deception'[8] – a comment surely not lost on Mackintosh.

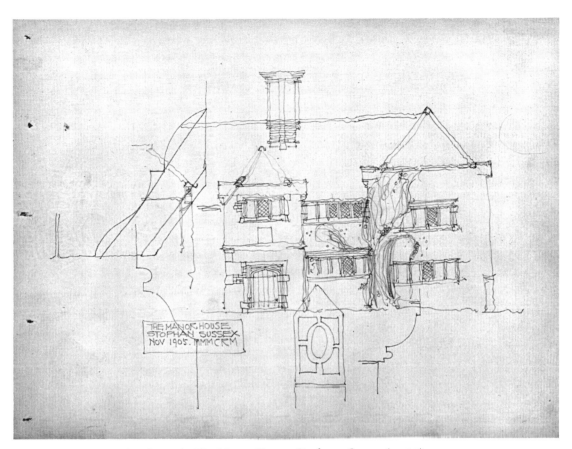

40. C. R. Mackintosh: The Manor House, Stopham, Sussex (1905)
A view of part of the E-shaped front elevation of this sixteenth century manor
with some seventeenth century restoration.

As Pugin saw it, his mission was to eliminate falseness. Hence the clarion
call in the first paragraph of *The True Principles of Pointed or Christian Architecture*. '1st, that there should be no features about a building which are not
necessary for convenience, construction, or propriety; 2nd, that all ornament should consist of enrichment of the essential construction of the building.' By these criteria much current building was morally condemned since
'Architectural features are continually tacked on buildings with which they
have no connexion, merely for the sake of what is termed effect; and ornaments are *actually constructed*, instead of forming the decoration of construction.'[9] While Pugin advocated specifically the use of Decorated of the late
thirteenth and fourteenth centuries, he was enough of a pragmatist to adopt
later modes for his secular compositions. 'What can be more absurd than
houses built in what is termed the castellated? . . . as models for our imitation
they are worse than useless.' The dilemma could be overcome by moving on

to the early Tudor age. 'The old English Catholic mansions ... were substantial appropriate edifices, suited by their scale and arrangement for the purposes of habitation.' Pugin next elucidated another article of faith in his design creed. 'Each part of those buildings indicated its particular destination.' Unfortunately, in contemplating the many newly-sprung Gothic Revival mansions, Pugin was forced to conclude: 'There is a great reviving taste for ancient domestic architecture, but a vast many ... instead of imitating the Tudor period, when domestic architecture was carried to a high state of perfection, stop short at the reign of Elizabeth, the very worst kind of English architecture.'[10] While Pugin's Catholic sympathies inhibited his appreciation for Elizabethan architecture there could also be criticism of its excessive ornamentation, such as strapwork, and the assimilation of Italian principles in the introduction of the orders and symmetry in plan and elevation.

Although there is no evidence that Puginian doctrine was taught in the classes which Mackintosh attended as a student, there can be no doubt that the theory was accepted by him. An examination of his sketchbooks, spanning the years from 1886 to 1921, albeit intermittently, reveals not only what Mackintosh considered to be of architectural worth but what, by its absence, he dismissed.[11] The first, rather earnest, surviving compositions, are seventeenth century mural tombstones, in the graveyards of Elgin and Glasgow Cathedrals, with colonettes upholding strapwork enclosing heraldic tablets. Strapwork would remain one of Mackintosh's abiding interests presumably because the abstract curves could easily become organic Art Nouveau forms. From Elgin Cathedral, too, there are watercolours of the ruined mediaeval chapter-house with broken Decorated tracery in the gashed windows. A more ambitious study in 1890 is the thirteenth century east end of Glasgow Cathedral against a vivid orange and yellow sunset.[12] Glasgow Cathedral had powerful associations for Mackintosh. Not only was it the largest and finest surviving ecclesiastical edifice in Scotland but when Mackintosh was young it was still the largest building in Glasgow, besides being just over the hill from his home in Firpark Terrace in Dennistoun. Later, Mackintosh would work with Honeyman, an acknowledged expert on mediaeval Gothic, who as the architect of the Cathedral contributed a chapter on its architectural development in *The Book of Glasgow Cathedral* (1898).

Like Pugin, Mackintosh's preference was for Decorated. Perhaps, therefore, it is no coincidence that his sketching tours were to the Cotswolds, Dorset, and Hampshire and to other areas in England which were richly stocked with Decorated architectural sources, both secular and ecclesiastical. So the sketchbooks record houses and churches alongside numerous ogees, undulating like seaweed, as well as stone and wooden panels, filled with burgeoning tracery, which would be revived in Mackintosh's own designs, as in the gallery pendants at Queen's Cross Church and in the library of the Glasgow School of Art. Early English evidently held no attrac-

WINDOW. SOUTH AISLE
. ELGIN CATHEDRAL.

41. C. R. Mackintosh: Window, Elgin Cathedral (1889)

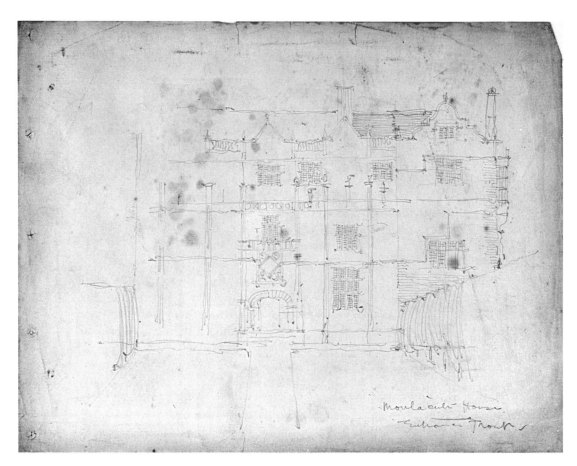

42. C. R. Mackintosh: Montacute House, Somerset – front elevation (1895)

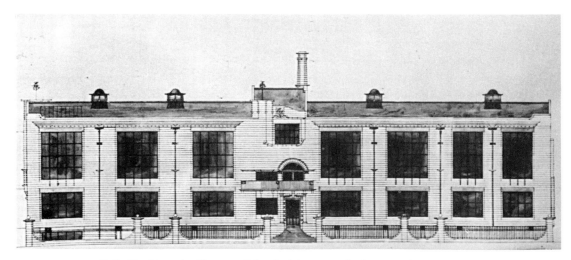

43. C. R. Mackintosh: Glasgow School of Art – north elevation (1897)

tion although there is an occasional Romanesque water-leaf capital, the flowing lines of which would be utilised later in ironwork or a poster design.

The choice of domestic work is just as limited. Although Mackintosh would have received a thorough training in the principles of classical architecture, so that he could turn out a competent academic exercise, such as the Science and Art Museum design in 1890,[13] he never showed a later predeliction for classicism, unlike his Glasgow contemporary, J. J. Burnet. No great country-houses are recorded except for two pencil drawings of Montacute House, Somerset (1580-99) which Mackintosh visited in 1895.[14] The date may be significant, for with its steep gables, gridded windows, an almost continuous band of glazing along the top storey and an oriel on the side elevation dropping through several floors, Montacute House could have been seminal in the conceptualisation of the north elevation of the Glasgow School of Art in 1896.

In his paper on Elizabethan architecture Mackintosh was selective in his choice of Elizabethan models, omitting, for example, Hardwick Hall, Derbyshire, which Fergusson admired.[15] Mackintosh begins his list of buildings with Warwick Castle and with Haddon Hall, Derbyshire, both dating in their major parts from the fourteenth century and notable for their ranges of domestic buildings. At Warwick Castle the mullioned and transomed windows play against low horizontal lines emphasised by string courses and crestings of ornamental parapets, while on the river front large Decorated windows are dominant. At Haddon Hall there are the same effects in addition to an Elizabethan long gallery, with an almost unbroken line of gridded windows, and an earlier great hall where the oak panelling, with plaster above, and the simple construction of the oak roof are indicative of interiors in the Glasgow School of Art. Indeed, there may be more than a passing interest in Mackintosh's comment on oak panelling: 'I doubt if full justice has been done to its merits and possib[il]ities' [D 19].

Not only did Warwick Castle and Haddon Hall represent centuries of building accretion but, overlaid with the patina of time, they had an appeal to those brought up to follow the tenets of William Morris and the Arts and Crafts movement. Thus, Haddon Hall could be eulogised as 'not spoilt or falcified by the modern restorer' [D 4]. Mackintosh's next choice was very different. Longleat House, Wiltshire, was not only the first of the Elizabethan prodigy houses (a term illustrative of the palatial residences built to receive and entertain Queen Elizabeth and her court during her annual summer progresses through the countryside) but is rated by Sir John Summerson as 'the first great monument of Elizabethan architecture and perhaps, indeed, the greatest'.[16] Unfortunately for Mackintosh the lack of critical historical research meant that he fell down on his facts. Longleat House was not built by a visiting foreigner, John of Padua, as stated by Fergusson and other writers,[17] but by Robert Smythson, whom Fergusson mentions as a 'Free master mason' but whom Summerson ranks as 'one of the great geniuses of English architecture'.[18] Smythson was engaged by Sir John Thynne to remodel the exterior of Longleat House after a fire in 1567; thirteen years later he moved to Wollaton Hall, Nottinghamshire. 'But when we compare the designs', says Mackintosh, quoting verbatim from Fergusson, 'instead of the almost Italian purity of the latter, we find a richer gothic feeling pervading Wollaton sometimes running into excesses bordering on the grotesque' [D 8]. Perhaps Mackintosh would have been surprised to learn that Wollaton has a truer Italian ancestry, albeit through Serlio, from the Poggio Reale built for King Alfonso V at Naples in the middle of the fifteenth century.[19] Apart from its striking silhouette, Wollaton Hall may have appealed to Mackintosh, as the late Gothic window tracery, lug turrets and strapwork were all replicated in Scottish sixteenth and seventeenth century architecture.

Strangely, Mackintosh set Crewe Hall, Cheshire, long regarded as 'a noble example of the mansion of the old English gentleman' [D 8], between the two prodigy houses. Mackintosh placed Crewe Hall in the sixteenth century when, in fact, it was begun in 1615 with a completion date in 1636. But did Mackintosh know just how much was restored by E. M. Barry following a fire in 1866?[20] Perhaps he did, since in admiring the hall, almost completely restored by Barry, he confines his comments to the planning arrangements.

44. Crewe Hall, Cheshire – main staircase

For anyone interested in late Elizabethan or early Jacobean work the staircase at Crewe Hall is pre-eminent. There is, however, a further interest in Mackintosh's description of the stair: 'It is a neuel stair built round a central well hole, and is of oak ... it is easy and convenient, and occupies but little space, being not more than 24 ft square from wall to wall while the storey itself is 20 feet high' [D 7]. That evokes the main staircase at the Glasgow School of Art where the dimensions are little short of those at Crewe Hall.

45. Glasgow School of Art – main staircase

46. Haddon Hall, Derbyshire – garden elevation

Also in Cheshire is Little Moreton Hall, dating from the sixteenth century, which was Mackintosh's exemplar of the timber-framed houses in the English West Midlands. Such houses probably interested Mackintosh because, as he says, of 'a peculiarity in construction' where 'carved pendants and the barge board[s] of the roofs and gables were executed in oak or chestnut with much beauty of design' [D 10], which demonstrated the Puginian ethic of ornament allied to design. Mackintosh's account was taken, much of it word for word, from the closing pages of Dallaway's *Discourses upon Architecture in England* (1833)[21] and from William Harrison's *Description of England* (1889).[22]

To a modern scholar it is an anachronism that Mackintosh should discourse on Heriot's Hospital, Edinburgh, 'so essentially in the Transitional style', according to Fergusson,[23] but lacking the horizontality, gridded windows, gables and projecting bays which characterised Mackintosh's English models. Nevertheless, as MacGibbon and Ross had pointed out, Heriot's Hospital 'now that Glasgow College has been demolished, is the finest and most important public building erected in Scotland during the seventeenth century';[24] and, indeed, one has the impression in reading Mackintosh's account, especially of the exterior of the chapel, that he had looked at MacGibbon and Ross's description. What Mackintosh most admired at Heriot's Hospital, as did Fergusson, was the Anglo-Flemish strapwork, 'a rich complicated piece of blind tracery if it may be so called', its sinuous forms allowing for 'an infinite variety', a 'form of ornament which is so singularly characteristic of this country. (Scotland)' [D 9].[25] Other examples cited by Mackintosh, again following Fergusson, were at the Old College of Glasgow (these were recorded by him in 1886,[26] prior to its final demolition), and at Moray House in Edinburgh, which Mackintosh refers to, mistakenly, as 'Regent Murrays House'.

Yet the question remains. Why was Mackintosh interested in Elizabethan architecture? A clever young architect of today would concentrate on contemporary work whereas Mackintosh's lectures and writings largely deal with the past, though that was perhaps inevitable given the eclecticism of the age. Nevertheless, Mackintosh was no mere stylist and it is informative that almost half his paper is an analysis of the principles of Elizabethan architecture. While there was an undeniable grandeur in the prodigy houses, Mackintosh saw in Crewe Hall 'a home like character' [D 6]; indeed, what he found most pleasing in the Elizabethan mansions was 'that air of mingled dignity and homeliness, which has ever been considered their most pleasing characteristic' [D 2]. That others thought likewise can be demonstrated by glancing at Mark Girouard's *The Victorian Country House* where the greater number of examples are Tudor or Elizabethan. Most of these nineteenth century prodigy houses would have displeased Mackintosh since their exuberant ornament 'often offends the eye, which will be better pleased

47. C. R. Mackintosh: Window, Old College, Glasgow, detail (1886)

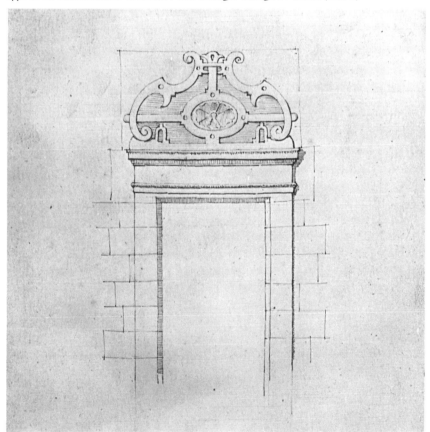

with the quaint though simpler treatment of the grange farmhouse or cottage' [D 10]. These humbler structures had become the preferred model when architects such as William Butterfield and Philip Webb began searching for a non-historical architecture, so that the Arts and Crafts movement became what Mackintosh, by implication, saw as 'a fusion between the new and the old in Archi[tecture]' [D 13] allied to honest and visible construction. As a follower of Pugin, Mackintosh criticised work of the past: 'The old energy of Construction appears to have died away, and its place to be imperfectly supplied by applied decoration' [D 14]. On the other hand, structural and needful elements could evoke admiration. Thus, with chimneys, 'the stacks of massed and clustered shafts became one of the most striking architectural features of the time' [D 14].

Although Glasgow was a stone-built city, Mackintosh could not but be aware that in England 'the increased intrest in brick architecture and the employment of moulded brickwork, are noticable signs of the present time' [D 15]. Mackintosh, however, had reservations about the use of polychromatic brickwork: 'In some of our recent revivals this treatment has been too freely indulged in' [D 16] – which may have been a reference to William Butterfield's Keble College in Oxford (1867-83), a notable example of the streaky bacon style. More significant in the forward development of architecture were Norman Shaw's country-houses, such as Leyswood, Sussex (1868), where brickwork and half-timbering were combined with gables, and elongated chimney-stacks and expansive oriels were introduced 'with the greatest freedom' [D 16], to admit the maximum of light. In all this Shaw was following the dictum of Kerr that 'the native English model of three hundred years ago seems now as fit as ever, at least in the country, for English uses'.[27] Shaw successfully removed his Old English style to town with the New Zealand Chambers, London (1871), and it was further developed by J. D. Sedding as in All Saints Vicarage, Plymouth (1887), both of which have compositional affinities with the entrance of the Glasgow School of Art.

That Mackintosh should have looked to such Elizabethan pastiches neither denigrates his genius nor lessens his achievement, since no less an authority than Sir George Gilbert Scott had written that 'we aim not at a dead antiquarian revival, but at the developing upon the basis of the indigenous architecture of our own country, a style which will be pre-eminently that of our own age'.[28] In seeking compositional principles rather than historical exactness, there emerged what Summerson has described as 'This free Tudor ... the most profoundly characteristic and most distinctly unifying architecture in Britain around 1900.'[29] Indeed, it was Summerson who first drew attention, though that has been overlooked, to the impact of that movement on Mackintosh,[30] although the latter's one overt experiment with the Tudor style, Auchenibert at Killearn (1906), ended unhappily with his withdrawing from the commission.[31] Yet others, too, were interested. In the late summer of 1887 a party from the Glasgow Architectural Associ-

48. R. Norman Shaw: Leyswood, Sussex (1868)
49. R. Norman Shaw: New Zealand Chambers, London (1871)

ation visited Helensburgh to inspect a number of the mansions erected on the littoral of the Clyde estuary by William Leiper (1839-1916) including the half-timbered Aros House at nearby Rhu.[32] Within a few more years Leiper, who had cornered the market in Helensburgh in providing for the well-to-do, had built Brantwoode (1895), Red Tower (1900) and Druma-doon (1901), all with some Elizabethan characteristics.

As with Scottish Baronial, Mackintosh accepted Elizabethan as a native architecture, untainted by external influences, which had developed in re-sponse to indigenous social change and been tempered by an 'intuitive affection which springs from use and tradition' [D 2]. Perhaps, therefore, the Glasgow School of Art, with its mullioned and transomed studio windows, its gabled oriels and lattices, may be seen not so much as the product of an imagination fired by the romanticism of past Scottish architecture but as a calculated reappraisal of the principles of Elizabethan architecture trans-posed to Scottish soil.

NOTES

1. Mackintosh's text shows a knowledge of David MacGibbon and Thomas Ross, *The Castellated and Domestic Architecture of Scotland* iv (Edinburgh 1892): see n. 24.
2. James Macaulay, *The Gothic Revival, 1745-1845* (Glasgow & London 1975) p. 148.
3. Macaulay (n. 2) p. 214.
4. Sir Walter Scott to Daniel Terry, 28 Dec. 1816. H. J. Grierson, ed., *Letters of Sir Walter Scott* (London 1932-7) iv p. 333.
5. See Macaulay (n. 2) p. 227.

6. Robert Wallace of Kelly to Sir John Forbes of Craigievar, 9 July 1828: Scottish Record Office GD250/41/3.

7. Robert Kerr, *The Gentleman's House* (London 1864) p. 57.

8. A. W. N. Pugin, *The True Principles of Pointed or Christian Architecture* (London 1841) p. 2.

9. Pugin (n. 8) p. 1.

10. Pugin (n. 8) pp. 69-70.

11. Four sketchbooks covering Mackintosh's British tours survive (H.A.G).

12. H.A.G.

13. Thomas Howarth, *Mackintosh and the Modern Movement* (2nd edn, London 1977) p. 11.

14. H.A.G. and Dr Thomas Howarth.

15. James Fergusson, *History of the Modern Styles of Architecture* (3rd edn, London 1891) ii p. 15.

16. John Summerson, *Architecture in Britain, 1530-1830* (4th edn, Harmondsworth 1963) p. 29.

17. Fergusson (n. 15) ii p. 13.

18. Summerson (n. 16) p. 31.

19. Summerson (n. 16) p. 32.

20. Nikolaus Pevsner and E. Hubbard, *Cheshire* (Harmondsworth 1978) pp. 191-2.

21. James Dallaway, *A Series of Discourses upon Architecture in England* (London 1833) pp. 369-71.

22. William Harrison, *Elizabethan England*, ed. L. Withington (London 1889) pp. 197-8.

23. Fergusson (n. 15) ii p. 16.

24. MacGibbon and Ross (n. 1) iv pp. 138-55.

25. Fergusson (n. 15) ii p. 18.

26. H.A.G.

27. Kerr (n. 7) p. 347.

28. G. G. Scott, *Remarks on Secular and Domestic Architecture* (London 1858) p. vii.

29. John Summerson, *The Turn of the Century: Architecture in Britain around 1900* (London 1976) p. 24. I am grateful to Mr William Buchanan, Glasgow School of Art, who drew my attention to this paper.

30. *Ibid.*

31. See Howarth (n. 13) pp. 109-11.

32. *British Architect* 38 (1887) p. 183.

CHARLES RENNIE MACKINTOSH

# D. *Elizabethan Architecture (c. 1892)*

D 1    Elizabethan Architecture.

At a period so famed in the history of our country, as that, the Architecture of which I propose to speak of to night, it is a matter of intrest to know the characteristics of the domestic edifices of an age which immediately preceeded the introduction of the classic style of buildings.

In such an enquiry will be found traits of that jenius which distinguished the times and features which marked the taste of the age.

As learning achieved her triumphs over the barbarism in which the middle ages had held her, so did utility and comfort proclaim their victories in the domestic buildings, which had hitherto been marked by strength and rudeness, rather than distinguished for comfort & convenience[1] The same features which distinguished the literature of the time, became the prevailing marks of its architecture for poetry was as little confined to fields of battle to deeds of heroes & sufferings of heroines, as the genius of architecture to the erection of monuments and cathedrals

The Elizabethan, may be more properly called Transitional Architecture,[2] for while it clung to Medeaevalism in its affection for mullions gables and general picturesqueness it aimed at the regularity and measured symmetry and details of Italian practice.

D 2    A careful study of the domestic architecture, will show a steady though gradual Transition from the Medieaval castle to the peaceful manor house of the English Squire  Features originally devised for defence, were clung to with that intuitive affection which springs from use and tradition, and such details, then survived as Architectural ornaments long after the reasons for their existance had entirely passed away.

The castles in being transformed into pallaces lost but little of their grandeur, while they gained in Architectural beauty of detail. They (the castles) could accomodate, and to some extent protect large bodies of retainers, but the necessities of warfare were gradually passing away, before the advances of civilization.

The great English mansions thus came to asume that air of mingled

1. *Cf.* James Dallaway, *Discourses Upon Architecture in England* (London 1833) p. 360: 'There was a transition from rude and massive strength to light and comparative convenience.'

2. 'Transitional Architecture' derives from James Fergusson's chapter 'Transition Style' in *History of the Modern Styles of Architecture* (3rd edn, London 1891) vol. ii, the major source for Mackintosh's lecture.

dignity and homeliness, which has ever been considered their most pleasing characteristic.

The walls still encompassed large open spaces and could be defended in case of need. The drawbridge was often maintained, bastions, battlements, and other features of earlier times were preserved, but the character of the enclosed buildings was altered.

We may trace the conflict of principles very clearly at such castles as Kenilworth and Warwick.

D 3     Warwick Castle was built at the beginning of the 15th Century. The keep is irregular in form, gateways, / wallturrets, and other defences are to be found, but the character of the enclosed buildings are greatly altered  The dwelling of the owner has a new significant prominence, it interrupts the continuity of the walls, and refuses to be cooped up in dull courtyards. It is built against the river and overlooks the country, while the various offices are aggregated in one mass, with every regard for dignity and convenience.

From such an arrangement it was only a step to the altogether unforti-fied mansion, although on the borders of Scotland and Wales and near the coast the old systems of construction lingered longer than they did in the midlands of England.

Haddon Hall  Derbyshire,[3] will illustrate the state of Transition. At a distance (see ill)[4] it presents a castleated appearance, but on closer inspection very little real fortification can be seen. The gateway with its tower is part of the 15th Century building, and displays a characteristic compromise between details of defence and ornament. There are two open courts with the hall in a central position. The Hall itself is perpendicular in style, the offices attached are spacious and well arranged and suited to advancing ideas of comfort.

On the exterior are remains of fortifications in the crenellated parapets, but in the late additions domestic influences are paramount.

D 4     The Elizabethan wing consists of a long gallery, a parlour, or drawing room, for the family, and other reception rooms with a range of servants rooms below.

Thus at Haddon[5] we find a history in stone not spoilt or falcified by the modern restores, although the older builders have worked their will upon the pile paying little regart to the work of their predecessors. Each phase of architecture has left its mark. There is Norman work in the Chapel, an Early English window in the nave, a perpendicular one adorns the chancel while the entrance gateway, Hall, and offices are of similar style,

3. Haddon Hall, Derbyshire is not cited in Fergusson (n. 2). It dates from the 12th to 16th centuries. No major restoration was undertaken until 1912. See fig. 46.

4. The text refers to illustrations of Haddon, Wollaton Hall and Little Moreton Hall, but there is no evidence that Mackintosh visited these sites and that the illustrations were by him.

5. Mackintosh here scored out '(says Mr Ferguson)' realising his error: see n. 3.

and at last there are the purely domestic buildings of Elizabethan Architecture.

Here we have large windows, spacious rooms, with elaborate internal decoration of oak panelling and plaster work together with wide fireplaces and other evidences of the comfort and refinement of English home life. Let us in illustration pass in review the work of some of the most noted Elizabethan Architects.

Longleat Hall. This Hall was built between 1567 & 1569 presumably by one John of Padua (a foreigner who visited this country (that is England) at that time). which would account for the greater purity which pervades its classical details, than is to be found in most buildings of that age[6] There is much in the design and arrangement of Longleat which shows italian influence.

D 5     Thus, it is quadrangular in plan, with the buildings arranged round inner courts of moderate dimensions. In making the quadrangles but secondary features Italian precedent was followed, but this mansion differs from them in this that the aspect is out ward, not into the court yard, and the windows are so placed as to command a view of the surrounding country.

We find in the exterior unmistakable evidences of Italian taste. It consists of 3 storeys, each ornamented with an order,[7] in the ordinary Italian manner. First the doric then the Ionic and lastly corinthian. The pilasters are well executed, each of which tapers gradually from the base to the summit in a very pleasing manner.[8] Each order is surmounted by its appropriate entablature of Architrave Frieze & Cornice, designed with due subordination of parts, and the whole is surmounted by a regular balustrade.

The prevailing principal of design is horizontality. There is a central entrance in a symmetrical front, and a very few additions and suppressions would give a complete Italian character to the whole composition. On the other hand we have the mullioned windows and the projections common in Elizabethan work serving to redeem the front from flatness and insipidity. Taken as a whole Longleat is one of the most

D 6     remarkable and beautiful buildings of the period and the details / indicate a purity of taste rarely found.

The design is obviously by an architect of taste & refinement and well accustomed to Italian work.

6. 'which would account ... buildings of that age', Fergusson (n. 2) p. 13, giving the dates as 1567-79. Longleat House, Wiltshire was in fact designed by Robert Smythson (c. 1536-1614): see Mark Girouard, *Robert Smythson & the Elizabethan Country House* (Yale 1983).

7. 'It consists of 3 storeys, each ornamented with an order', Fergusson (n. 2) p. 13.

8. 'each of which tapers gradually from the base to the summit in a very pleasing manner.' Fergusson (n. 2) p. 13.

Crewe Hall is a much later example,[9] but shows some coincidence in principle mixed with conciderable individuality. Crewe Hall is much smaller and less imposing than Longleat, but there is the same grouping together in one large block, the same projections of bays and oriels, the same welth of mullioned and transomed windowes, and the same horizontal spirit of design  On the other hand there is more English feeling pervading this Hall. Here at Crewe the use of the pilaster is confined to the principal entrance, and the gable is retained (in a subordinate form in the main building, but freely used in the offices) which with the red moulded brick chimneys and the mixture of brick and stone in the Elevations, give a home like character to the building. Internal lighting is obtained by means of a small central court. The chief feature, is the hall, a room of great dignity & importance, marked by the oriel & dais at the upper end, and having an elaborately carved oak screen at the lower end with the Mediaeval arrangement of passage and buttery hatch.

Close to the Hall is the with-drawing room for the family (here traditionally known as the carved parlour.) The chapel is of small dimensions D 7    and constructed in accordance with precedent although it stands / North and South.

Crewe Hall is rich in the posession of one of the finest existing specimens of a Transitional Staircase. It is a neuel stair built round a central well hole, and is of oak, elaborately worked and carved. Elegant in design and sound in construction according to a well known authority,[10] it is easy and convenient, and occupies but little space, being not more than 24 ft square from wall to wall while the storey itself is 20 feet high. The shortness of flights and frequency of landings, secure great ease in ascending and from the compactness of the plan no unnecessary distance is traversed. With its handsome newels, carved and panelled surmounted by quaintly carved animals with heraldic cognicences, its nicely wrought balusters, and picturesque arrangement this staircase is one of the most interesting examples of the 16th Century. This staircase at Crewe led to the great reception rooms and principal guest chambers. These were all on the first floor and looked outwards in the English manner. The whole of the North side was occupied by the usual long gallery  The other appartments were principally sitting rooms and were approached through each other.

The ceilings are generally of great elaborateness and in some cases of much beauty, and large and curious chimney pieces reach up to the ceiling. We find in the whole arrangement a highly characteristic amount D 8    of / domestic comfort. The execution of the ornamental details is good, particularly the carpenters work, although the representations of the

9. Crewe Hall, Cheshire, was in fact constructed between 1615 and 1636. Crewe like Haddon is not cited in Fergusson (n. 2).
10. The 'well known authority' is so far unidentified. See fig. 44.

human figure are strained and uncouth  Notwithstanding all drawbacks
Crewe Hall was a splendid example, of the taste, and ability, of the
architects of the Transitional epoch, and a noble example of the mansion
of the old English gentleman.

Wollaton Hall. of which you will get a better idea by looking at the
illustrations than by an description I could give, was built immediately
after Longleat was finished.[11] In it we find the orders used in about the
same manner as at Longleat, but when we compare the designs instead of
the almost Italian purity of the latter, we find a rich gothic feeling pervading Wollaton sometimes running into excesses bordering on the
grotesque  The great hall which rises out of the centre of the whole block
(see ill) is plain in outline and gothic in detail, and overpowers the lower
part of the design by its mass, and thus detracts very much from the
beauty of the whole. But the lower part of the design is probably the
happiest conception of the age.[12]

Herriots Hospital Edinburg. Though late in date this building is so
escentially in the Transitional style that it must be classified among these
buildings which were erected before the reform introduced by Inigo Jones.

D 9      It was commenced in 1628 and completed in 1660. The chapel / The
chapel and other parts of this building not only retain the mullions and
foliation of the Gothic period, but, the window heads are actually filled
with tracery, which had long been abandoned generally. But these
features are mixed with classical details treated in the Elizabethan form,
with a grotesqueness which the age has taught us to tolerate, but which
have not in themselves any beauty or appropriateness, which can render
them worthy of admiration or imitation.[13]

Generally the windows are adorned with a pilaster on each side,
supporting a richly ornamented entablature, but, above that instead of
the usual straight lined or curved pediment used in England the Scotch
Employed a rich complicated piece of blind tracery if it may be so called.

As used by them (says Mr Ferguson) the Effect is not always pleasing,
the design being frequently ungraceful, and the ornaments grotesque, but
it is questionable whether in principle it is not a more legitimate form of
adorning a window head than the one that was generally made use of
in England. It admits at all events of an infinite variety. Some of those
that were at the Old College Glasgow or at Regent Murrays House in
the Cannongate of Edinburg are as elegant as any. But there is scarcely

11. Wollaton Hall, Nottinghamshire, designed by Robert Smythson in 1580-8 (see
n. 6).

12. 'but when we compare ... conception of the age.' Fergusson (n. 2) p. 15.

13. 'Though late in date [D 8] ... admiration or imitation.' Fergusson (n. 2) pp. 16-17.
In the last sentence Mackintosh substitutes 'Elizabethan' for 'Jacobean' to sustain his
argument and cover his omission of Fergusson's description of Jacobean architecture.
Heriot's Hospital evidently arose in the discussion following Mackintosh's lecture on
Scottish Baronial Architecture: see A n. 61.

a Scotch House of this period which has not some specimens of this form of ornament which is so singularly characteristic of this country. (Scotland).[14]

D 10    But the principals which governed Transitional construction were not confined to great pallaces and mansions, many of the examples to be found in less pretentious houses being of equal intrest. The exuberance of ornament to be fount in many of the former often offends the eye, which will be better pleased with the quaint though simpler treatment of the grange farmhouse or cottage. Before proceeding further it will perhaps be my duty to notice a peculiarity in construction which prevailed in some large houses of the provinces more particularly in the counties of Salop. Chester and Stafford the memery of many whereof (though several are still to be seen) is chiefly preserved in engravings[15] I alude to these houses of timber frame work in places where the supply of stone or brick was scanty. The carved pendants and the barge board of the roofs and gables were executed in oak or chestnut with much beauty of design, and often with a singularly pleasing effect.

The timber style reached its zynth in the reign of Elizabeth and is thus illustrated in Harrisons description of England. "Of the curiousness of

D 11    these / piles I speak not, sith our workmen are grown generallie to such an exelance of device in the frames now made that they sine pass the finest of the olde.[16]

And again, "It is a wonder to see how divers men, being bent to buildage, and having a delectable view in spending their goodes by that trade, do dailie imagine new devices of their owne, to guide their work-men withall, and those more curious and exelent than the former.[17]

The fashion was no less prevelent in the cities and towns than in the country, for in them we find that timber framed houses abounded, and that they also were highly ornamented with carvings and exibited in their street fronts an exuberance of extremely grotesque figures performing the office of corbels.[18]

The fashion was imported from the continent where there are numer-ous examples especially in Rouen Burges Antwerp, Brussels, Nuremberg & Strasburg very far surpassing any that this country can boast.

We have however sufficient remains of them in England to show that the wealthy burgess affected an ornamental display in the exterior of his

14. 'Generally the windows . . . characteristic of this country. (Scotland).' Fergusson (n. 2) pp. 17-18. In the last sentence Mackintosh substitutes 'this country. (Scotland)' for Fergusson's 'the age' as if to stress Scotland's distinct characteristics.

15. See Dallaway (n. 1) pp. 370-1: 'Such occurred more frequently in manor-houses in the counties of Chester, Salop and Stafford.'

16. William Harrison, *Elizabethan England*, ed. L. Withington (London 1889) pp. 197-8. Harrison's chronicle was compiled in the last quarter of the 16th century.

17. Harrison (n. 16) p. 198.

18. Corbel: projecting stone or piece of timber supporting a superincumbent weight.

D 12 dwelling rivalling that of the country squire and wanting neither elegance / or elaborate finishing, while it was productive of a highly picturesque effect in the street architecture of the day. This manner (says Dalleway) was much better suited to the painters eye, than to comfortable habitation, for the houses were lofty enough to admit of many stories and subdivisions, and, being generally in narrow streets, were full of dark and gloomy apartments overhanging each other; notwithstanding that they had fronts which with the projecting windows and interstices were filled for nearly the whole space with glass.[19]

Moreton Old Hall (see ill) Chester is one of the finest examples of the timber style.[20]

D 13 The principal peculiarities of Elizabethan Architecture which distinguished it from the Medieaval styles which it succeeded is the admixture of Classical details with general forms of a Gothic Character. Thus the gable an escentially gothic feature was retained, though masked, deprived of its importance and broken up into forms more or less fantastic.

Mullioned windows were still employed but in combination with pilasters and with a complete change of mouldings The windows were indeed so varied and fanciful that it is not easy to define with precision, the forms of so called Elizabethan Archi. For we may find in one example, a roughness, and vulgarity of execution, almost deserving the title of barbarous, while in other buildings of the same style we can detect evidences of a purity of taste together with a beauty of detail, almost equal to many examples of good Italian work.

In the interior, the Hall and other arrangements of the Medieaval House were for a long time to be found, but with numerous additions and modifications.[21]

The Elizabethan was a fusion between the new and the old in Archi., and in this character has not been sufficiently considered, a neglect due to a great extent to the rude execution of much of the detail, and more particularly to the badness of the representations of the human figure. These defects were the effect of a development too sudden for the available

D 14 number of competant workmen to execute. Hence the / grand ideas and the bad workmanship.

The use in the same building of different materials, and the combination of labour are noteworthy. To the mason, bricklayer and carpenter, is now added the plasterer, whose work on wall and ceiling, is among the most interesting peculiarities of the style. Elizabethan masonry is highly elaborate, as in the curious and ornamental scrolls which abounded, the fantastic gables and the turrets: but the elaboration is of ornament only.

19. See Dallaway (n. 1) p. 370.

20. Little Moreton Hall, Cheshire, a courtyard house which dates back to the late 15th century, with a great variety of Elizabethan black and white decorative motifs.

21. Mackintosh here scored out 'But the principals which governed this Style of Architecture'.

The old energy of Construction appears to have died away, and its place to be imperfectly supplied by applied decoration.

As the mason lost in importance, the bricklayer advanced the two commonly working together. In the late examples are to be found moulded bricks, and terra cotta which played an important part in certain Elizabethan Types.

For chimneys brickwork was generally used, and the stacks of of massed and clustered shafts became one of the most striking architectural features of the time. Sometimes square, sometimes circular, polagonal or octagonal on plan they were for the most part grouped together, and were frequently placed in internal walls  The capitals were in some cases single and in others continuous like the base. There are numerous examples of such chimneys in which the moulded bricks are of the most elaborate description as at Hampton Court Palace (see ill).

It is evident the designers of these works delighted in the use of moulded bricks and devoted themselves to their study and manufacture.

D 15    In cases where the supply of stone was limited or not easily attainable the walls were built of bricks frequently of red colour with dressings of stone the mullions of windows, string courses, parapets and copings being constructed of the same material  The bricks were usually smallar than the regulation size is now, they were not very regular in shape, and consequently the joints were large with a good deal of mortar, but as it (the mortar) was usually good the walls were not altogether destitute of solidity or strength.

The custom (that is of using bricks) declined somewhat in consequence of a tax being put on bricks, but has again revived, and the increased intrest in brick architecture and the employment of moulded brickwork, are noticable signs of the present time. But the ligitimate use of moulded bricks is limited and needs both taste and judgement.[22]

The bricklayers seemed to think that the surface of their walls needed ornament, for they were very fond of using a few black bricks with those of different colors, so disposed as to give the well known diagonal patterns on their walls. This treatment is undoubtedly pleasing when not used to excess, it breaks the effect of monotony which to much plain surface is apt to produce. It is unobtrusive and while it is an evidence of care & thought on the part of the work men, it does not when sparingly em-

D 16    ployed chalange attention or arrest / the eye by startling contrast. In some of our recent revivals this treatment has been to freely indulged in often with the effect of minimising buildings which could not afford to trifle with the element of size.

22. Mackintosh here scored out 'Terra cotta redily  The bricks used by Eliz builders were usually red, and a few black ones were often introduced so disposed as to give the well known diagonal patterns on the walls'.

Perhaps the most noticable development of this period was the treatment of the windows. The few and small windows of the castle have been increased and enlarged untill (in some cases) we have a perfect blase of light. Oriels and Bay windows are used with the greatest freedom, and we have projecting windows of all kinds of design with canted, square or curved sides, and even semi circular on plan, and of such height that they need to be devided by horizontal transoms. This change from Medieaval economy to Elizab- exuberance in windows forshadowed by Tudor work, is very remarkable.

The Elizabethan builders however, went beyond their Tudor predecessors, they widened the bays and increased the projections they lengthened the lights discarding tracery, and even the flat four centred arch. The windows were usually made up of rectangular divisions, and arches now semi-circular were reserved for doors. The window sills were made higher than modern taste approves.

The Elizabethan was not a tower building style, at Wollaton however the traditions of the keep of the old castles, survives in the elevated mass of the central hall. Turrets abounded thus keeping up the statliness of earlier times but were usually finished with depressed ogee of wood covered with lead. / A horizontality of treatment was aparent throughout the buildings the floors ascerting themselves externally. Cornices and parapets were used and roofs of moderate pitch and span replaced the high coverings of earlier times. Although the gable thus lost its original importance it was not neglected, indeed, it was regarded with special favour, and great care was given to its varied outlines. For farm houses and structures of moderate pretensions the gable still kept much of its old prominance, but for mansions such as Crewe Hall, and still more Wallaton it was only represented by scrolls and ornaments recalling in an indirect manner its former outline

D 17

The taste for more formal design which was becoming fashionable not only pervaded the houses of this period but extended to the adjoining grounds, which were laid out in plantations and terraces gardens of stiff forms and patterns, bowling greens, labrynths and mazes, hedges becoming walls, streams canals, and nature itself being put in fetters. At most of the Elizab. pallaces & mansions the gardens have been replanned; but a very interesting example still remains at Levens in Westmorland, where the aspect of things have been maintained by the owners, without alteration from the time of the original foundation of the place.[23] The terraces at Haddon Hall (see ill) exibit some original details, but the Elizab. Architects usually borrowed their ballusters from foreign examples. Thus at Crewe Hall we find a terrace with a ballustrade of forms common in

23. Levens Hall, the largest Elizabethan house in Westmorland. The topiary of the garden is renowned, created for James Graham between 1689 and 1712 by M. Beaumont. In the 1890s the house was owned by the Howards, Earls of Suffolk.

D 18 Italy and divided into bays according to the methods of the same country / All the peculiarities, eccentricities, and characteristics of the Eliz. Architecture are so consentrated in their sculptured tombs & monuments, that no better idea of the leading principals of the style could be got than by studying these monuments and more particularly the one erected to perpectuate the memory of Elizabeth herself.[24]

A taste for Internal decoration prevailed at this period. "A decoration (says Ferguson) not of the true artistic character which calls for the co-operation of the sister arts of painting and sculpture, but a decoration of masons, plasterers, and carpenters, with much striving in the dark and half realization of good intentions.[25]

The walls of rooms were handed over to the carpenter and he covered them with oak panelling, generally extending from floor to ceiling. In some cases he shared his task with the plasterer, and allowed his comrade space for a deep and elaborate frieze. There was frequently much grace and skill in the whole design, both in general composition and disposition of parts, and where scroll work was introduced, had a curious intracasy and a characteristic elaborateness.

The fireplace had become the most conspicuous feature of the living rooms. They were often massive structures extending to the ceiling, and ornamented, with rich panelling, niches carving & sculpture. They illustrate very clearly the Transition that was in progress, and the taste that was opening up for Italian detail & style.

D 19 The earlier examples of Elizabethan fireplaces have projecting hoods and follow the ancient forms of construction. Gradually departing from this tipe we come to designs of a less prominent character as regards shape and more decorated in detail. The chimney pieces became import-ant architectural compositions built against the side of the rooms and forming their chief ornament.

The material used was usually stone, but the upper part was often of wood and even plaster was used

The amount of woodwork used for internal decoration was very great. Panelling was not only plentifully used for window and door furnishings but extended from floor to ceiling in the galleries and principal rooms. The panels were designed with numerous mouldings of a shallow section, often very roughly worked.

In the best examples the mouldings were wrought on the solid rails and in the earlier work were combined with chamfered top & bottom rails in accordance with the custom of Medieaval workmen The wood used was usually oak, and the grain upon it was very distinct. and far more

24. Elizabeth I's marble tomb, carved by Maximilian Colt and completed in 1606, is in Westminster Abbey.

25. This quotation is not from Fergusson's chapter 'Transition Style' (n. 2) but may be a reformulation by Mackintosh of comments found in Fergusson.

beautiful than we usually see now. While it is impossible to claim for the style a high artistic merit, I doubt if full justice has been done to its merits and possibities.

There was in Eliz. Buildings a care for architectural effect, the construction was generally sound and truthful, and there was an appropriateness in design which rarely fails to please. The style spoke of home life and comford, and was certainly more distinctly national than any that has followed it.

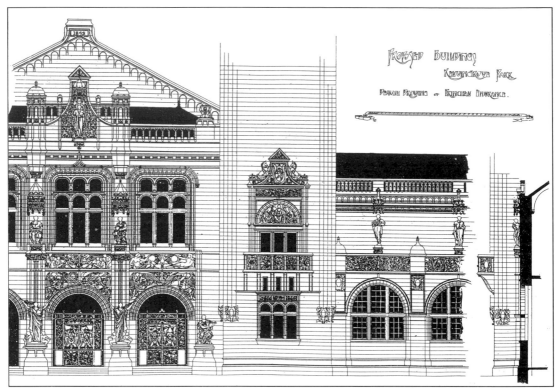

GLASGOW ART GALLERIES. FINAL COMPETITION
DESIGN BY HONEYMAN & KEPPIE

50. C. R. Mackintosh: Glasgow Art Galleries – competition design (1892)

DAVID WALKER

# Mackintosh on Architecture

It is a measure of the interest that Mackintosh commanded in artistic circles in Glasgow in the early 1890s that he should have been invited to deliver two papers on the subject of architecture. He was still only a relatively junior assistant in the office of Honeyman & Keppie, known to the profession at large by just a handful of published student competition designs. Closer observers of the Glasgow art and architectural scene would, however, have recognised his distinctive draughtsmanship in the designs submitted by his firm in the competitions for the new Glasgow Art Galleries and Museum at Kelvingrove (1892) and the Manchester Technical Schools (1892), and foreseen that he could shortly become the most important Glasgow architect of his generation.

Neither lecture is what his listeners are likely to have anticipated at the time. Only the first discusses actual buildings and then only rarely, concentrating on definitions and principles and attempting to discriminate between the right and wrong in architecture. The second represents the discovery of answers to issues not resolved to Mackintosh's own satisfaction in the first. The sources from which his ideas were drawn, particularly in the first lecture, must sometimes have seemed to his listeners strangely old-fashioned. To the informed Glaswegian of the early 1890s the future of architecture, as of painting, lay with those who had studied in Paris, and those who had absorbed the teaching of the Ecole des Beaux Arts at second hand through working under them. Mackintosh himself fell into the latter category. His master and early mentor, John Keppie, had studied under the great Jean-Louis Pascal until James Sellars recalled him to help with the Glasgow International Exhibition of 1888, and Mackintosh's own South Kensington Silver Medal design for a Museum of Science and Art is doubtless the result of a perusal of the portfolios Keppie had brought home.

Both lectures show that by the time they were given, Mackintosh had begun to seek ideas elsewhere. Except perhaps for passing references to 'essentials' there is not a single hint of Beaux Arts teaching in either of them. The first paper, delivered to an unknown literary society, possibly the Scottish Society of Literature and Art,[1] is undated, and such references as there are to the contemporary scene do not offer much guidance. A date in spring/summer 1892 and certainly before February 1893 does, however, seem likely. The familiarity with regional characteristics in Italian mediaeval architecture suggests that it was delivered after his Italian tour, i.e. some time after July 1891; while some elements of the paper appear to be indebted to Gerard Baldwin Brown's lecture 'Beauty and Utility in Architecture', delivered to the Architectural Section of the Glasgow Philosophical

51. C. R. Mackintosh: Science and Art Museum – competition design (1890)
A full-blown exercise in Beaux Arts design, probably inspired by the designs
Keppie had made in the atelier of Jean-Louis Pascal.

Society in February 1892, and possibly also have some relevance to the
veteran architect John Gordon's paper on 'Utility in Architecture' given to
the same body a year earlier. 'Utility' was evidently a particularly topical
subject at the time, although the word had been in use as an architectural
term since Pugin's writings. The only other guidance Mackintosh's paper
provides as to its date is the reference to the Conservative Club, which is
clearly to the old clubhouse on West George Street, a palazzo by David
Bryce, and not to the new free early Renaissance one on Bothwell Street
designed by Colonel R. W. Edis (since demolished), which was well in hand
by the end of 1892, indicating a date rather earlier in the year.

Mackintosh drew heavily on the writings of John Ruskin for both the text
and the ideas presented in the first paper – even more so than the text
acknowledges – although he was careful to distance himself from Ruskin's
more dated architectural principles by declaring that he did not consider
him by any means the architectural critic, criticising his writings with a
quotation from a review by H. H. Statham of *The Stones of Venice*[2] as being
'crammed full of paradoxes, eccentricities, and rhetorical claptrap: at one
time presenting accidentals as if they were essentials, at another exibiting
absolute ignorance where knowledge & science are pretended, and diffuse
and rambling to a degree that may truely be called protentious' [E 7b].
Mackintosh defended his choice of Ruskin on the ground that his 'writings

are more poetical & captivating to the ordinary listener, than the dryer but more truthful treatment of other Architectural critics and historians' |E 7a|. While Ruskin's social, educational and political ideas would still have been matters of interest, Mackintosh's listeners must have been surprised by the choice of a writer whose direct influence on architecture might seem to have faded a decade and a half earlier. Some at least would know that Ruskin himself had now entered into his final eleven-year silence at Coniston in the custody of the Severns, unable to undertake the radical revision that he had recognised his architectural writings to require.

But there are likely to be deeper reasons for Mackintosh's choice of Ruskin as his text. By the early 1890s Ruskin had become the prophet of the Arts and Crafts movement, partly because of his fusion of political and artistic theory and partly because a new significance had been found in some of his writings, particularly the wonderful central chapter of *The Stones of Venice*, 'The Nature of Gothic'. In 1891 William Morris reprinted this chapter as a separate Kelmscott Press book presenting it as 'one of the very few necessary and inevitable utterances of the century' and identifying as its key the passage on the mistaken suppositions 'first, that one man's thoughts can be, or ought to be, executed by another man's hands ... second that manual labour is a degradation when it is governed by intellect .... We are always in these days endeavouring to separate the two, we want one man always to be thinking and another to be always working. Now it is only by labour that thought can be made healthy, and only by thought that labour can be made happy; and the two cannot be separated with impunity.'

In 1889 at the National Association for the Advancement of Art and its Application to Industry meeting in Edinburgh, which was attended by Mackintosh's senior partner, John Honeyman, the Arts and Crafts architect J. D. Sedding took as his text 'Had you been, in fine, anything else in the world but architectural designers, you might have been of some use and good to people' from Ruskin's *Two Paths*. In his paper Sedding was merely critical of Ruskin's views on the role of sculpture as the alpha and omega of architecture, pointing out that the subject of the Ruskin lecture he was quoting from *Two Paths*, 'The Influence of Imagination in Architecture', had been conspicuous only by its absence. But at least by 1891, the year of his death, Sedding had found a deeper meaning in his Ruskin text and in his further quotation: 'Shall we, then, abandon this theory of the soul of architecture being in proportional lines?' Like Morris he found new significance in 'The Nature of Gothic', neatly summarising its message – curiously enough, in a short essay on design in embroidery rather than architecture – as 'we shall have designs *by* living men *for* living men – something that expresses fresh realisations of sacred facts, personal broodings, skill, joy in Nature – in grace of form and gladness of colour ... we must clothe modern ideas in modern dress; adorn our design with living fancy and rise to the height of our knowledge and capacities .... Still there is hope in honest error: none in the icy perfections of the mere stylist.' It was published in *Arts*

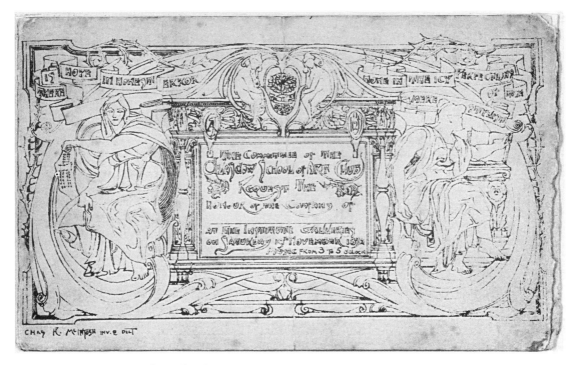

52. C. R. Mackintosh: Glasgow School of Art Club At Home Invitation (1892)
J. D. Sedding's aphorism 'There is hope in honest error . . .' is incorporated into
the design with two Michelangelesque sibyls.

*and Crafts Essays* (1893) but had been in print earlier.[3] Mackintosh made
the last sentence of it – a paraphrase of one of Ruskin's in 'The Nature of
Gothic', 'For the best that is in them cannot manifest itself but in company
with much error' – the text of his invitation to the Glasgow School of Art
Club meeting of 19 November 1892.

From that invitation card we can be certain that Mackintosh was well
aware of this Arts and Crafts debate. He read, or rather reread, Ruskin
whose Italian Gothic related writings he had probably studied as part of his
preparation for his travelling studentship, but it cannot be said that he spelt
out the Arts and Crafts message of 'The Nature of Gothic' so clearly in his
first paper as he did in his second. His definition of architecture as against
building, a term which he reminded his audience included shipbuilding and
carriage building, is an unabridged quotation from 'The Lamp of Sacrifice' in
Ruskin's *Seven Lamps of Architecture*. It is not acknowledged in the paper,
although it may have been when delivered, since he proceeds to a second
quotation which he does acknowledge and which is in fact Ruskin's introduction, in its later expanded form, to his first quotation. In this second
passage Ruskin defines architecture as proposing an effect on the human
mind and not merely a service to the human frame. This is made the
occasion of Mackintosh's contempt for critics who condemn designs without

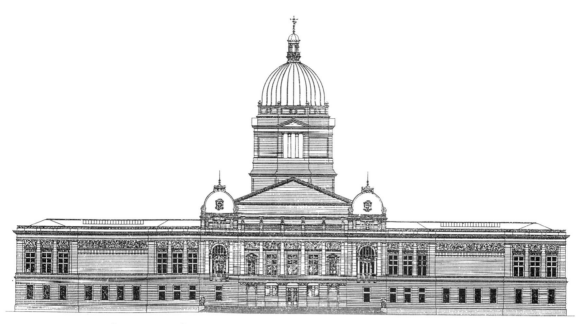

53. John Keppie: Glasgow Art Gallery – competition design (1892)
This was undoubtedly the design Mackintosh had in mind when he complained
of critics seeking windows where none was functionally appropriate: 'to have
openings for no use but effect would be to construct the decoration not decorate
the construction' [E 9].

considering their function, taking as his example those who appear to have
complained of the lack of windows in an art gallery where none was functionally required. Presumably, since he felt it so keenly, the art gallery
referred to was one of the Honeyman & Keppie Kelvingrove competition
designs of that year, all three of which had windowless upper floors. This led
him to a justification of diversifying the plainness of necessarily windowless
walls by ornament since 'to have openings for no use but effect would be
to construct the decoration not decorate the construction' [E 9]: his word-
ing appears to be adapted from a passage in Sir George Gilbert Scott's
Royal Academy lectures which in turn had been derived from Pugin.[4]
Mackintosh's rejection of the utilitarian-functionalist argument that such
ornament was unnecessary waste brought him to an assault on utilitarianism generally which has overtones of 'The Virtues of Architecture' in *The
Stones of Venice*. He found his targets locally in the Caledonian and Glasgow
and South Western Railway viaducts across the Clyde in central Glasgow,
the design of which had been put beyond the reach of the Dean of Guild by
parliamentary powers, and, more challengingly, the desirable suburban
family residence, 'square as a band box' [E 14], such as was no doubt owned
by a good many of his listeners. Fleetingly he declared his allegiance to the
architecture of Devey, Shaw, Nesfield and Godwin in pointing out that in the

centre of these houses 'the light … is got by a skylight which prevents the comfort as well as the appearance of a fine Hall window. The rooms have no pleasing projections giving variety to the view of nature seen from them and pleasing effects to the house itself no picturesque chimney stalks like what are to be found in old english work, no projecting eaves, no all substantial symmetry and cheerful as a prison or infirmary' [E 14].

Of the Seven Lamps proposed by Ruskin – Sacrifice, Truth, Power, Beauty, Life, Memory and Obedience – Mackintosh adopted only one, Beauty, in his three main architectural attributes, substituting Strength or Stability, and Utility for the other six, although many of the ideas expressed were still Ruskin-derived. His restructuring of Ruskin's lamps was not entirely original. Strength or Stability was of his own choosing although it was a quality on which Ruskin had laid emphasis; Beauty and Utility derived not from Ruskin but the Baldwin Brown lecture of that name referred to earlier. As for Stability, Mackintosh held that it must be apparent as well as real and – perhaps with Burnet's newly-completed Charing Cross Mansions, in Glasgow, in mind – that the practice of raising tall façades on plate glass was to be avoided. His own Willow Tea Rooms were later to be an object lesson in how to give such a frontage the appearance of stability: so indeed were Burnet's

54. John J. Burnet: Charing Cross Mansions, Glasgow (1891)
'… the eye is distressed at huge lofty tenements resting to all appearance on nothing more stable than plate glass for the real actual supports are easily overlooked' [E 16].

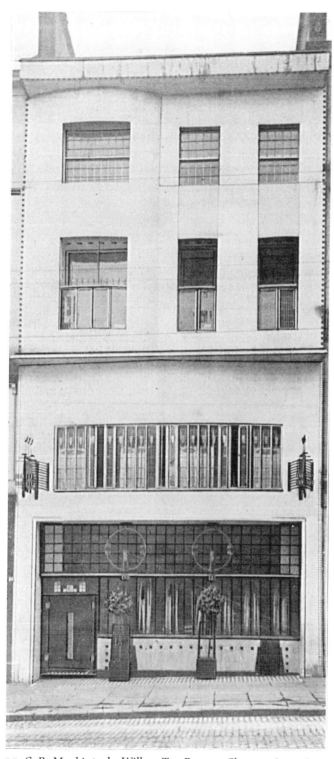

55. C. R. Mackintosh: Willow Tea Rooms, Glasgow (1903)

later department store façades in Glasgow, Edinburgh and London. Perhaps not surprisingly for a man who was fundamentally an Arts and Craftsman, Mackintosh took the opportunity to return to the charge against utilitarianism, rejecting, on the same ground of lack of apparent stability, the claims of architectural writers such as James Fergusson that Crystal Palace-derived buildings such as the Iron Building in Jamaica Street, Glasgow, represented the invention of a new style. He dismissed such buildings as foundry repetition without limit 'minimising of intellectual labor and ... the payment of it' [E 16].[5] Some, perhaps, may see that as a long-range prophecy of the current reaction against commonplace post-war curtain-walled modernism.

Mackintosh's discussion of the attribute of utility must have left those of his audience who had not heard either the Gordon or the Baldwin Brown lectures, the first of which dealt with temples and the second with basilicas, somewhat mystified. While acknowledging the potent influence of the employer he did not venture any general principles of planning as Burnet would have done. Nor did he quote – as most other Arts and Crafts architects of the early nineties would have done – from paragraph 38 of 'The Nature of Gothic' where Ruskin finds that:

Gothic is not only the best, but the *only rational* architecture, as being that which can fit itself most easily to all services, vulgar or noble. Undefined in its slope of roof, height of shaft, breadth of arch or disposition of ground plan, it can shrink into a turret, expand into a hall, coil into a staircase, or spring into a spire with undegraded grace and unexhausted energy: and whenever it finds occasion for change in its form or purpose, it submits to it without the slightest sense of loss either to its unity or majesty – subtle and flexible like a fiery serpent but ever attentive to the voice of the charmer. And it is one of the chief virtues of the Gothic builders that they never suffered ideas of outside symmetries and consistencies to interfere with the real use and value of what they did. If they wanted a window, they opened one; a room, they added one; a buttress, they built one; utterly regardless of any established conventionalities of external appearance knowing (as indeed it always happened) that such daring interruptions of the formal plan would rather give additional interest to its symmetry than injure it.

Although nothing could better have described the principles on which he was to design the Glasgow School of Art than the latter half of that passage, Mackintosh's preoccupation was then with his firm's competition designs for the Art Galleries at Kelvingrove referred to earlier. His discussion of Utility is a reflection of his studies for the central hall of that design. For the Kelvingrove competition Honeyman and Keppie had at first competed separately, Honeyman producing a superb neo-classical design[6] with elements reminiscent of Thomas Hamilton's Edinburgh Royal High School (1825-29)[7] and Alexander Thomson's South Kensington design (1864),[8] while Keppie produced a Beaux Arts design[9] with a dome similar to Rowand Anderson's at the Old College of Edinburgh University. These secured separate places in the final competition but in the event Honeyman and Keppie submitted a single design which was largely, if not wholly, the work of

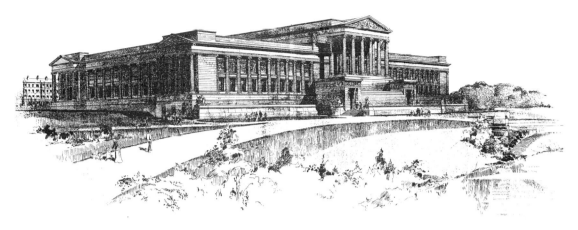

56. John Honeyman: Glasgow Art Galleries – competition design (1892)
'How absurd it is to see modern churches theatres Banks, Museums, Exchanges Municipal Buildings, Art Galleries &c &c made in imitation of greek temples'.

57. C. R. Mackintosh: Glasgow Art Galleries – competition design (1892)
Mackintosh's eclectic design integrates mixed Renaissance with the late Gothic motifs of the Sedding school in the exterior, and contrasts this with an Italian Romanesque interior.

Mackintosh.[10] The assessor was Alfred Waterhouse. Mackintosh took a good look at Waterhouse's own work and recent competition decisions, noted his recent transition from Franco-Italian Romanesque and Gothic to late Gothic and early Renaissance, and based the planning of his galleries on Waterhouse's Natural History Museum at South Kensington with its twin-towered cathedral-like central hall. His studies for this design can be linked with his reading of Ruskin – who had advocated North Italian Romanesque as a style suitable for modern uses – and coincided with Baldwin Brown's lecture on 'Beauty and Utility in Architecture' which was developed from his book *From Schola to Cathedral*, published in 1886. In his Kelvingrove design Mackintosh put his Italian sketchbooks to effective use: the interior detail of the basilican central hall – which probably owed as much to Baldwin Brown's theories as Waterhouse's at South Kensington – can be directly related to his sketches of Italian Romanesque church interiors at Pavia and Verona, while the apsidal feature on the end elevation was directly adapted from his sketch of that at S. Fedele Como.[11] In that context Mackintosh's particular interest in the development of temple to basilica, and basilica to cathedral and secular buildings such as college and manorial halls and the great mediaeval barns – all doubtless based on notes made at Baldwin Brown's lecture – is easily comprehended. It was used to demonstrate to his audience that in ancient examples, notwithstanding the similarity of plan and a certain continuity of architectural character, no one would mistake the purpose for which the building had been erected, whereas in modern work a villa might be differentiated from a temple or a monastic establishment only by the chimneys. Mackintosh's message to his audience, unaffected fitness for purpose, was thus similar to Ruskin's, but made in relation to a single basic plan-form. Brown's lecture probably also contained the echoes of Ruskin's 'Lamp of Truth' in the discussion of construction and materials, and the subsequent discussion of the effect of differences of religion, climate and national sentiment on basic religious plan types.

In his discussion of Beauty, Mackintosh again deserts Ruskin's Lamp of that name for a discussion of taste based on a passage from C. L. Eastlake's *Hints on Household Taste* and gently teases the ladies in his audience with a further quotation from the same book, complaining of the lack of any teaching of even the simplest principles of architecture in the day schools [E 26]. He then proceeds to seek his material not in 'The Lamp of Beauty' but in 'The Lamp of Truth', finding, as Ruskin did, that the veneers of marble applied to brick buildings were acceptable whereas artificial graining and marbling were not. His dislike of gables not answered by the roofs behind them and of the screen wall upper storey of Wren's St Paul's derive from other writers (presumably principally Fergusson),[12] while his distaste for the late Georgian neo-classical habit of applying pilasters to the façade rather than enriching the openings with aedicules or rich architrave frames – as at Bryce's Conservative Club (now the Scottish Widows Building) on West George Street, or Rochead and Sellars' Bank of Scotland Buildings in George Square, both in Glasgow – are personal observations which reflect the practice of his own time. Venturing further on his own account he also includes, under the heading of Beauty, the attributes of Association or Tradition – to some extent the equivalent of Ruskin's 'Lamp of Memory'.

At the conclusion of his first lecture is a plea, perhaps aimed at the Glasgow Beaux Arts group, for architecture to be a little less cosmopolitan and rather more national in character – as it was to be in his own Glasgow Herald building of the following year. While he recognised the possibilities of modern civil engineering he did not see as much hope in the engineers themselves as John Gordon had done in the previous year, criticising their lack of imagination and respect for truth in reproducing stone detail in cast metal, and urging them to think more in terms of the designs which could be moulded on a plate. Developing his thoughts on what modern architecture should be, he bemoaned the fact that it 'would be a difficult task to read a history from the architecture of this nation at the present time' [E 36]. Echoing to some degree the thoughts of Gordon's paper, he complained that 'We do not build as the ancients did who in each succeeding building tryed to carry to further perfection the national type', but 'build now in Greek if we love the Classic, now in Norman if we doat on the romantic, or if we have travelled show their [our] ill regulated admiration for foreign beauties by reproducing Swiss Chateau, &c &c in the most inappropriate positions' [E 36]. These views are a distant echo of Pugin's *Apology* in a stylistic dilemma which had been made infinitely more complex than that of the 1840s by continental influences. In his next paragraph Mackintosh gives a few hints on his thoughts as to what modern architecture should be. After telling his audience that as far as possible he had avoided a discussion of styles as they were too apt to be used as recipes which ensured some sort of a result without overmuch discrimination, he then weakened his stance on cosmopolitanism and ventured to say 'Not that I would slight or ignore styles & say with many why not unite the beauties of all in one modern style, for each style has an expression peculiar to itself' [E 37]. That statement may be assumed to be the background to the third Kelvingrove competition design, in which early sixteenth century north European Gothic and early Renaissance elements intermingled with Italian Romanesque; or the Glasgow Herald Building, in which a few Romanesque details at the corner tower introduced novel elements into what was otherwise an early modern design with a Scots Renaissance skyline. The fashion for such eclecticism had been commenced by Alfred Waterhouse at his National Liberal Club in Whitehall Place, London (1885-7) and was to reach its climax in Aston Webb's designs for the Victoria and Albert Museum (original competition design assessed by Waterhouse 1891, built to revised design 1899-1909). In these, as in Mackintosh's Glasgow Herald design, the motifs are integrated. In Mackintosh's Kelvingrove design early and late mediaeval features were deliberately contrasted, following the lead of John Belcher in his design of 1889 for a church at Maida Hill, London (presumably a competition design for the Catholic Apostolic Church), in which a Provençal Romanesque portal was inserted into an otherwise English neo-Perpendicular façade.[13] But Mackintosh had now begun to think that the expression of one style was weakened by the introduction of another, supporting his view with a passage from Reynolds' *Discourses* on the combination of incompatible elements in sculpture. Clearly this was an important statement on current architec-

58 (*opposite*). C. R. Mackintosh: Glasgow Herald Building (1893)
Italian Romanesque details are combined with sixteenth and seventeenth
century motifs.

59. John Belcher: Church, Maida Hill, London (1889)
Belcher's design provides a precedent for Mackintosh's combination of Romanesque and late Gothic in his Art Gallery designs.

ture: he had begun to have doubts about the wisdom of this type of design
and he may even have been telling those who knew the Kelvingrove designs
that the mixed motifs in the third design were not his idea. His message to us
appears to be that the integration of styles was an acceptable course of
design, as exemplified in his Glasgow Herald design of the following year,
but that the deliberate contrast of incompatible elements was not.

Shrewdly picking up the relationship of Reynolds' *Discourses* to James
Fergusson's *An Historical Inquiry into the True Principles of Beauty in Art*
(1849), as Nikolaus Pevsner did ninety years later, Mackintosh then proceeded to a discussion of the Phonetic in architecture, which he defined as
explaining its purpose or illustrating history. This curious term derived from
Fergusson's attempt to systematise and evaluate architecture with tables
and graphs by putting values on the anthropic arts: technical beauty (tools

etc.) I unit; aesthetic beauty (senses) 2 units; and phonetic (speech, intellectual beauties) 3 units. Architecture, Fergusson held, could only become 'phonetic' and reach the highest levels by the addition of painting and sculpture, a very Ruskinian pronouncement.[14] Mackintosh then proceeded to explain the Phonetic as what is more familiar to us as *l' architecture parlante*, i.e. that 'a Temple should aim at sublimity, a villa at domesticity, a Palace of Justice at dignity & so forth' [E 37]. But, very sensibly, Mackintosh advised his audience that 'a building can not really be phonetic, merely expressive, for it is generally only association of ideas which has given these attributes any standing' [E 37]. Mackintosh is here referring to a passage from Reynolds' *Discourses*, and a still more telling one from Ruskin's 'Virtues of Architecture' in *The Stones of Venice* in which he demonstrated that architectural sculpture is meaningless if the spectator does not know enough of its subject matter to be able to read it.

Mackintosh had thus developed, no doubt with some help from the younger generation of architectural critics, a healthy scepticism for received architectural thinking. But his approach to innovation was still basically cautious: while calling for an end to mediocrity in design in 'the senseless & increasing repetition of features which have only their age to recommend them', he could still hold that 'Variety & Novelty if not carried to far are qualities both allowable & desirable, but by ignorance often clamoured for most unreasonably' [E 34]. Nevertheless the lecture had earlier contained a few hints of Mackintosh's future style. Not only did he admire old English houses, he could find old English barns among the most picturesque buildings extant, and, presumably with such buildings as these in mind, could observe that a building could be artistic and truly architectural and yet not have a single cornice or moulding. While it was not until his Lennoxtown Inn of 1895 that Mackintosh was able to begin experimenting with a vernacular-based architecture, the concept of houses such as Windyhill and The Hill House appears to have begun to take shape in his mind.

By February 1893, when Mackintosh gave his second lecture on the subject, he had acquired a much more confident outlook even if much of what he had to say was adopted from William Richard Lethaby, as Robert Macleod first pointed out, and some of it from Sedding.[15] The precise circumstances in which this lecture was given have not yet been established. The introduction and the conclusion suggest that it may have been given at the Glasgow Art Club, on the reconstruction and extension of which Keppie and Mackintosh were then engaged. Or it might equally have been given at Glasgow School of Art as a result of a lecture invitation from the painters to the architects, as the reference to Fra Newbery, Director of the School, suggests. Whatever the circumstances, it was an invitation to which Mackintosh responded with an appeal to the painters, sculptors and artist craftsmen to join in architecture as the commune of all the crafts.

Like the first lecture, the second is a search for the 'basis of certain ideas common to the architecture of many lands & religions' [F 1], and in fact

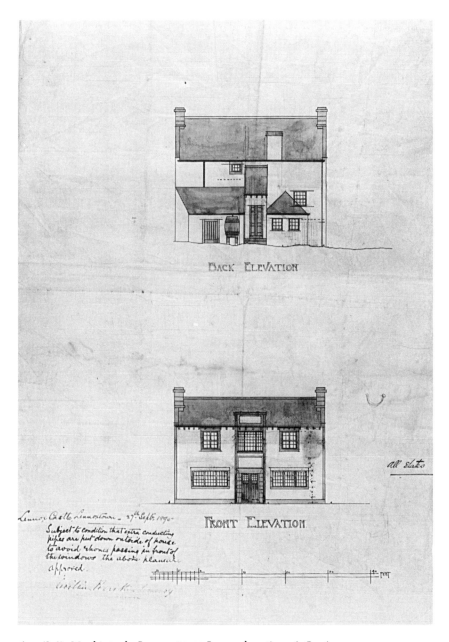

60. C. R. Mackintosh: Lennoxtown Inn – elevations (1895)

repeats three paragraphs from it, one quoted from Reynolds, one from Ruskin and a third on music from an as yet unidentified source. These are, however, merely used as incidental illustrations to a text taken from Lethaby's *Architecture, Mysticism and Myth*, which had been published in 1891, and in which Mackintosh found the answers he had been seeking. It

61. C. R. Mackintosh: Glasgow Art Club – details (1893)
Glasgow Art Club may have been the venue for Mackintosh's second lecture on
'Architecture' [F]. These details illustrate his decorative design style at that time.

was not the sort of book which would normally have attracted a practising architect, small in format with tiny diagrammatic illustrations. It did, however, have a magical effect within the circle of artists and craftsmen in which Lethaby moved: May Morris, Mary Watts, Henry Wilson and R. Weir Schultz all drew inspiration from it, Schultz recalling later that the book 'had opened up to us younger men a hitherto undreamed of romance in architecture'.[16] The probability is that Mackintosh's attention was drawn to Lethaby, not then well-known outside his own circle in London though probably known to Newbery, by J. A. Slater's 'Town Mansion' design which the Architectural Illustration Society had published in 1891. This was dedicated to Lethaby and is believed by Lethaby's biographer, Godfrey Rubens, to have been inspired by *Architecture, Mysticism and Myth*, although from notes to the plates provided later in 1892 we learn that this austere non-period design, with hints of H. H. Richardson and Louis Sullivan in some of the details, had been made as long ago as 1885.

Lethaby was eleven years older than Mackintosh and, like Voysey, had come of a household with deeply felt non-conformist religious beliefs, if of a very different kind, his father being a member of the fundamentalist Bible Christian Society, a politically radical Wesleyan sect. His early education had been put in the hands of a Plymouth Brother. Lethaby's draughtsmanship had attracted Norman Shaw, to whom he was chief assistant from 1879 to 1889 before setting up on his own, his first large work being Avon Tyrrell, Hampshire, for Lord Manners, a major commission generously

62. W. R. Lethaby: Avon Tyrrell, Hampshire (1891)

passed on to him by Shaw. From about 1885 he had begun to explore the mythical origins of architecture, especially those which regarded the temple as a microcosm. His theory that ancient architecture in all its differing forms represented man's conception of the Universe was guided by Herbert Spencer's thesis that, on the basis of the data available to him, primitive man made essentially reasonable inferences about his world.[17] The actual content of the book, detailed studies of the origin of motifs, suggests that he may also have been influenced in his search by one of Ruskin's more challenging dicta, that no man can be an architect who is not also a metaphysician; but, as Rubens has shown, Lethaby found its immediate origins in his reading of Anna Jamieson's *Sacred and Legendary Art* (1848) and in Francesco Colonna's Italian Renaissance romance, *Hypnerotomachia Poliphili* (1499), the woodcut illustrations of which provided the source of some of his early designs.

Lethaby's introduction provided, with only minor adjustments for a spoken rather than a written paper, nineteen of Mackintosh's fifty paragraphs. Whether or not he acknowledged his indebtedness when the paper was given we do not know, but very probably he did since in the second paragraph he apologises for his presumption in quoting unfamiliar matter at second hand. But, as Robert Macleod has observed,[18] one should avoid being distracted from the main ideological issue, which was that Mackintosh was prepared to subscribe to Lethaby's ideas and adopt them in his own practice. In Lethaby, Mackintosh found more fundamental answers than Ruskin or Baldwin Brown could provide to the issues he had struggled with in his first paper: 'the distinction between architecture and building finds its answer in building being the medium of the architect like pigments in painting ... architecture interpenetrates building not for the simpler needs of the body but for the complex ones of the intellect ... architecture and building are quite clear and distinct as ideas, the soul and the body' and, most importantly for Mackintosh's own practice, 'architecture is the synthesis of the fine arts, the commune of all the crafts'.[19]

After a digression into the three paragraphs from his earlier paper, where he found in Reynolds and Ruskin parallels to Lethaby's thoughts on iconography and symbolism, he returned to Lethaby's text, finding in his conclusion that all architecture was one when traced back through the civilisations as they followed or influenced one another, a deeper answer to the origins of architecture and its basic architectural principles than in Brown's discussion of the basic aisled building type. The ultimate facts behind all architecture were identified as the similar needs of men, the necessities of materials and the physical laws of their erection and combination, and nature, which Lethaby identified as having provided the stylistic element. Thus the early ships took their form from fishes, and tables and chairs from quadrupeds, while the temple was a local reduplication of the World's Temple as perceived by ancient man, a great domed chamber lighted by the sun, the moon and the stars.

From all this Lethaby deduced that old architecture lived because it had a purpose and that, to be real, modern architecture must not be an envelope without contents. He held that it could not be the architecture of the past, for its aim had been to crush life, and that the message of the new architecture should still be nature and man but should also be 'sweetness, simplicity, freedom, confidence and light' – an expansion of the 'Sweetness and Light' of Matthew Arnold's appeal to cultivate the Hellenic virtues in his *Culture and Anarchy* (1869), which became the motto of the Aesthetic Movement, and more recently the title of Mark Girouard's history of the 'Queen Anne' movement in later nineteenth century architecture.

The message of Mackintosh's final fifteen paragraphs, which appear to be mainly original, although probably incorporating some as yet unidentified elements adapted from other writers, is not less important than Lethaby's, and one can even now feel the power of his appeal to his audience. From *Architecture, Mysticism and Myth* he concluded that architectural styles had not been made purposely. He launched into an eloquent plea for modernity, arguing that all great and living architecture had been the direct expression of the needs and beliefs of men at the time of its creation, and that, if we would have great architecture created, it must still be so. Treading rather dangerously if the audience included his principal, John Honeyman, he observed how absurd it was to see modern churches, theatres, banks, museums, exchanges, municipal buildings, art galleries etc. in the form of Greek temples, holding that the temple form must lose all dignity when imported and set up for such varied purposes – i.e. Lethaby's envelope without the contents appropriate to it. At the same time he conceded that an art gallery copied from a Greek temple could have the same charm and dignity as the original. When he spoke with such feeling of the absurdity of the modern architect having to make-believe that he was living four

63. John Honeyman: Paisley Museum (1868)

64. Leonard Stokes: A New Town Church (1893)
Stoke's designs reveal an original handling of English late Gothic.

hundred to a thousand years ago, he was speaking – as many in his audience would know – from the standpoint of an architect whose principal
had actually built a Greek temple as a library, museum and art gallery at
Paisley in 1868; and who had himself – with evident enjoyment – drawn
out the same principal's competition design for that at Kelvingrove within
the last few months before superseding it with his own eleventh to sixteenth
century freestyle design in the second tier of the competition. He proclaimed
as his current heroes Shaw, Bentley, Belcher, Bodley, Stokes and perhaps
above all Sedding, quoting, with slight variations, the passage from his
'Design in Embroidery' essay referred to earlier on 'clothing modern ideas in
modern dress – and adorning design with living fancy'. Surprisingly he
omitted '[still] there is hope in honest error: none in the icy perfections of the
mere stylist', although it was to remain something of a personal motto,
being made the subject of a panel of lettering as late as 1901 (fig. 7). In his
final appeal to the painters he ends with a plea for originality – 'magic' – the
idea of beauty in the artist's own mind, not the servile imitation of nature of

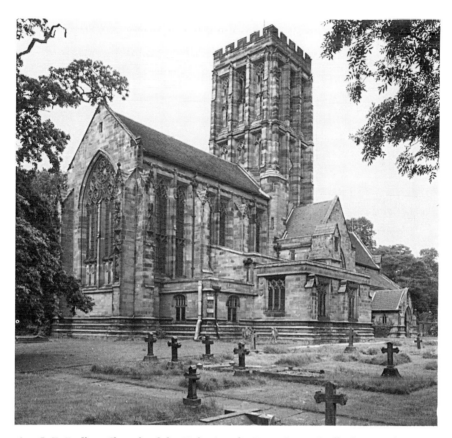

65. G. F. Bodley: Church of the Holy Angels, Hoar Cross, Staffs. (1872-6)
The rectilinear design of the tower and the absence of pinnacles hints at the
western towers Mackintosh later proposed for Liverpool Cathedral (see fig. 77).

'small-minded men', the quality which takes 'architecture above building &
painting beyond paint' [F 27].

Mackintosh's select list of the most imaginative contemporary architects
was well chosen. Bentley was a particularly perceptive inclusion as he did
not receive the Westminster Cathedral commission until the following year,
although one might also have expected Ernest George, G. G. Scott Junior and
Basil Champneys. Philip Webb, the architect who perhaps best represented
what he was seeking, he could not know about from Glasgow as Webb
built almost exclusively for private clients and would not allow his work to
be published. Ernest Newton, Halsey Ricardo, C. F. A. Voysey, Harrison
Townsend, Edgar Wood and Lethaby himself had all appeared in print and
must have attracted Mackintosh's attention, but had not perhaps published
quite enough to merit inclusion.

Mackintosh included no Scottish architects, presumably because their
firms were in direct competition with his own. But it is of interest that the
Scottish architects he is known to have admired most in his earlier years –

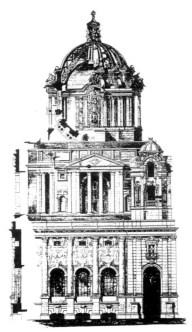

66. John Belcher: South Kensington Museum – competition design (1891)
67. Honeyman & Keppie: Royal Insurance Buildings, Glasgow – competition design (1895)
Mackintosh was undoubtedly involved in this project. His corner details show a knowledge of Belcher's cupola designs.

68. John Belcher: Institute of Chartered Accountants, London (1890-3)
69. W. F. MacGibbon: Corn Exchange, Glasgow (1895)
MacGibbon's design shows the influence of Belcher's Baroque in contemporary Glasgow.

James Sellars, who had died five years earlier, and John James Burnet[20] – were amongst the earliest Scottish architects to be influenced by Shaw and his school. Sellars had built a quieter version of Shaw's Cragside in his large mansion at Keil, Kintyre (1874 and later, demolished) and Burnet had built Shavian half-timbered Gothic houses at Corrienessan, Loch Ard and Nunholme, Dowanhill, Glasgow (both 1886, the latter now also demolished). Burnet had also been the first to use Shavian Baroque detail in his Athenaeum Theatre, Glasgow (1891-93) and was shortly to improvise brilliantly on themes from Shaw's Scotland Yard in his competition designs of 1891 for the Central Thread Agency in Glasgow's Bothwell Street and of 1895 for Edinburgh's North British Hotel. Although Mackintosh thought that most of his audience would never have heard of the majority of the architects in his select list, other Glasgow architects had begun to share his enthusiasm for them. Sedding had found another admirer in William Gardner Rowan whose Trinity U. P. Church, Glasgow (latterly Pollokshields – Glencairn Church of Scotland, recently burned down) had echoes of Holy Trinity, Sloane Street, Chelsea (1888-90) as early as 1891; Leonard Stokes' late Gothic domestic had found a follower in H. E. Clifford; and the style of

70. R. Norman Shaw: New Scotland Yard, London (1887-90)
71. John J. Burnet: Glasgow Athenaeum Theatre, Buchanan St (1893)
Burnet's design shows the influence of Norman Shaw's Baroque on
Mackintosh's Glasgow contemporaries.

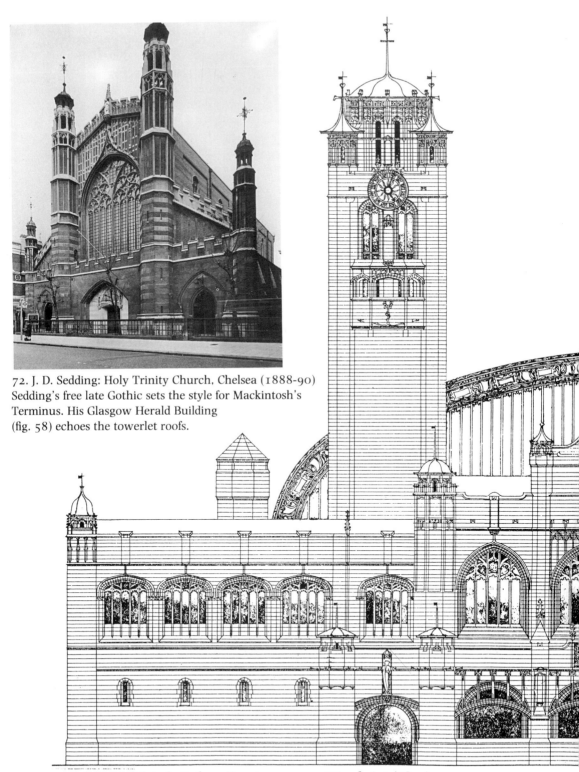

72. J. D. Sedding: Holy Trinity Church, Chelsea (1888-90)
Sedding's free late Gothic sets the style for Mackintosh's
Terminus. His Glasgow Herald Building
(fig. 58) echoes the towerlet roofs.

73. C. R. Mackintosh: Railway Terminus – competition design (1892)
Mackintosh's scheme shows the influence of both Sedding and his pupil, Wilson.

74. H. Wilson: New Cathedral, Victoria, Canada (1893)
Wilson, Sedding's pupil and assistant, further developed
Sedding's style after his untimely death in 1891.

Belcher's Institute of Chartered Accountants in London's Moorgate (1889-90) was to be brilliantly exploited by William Forsyth MacGibbon in his Glasgow Corn Exchange, now alas demolished, in the year following Mackintosh's lecture. Mackintosh's own Railway Terminus competition design of 1892 for the Soane Medallion shows a general indebtedness to Sedding and his pupil Harry Wilson. So does his Queen's Cross Church of 1895, which also has hints of Leonard Stokes, while the Baroque corner cupola of his competition design for the Royal Insurance Building (1894) was directly adapted from Belcher's much admired Victoria and Albert Museum competition entry of 1891.

Valuable though the second lecture may be as a guide to what interested Mackintosh most at the time, the significance of these lectures extends far beyond matters of detail. That the first is a ragbag assembled piecemeal, as the manuscript itself shows, from Ruskin, Reynolds, Scott, Baldwin Brown and Eastlake, and that the second is so heavily quoted from Lethaby, and in a lesser degree Sedding, may limit their value as original pieces of writing but has little bearing on their significance to Mackintosh's development. It is important to remember that these lectures were never intended for publication, and simply represent an empirical approach to his crusade for better architecture, or to teaching as the case may be, by presenting the best in contemporary architectural thought in the most eloquent and telling language to which he could lay his hand. The invitations to deliver them forced him to think beyond the everyday practice of architecture and concentrate his mind on seeking and developing answers to his quest for the fundamental principles underlying architecture, and in Lethaby and Sedding – even if the latter had been writing about embroidery – he found the best possible counsel. His findings from Lethaby in particular may well have prompted his study tours of the simple timeless English vernacular architecture, innocent of any stylistic or historic references, which began in the following year and had much influence on the dramatic simplifications of sixteenth, seventeenth and early eighteenth century vernacular Scottish forms at Glasgow School of Art, Windyhill and The Hill House. His reading of Ruskin and Lethaby is likely to have had an effect on his decorative art which went far beyond the ideal of architecture as the commune of the arts and crafts. From the writings of Ruskin he must have learned intensity of observation of natural forms and to think more deeply about their application as decorative detail; and, from Lethaby's detailed studies of the symbolic origins of architectural detail, an artist whose work, as in *The Harvest Moon* of 1892, already had affinities with the Symbolist movement must have drawn encouragement to think still deeper. We can only guess at the ultimate significance of these lectures: but from the way in which they chart the development of his architectural thought in the critical formative years it seems probable that they had a significant catalysing effect. Although primarily intended for the enlightenment of his audience, their preparation must have caused Mackintosh to pull together the essence of what he had thought and read into the basic principles which were to form the philosophical basis of his mature style of the later 1890s and early 1900s.

NOTES

1. Little is known of the S.S.L.A., founded in 1886, based in Glasgow. It was last entered in the Glasgow Post Office Directory for 1895-6.

2. *Builder* 55 (1888) pp. 131-3.

3. W. R. Lethaby, 'J. D. Sedding Obituary', *Builder* 61 (1891) p. 271.

4. G. G. Scott, *Lectures on Mediaeval Architecture* (London 1879) lecture 33 p. 292. For other adaptations of Pugin's phraseology see J. Mordaunt Crook, *The Dilemma of Style* (London 1987) p. 52.

5. Mackintosh was probably referring principally to the section on 'Ferro-Vitreous Art' in James Fergusson, *History of Modern Architecture* (London 1862) bk 11 pp. 482-3, in which it is described as 'a new style' which 'promises to have a still greater influence in the future'.

6. Illustrated *Builder* 62 (1892).

7. See J. Rock, *Thomas Hamilton, Architect, 1784-1858* (Edinburgh 1984) pp. 23-6; N. Allen, ed., *Scottish Pioneers of the Greek Revival* (Edinburgh 1984) pp. 18-20, 37-42; J. Mordaunt Crook, *The Greek Revival* (London 1972) pp. 98, 104-5, 146, 150.

8. Ronald McFadzean, *The Life and Work of Alexander Thomson* (London 1979) p. 147.

9. Illustrated *British Architect* 38 (1892).

10. Illustrated *British Architect* 37 (1892) and 38 (1892).

11. For further discussion of Mackintosh's use of his Italian sketchbooks in his architectural designs see Maria Cristina Finucci, 'Il Viaggio in Italia di Charles Rennie Mackintosh', *Critica d' Arte* 51 (1986) pp. 55-64.

12. See Fergusson (n. 5) pp. 305-6.

13. Crook (n. 4) pp. 85-6; N. Pevsner and J. M. Richards, eds, *The Anti-Rationalists* (London 1973) p. 120.

14. James Fergusson, *An Historical Enquiry into the True Principles of Beauty in Art* (London 1849) pt 2 sect. 8, pp. 115-24. For modern discussions of his theories, see chapters on Fergusson by N. Pevsner, *Some Architectural Writers of the Nineteenth Century* (Oxford 1972), and Maurice Craig in J. Summerson, ed., *Concerning Architecture* (London 1967).

15. Robert Macleod, *Charles Rennie Mackintosh: Architect and Artist* (1st edn 1968; 2nd edn, London 1983) pp. 33-8; and again in more detail in Patrick Nuttgens, ed., *Mackintosh & His Contemporaries* (London 1988) pp. 18-24.

16. See Sylvia Backemeyer and Theresa Gronberg, eds, *W. R. Lethaby, Architecture, Design and Education* (London 1984) pp. 38-41, 53, 56-63, 80-3; Godfrey Rubens, *William Richard Lethaby: His Life and Work, 1857-1931* (London 1985) pp. 79-84; Nuttgens (n. 15) pp. 18-24.

17. See Rubens (n. 16) pp. 80-4.

18. See Macleod (n. 15) p. 33; Nuttgens (n. 15) pp. 18-24.

19. W. R. Lethaby, *Architecture, Mysticism and Myth* (London 1891) pp. 1-2.

20. Thomas Howarth, *Charles Rennie Mackintosh and the Modern Movement* (2nd edn, London 1977) p. 55, quoting someone who knew Mackintosh, perhaps Herbert MacNair. Comments in 'Scotch Baronial Architecture' [A] suggest that Mackintosh also admired J. M. MacLaren and Dunn & Watson's buildings at Glenlyon, Perthshire, although the location of the buildings is not specifically identified. See Macleod (n. 15) p. 20-1, 27; Nuttgens (n. 15) pp. 32-8.

CHARLES RENNIE MACKINTOSH

## E. *Untitled Paper on Architecture* (c. 1892)

E 1   I feel that it is not an altogether happy circumstance that on this or any other tecnical subject a prifessional should expatiate, as there is the probility that even when he avoids the temptation to magnafy his office unduly, or publish private conviction as assured & self-evident truths, and really gives a fair & impartial statement of the claims and position of the subject under consideration, the ordinary listener even were he aware of this is apt to allow a liberal discount for supposed exageration or over estimation. I can but bring before you, as wise men, some facts regarding and principals which are considered essential to architecture, and submit them for your criticism, in all modesty admitting that in matters of taste when I say a thing is so & so, I only mean that I think it is so & so  Yet I make no apology for introducing this subject, tecnical as it is in some of its branches, to a literary society such as this, for architecture the Mother because the first of The Fine Arts whatever be her relative position in honour, is the one which every one should posess a knowledge of, as being by far the most pronimently before us in daily life, unlike Painting

E 2   or Sculpture which must[1] / generally be sought for, Architecture good or bad exists co-extensivily with civilized man; travelling in a strange country you may go to Galleries of Painting, and at even rarer intervals be favoured with a view of Statuary, but it is the Architecture of the country which surrounds you, prominent and characteristic as the people. Architecture is the work of nations but we cannot have nations of great sculptors.

   This feature alone, of national character entitles it to a consideration by a literary society, for you will perceive that if Architecture has national peculiarities impressed upon it, then it must be history – the worlds history written in stone  With such enduring documents there need be little fear of uncertainty or ambiguity from tampering or illegibility – unless indeed the falcefying restorationist has been at work – thus incidental to parchments – much of Assyrian life & manners, and the source of there decent is known from their ruins apart altogether from the inscriptions of more or less doubtful interpretation which cover the walls – the actual buildings themselves are histories. While of many other races now wholly extinct nothing but there architecture remains – such as those mysterious peoples of N & S. America especially the Astecs – our

E 3   sole knowledge is confined to / their buildings, and those scanty though

1. The verso of E 1 is inscribed with the following notes: 'Archi national exp.'; 'No exp in the age.' 'deception – what is the how[?]'; 'deception is possible how much?'; 'Although at first sight'; 'Dron.'; 'Ross.'; 'Donald'; 'Dron. Greek Temple.'; 'Allendarer'.

they are, tell of their history & position with a certainty beyond a chance
of the doubt inseperable from tradition or written documents. So much is
this the case that Ferguson considers that enquirers into the science of
Ethnography by hitherto neglecting the study of ancient Architecture
have overlooked their surest guide[2]

What then is architecture. When Gothe calls it a "petrified religion or
Madame de Stael "frozen music" they in common with poets & orators of
all times are only considering it as a Fine Art, but a fairer because a more
comprehensive description is given by Sir Gilbert Scott when he says
"Architecture differs from the sister arts of Painting & Sculpture in this,
whereas they arise directly from the artistic inspirations of our natures
apart from pratical necessity or utility it arises from the necessity & then
from the desire to clothe the result with beauty. It may be said that
the yearning after abstract beauty unlinked with utility is the higher
and more spiritful sentiment, but on the other hand if we look around
throughout the creations of nature we are prompted to reply that in
E 4    linking beauty with utility, we are / more directly imitating "him" who
made man in his own image & in whose works the union of the useful &
beautiful is one of the most universal characteristics.[3] Yes Archi is a Fine,
but also a useful art. And it surely needs no profound argument, or array
of facts, to prove that it is equally a science, that in great buildings
besides the artistic skill there has been sometimes more than brute force
employed if not in the rearing of Egyptian temples, surely in the soaring
arch of Medieaval times or still more recently in the Dome of St Pauls
Cath Lond –

In this paper I propose giving some of the elementary rules which
govern true architecture, a knowledge of which is necessary to the critic.
For I do believe that most inteligent people desire the capacity of discriminating between the right & wrong in architecture to the same degree
at least as they do in Painting, Sculpture or Music or poetry. Perceiving
differences of style in buildings both in their ornament & general
construction they acknowledge the existance of some ruling principals
although ignorant of their nature. Books on the subject though not
awanting are somehow little read and this is the more surprising as there
are many famous writers on this subject yet even of Ruskins works as
E 5    The Art Critic / which surpass those of his on social economy a general
ignorance seems to prevail. Few books can be more eloquent more
enthusiastic or more beautifully illustrated than his stones of Venice or
Seven Lamps of Architecture yet I believe the study of the latter by its
authors professed friends The Ruskin Society was but feebly entered upon

2. James Fergusson (1808-86). See Nikolaus Pevsner, *Some Architectural Writers of the
Nineteenth Century* (Oxford 1972). Fergusson was the major source for Mackintosh's
lecture 'Elizabethan Architecture': see D n. 2.
    3. Sir G. G. Scott, *Lectures on Mediaeval Architecture* (London 1879) lect. 23, p. 291.

and was finally abandoned for some of his more startling though perhaps less important and masterly works.[4]

E 6     I am really unacquainted with a definition of Architecture which is quite comprehensive.[5] / To begin with it is not building. To build, literally to confirm – is by common understanding to put together and adjust the several pieces of any edifice or receptacle of a considerable size. Thus we have church building, house building, ship building & coach building. That one edifice stands another floats & another is suspended on iron springs makes no difference on the nature of the art, if it may be so called, of building or edification. The persons who profess that art, are severally builders, ecclisiastical naval or of whatever other name their work may justify; but building does not become architecture merely by the stability of what it erects: and it is no more Archit which raises a church, or which fits it to accomodate with comfort, a certain number of persons occupied in certain religious offices, than it is Architecture which makes a carriage commodious or a ship swift

I do not of course mean that the word is not or may not be legitimately applied in such a sence (as we speak of Naval Architecture) but in that sence Archi ceases to be one of the fine arts, and it is therefore better not to run the risk by loose nomenclature of the confusion which would arise, and has often arisen from extending principals which belong altogether to
E 7     building into / the sphere of Architecture proper.[6] To take one of Ruskins aphorisms which is as good a definition as I am acquainted with "All Architecture proposes an effect on the human mind not merely a service
E 7a    to the human frame ... is the Art / which so disposes and adorns the edifices rased by man for whatsoever purpose, that the sight of them may contribute to his mental health, power, & pleasure,[7] so from its conception the general form as an object of beauty is aimed at, requiring it may be some consessions from convenience & parsimony, and still the building in grouping may be artistic and truly architectural and yet not have a single cornice or moulding, politeness in building that is Archi may be obtained without unnecessary feature but not without unnecessary

4. It is not certain to which Ruskin Society Mackintosh refers. Several cities had such societies: Glasgow's was founded in 1879.

5. Mackintosh scored out the following: 'It is not mere building, for if a house be erected on purely utilitarian principals then it is building or civil engineering, nor yet does ornament constitute Architecture for then we can conceive a bare naked shell run up and then clothed with ornamental decoration the most refined & beautiful it may be accomplished through a devision of labor – thought not only feasible but right and proper by ignorance but this is a severance of the artistic & practical & so the result would not be Architecture  No to take one of Ruskins aphorisms which is as good a definition as I am acquainted with "All Architecture proposes an effect on the human mind not meerly a service to the human frame, ... is the art'.

6. 'I do not ... architecture proper.' John Ruskin, 'The Lamp of Sacrifice', *The Seven Lamps of Architecture* ch. 1.

7. 'All Architecture ... power, & pleasure', Ruskin (n. 6).

design Let me state here that I shall refer frequently to Ruskin throughout the paper – not that I consider him by any means the Architectural
critic, but as one whose writings are more poetical & captivating to the
ordinary listener, than the dryer but more truthful treatment of other
E 7b     Architectural critics & historians. / The fine outbreaks of prose poetry
which occur from time to time in his volumes we can admire as much
as any readers (save perhaps for a kind of smothered suspicion that they
are not quite genuine) the frequent sarcasms at the expense of modern
Architects & Archi we can enjoy as those who are guiltless of any
connection with Archi: they are sometimes true, and almost always witty
and amusing. But passages of prose poetry and coruscations of sarcasm
will not serve to redeem a book or books professing to be an educational
tratese but crammed full of paradoxes, eccentricities, and rhetorical
claptrap: at one time presenting accidentals as if they were essentials, at
another exibiting absolute ignorance where knowledge & science are
pretended, and diffuse and rambling to a degree that may truely be called
protentious. In this respect Mr Ruskin does full justice to the Spanish
E 8     proverb as to writers who "leave nothing in the inkstand[8] / Mr Ruskin is
also unprofessional and so presumably better suited for such an audience
as this. I would further add that this latter fact is true generally, the
greatest writers on Architecture are not architects, Ferguson the historian
was trained as an indigo planter, Rickman the authority on old English
Work was a Quaker Merchant & Professor Willis a clergyman,[9] you need
E 9     not therefore be scared from the reading of these by the dread of / meeting
wearisome technical nomenclature & the practical rules of a profession-
ally interested coterie.

To return to Ruskins definition, let us consider it well, for it expresses
the true basis of Architecture namely – that not only must the body be
served but the mind pleased. This first condition no one for a single
moment would question you would imagine, yet aparently it is by the art
critic when he offhand condems the composition or appearance of a
building without knowing & so without making allowence for the purpose
it is designed to fulfill. As for example if a Picture Gallery which must be
lighted from the roof and have the wall space quite unbroken, be objected
to as jail like in appearance because it has no windows – this is not
common sence criticism the wall surface may be diversified by ornament
but to have openings for no use but effect would be to construct the
decoration not decorate the construction.[10]

The other condition of Mr Ruskins definition, that is it must please or at
least avoid offending the mind, while almost equally binding is one by no

8. 'The fine outbreaks ... in the inkstand', H. H. Statham, 'The New Edition of The
Stones of Venice', *Builder* 55 (1888) p. 133.

9. James Fergusson (1808-86), Thomas Rickman (1776-1841), Robert Willis (1800-
75): see Pevsner (n. 2).

10. *Cf.* Scott (n. 3) p. 292.

means universally accepted but decidedly objected to by the utilitarians.
"Why throw away money on ornamentation or meer appearance? if
E 10    protected from wind & weather what more do we want? / they say. and
very likely add that the necessity for beauty is urged by those who are
financially concerned in its production. Well even admitting the last
clause as incontrovertable, still, the fact remains that man in all ages has
desired and created what he at least considered beauty, and that not after
all his animal wants had been supplied but before – no race or nation has
ever accipted these utilitarian maxims and hence we may assume none
ever will, the rudest savage ornaments his war club & decorates himself
& his hut. Even the utilitarian objection can hardly be conceived existing
without color either in the form of paint on his dwellings & furniture or in
dyes on his raiment, and if he admits these as allowable because pretty
although not absolutely necessary, he admits the principal and then it is
meerly a matter of argument to prove that form is nobler than color. This
argument of the utilitarian is pure & unmitigated selfishness which says
in effect – if my animal wants are satisfied what matters it if a whole
lanscape is degraded & the feelings of others hurt (for he cannot deny that
history as we have seen proves man to be possessed of this sence of
E 11    beauty) if so be it suits his wretched ideas of parsimony / – or more often
his boorishness & want of culture. This spirit is most aggrivating and
actually provocative of ill-will when seen in some huge unsightly and
unfortunately it may be most enduring erection, a blot in the midst of
surrounding beauty whether of nature or art, for not to speak of the
moral laws of right & wrong, but taking lower ground mere politeness
requires that all source of irritation be removed if possible, is architecture
then, it may be asked, a concession to commonism, and a pampering to
the worst feelings of a mob? By no means: if it be so then is common
politeness the same, for its object is to avoid these same feelings, which be
it remembered bad as they may be are yet human & universal. It is not
courtesy that pampers them, but its absence that excites & exasperates
them. Politeness is altogether a negative art, and consists not in aiming at
a positive good, but in avoiding a posative evil: but as long as they exist,
that is as long as man is man, they will be excited at the idea of a great
property benefiting none but the owner. This utilitarian feeling when
carried to certain lengths is curbed by law, and most rightly. If a merchant were to propose to erect a shed or bare ungainly store in some
E 12    fashionable street or square the surrounding / propriators would object to
the amenity of the place being destroyed, and by power of the Dean of
Guild it would be prohibited.[11] Similarly when a district is fued[12] the
superior generally reserves the power of preventing any erection out of

11. Dean of Guild: prior to local government reorganisation the chairman of the court
responsible for building control.
12. Feu: lease, usually perpetual, of a piece of land at a fixed rent, normally, though not
necessarily, for the purpose of erecting a building thereon.

harmony with the surrounding ones. Now surely this is but reasonable when the objectionable element can be so redily removed  It is more difficult to act in instances where useful contrivances and buildings are almost unavoidably obnoxious, such as smoke chimneys, railways & huge bridges but in all these there might be shown at least an acknowledgement of this obligation, and not the high handed action of many railway companies who scoff at the sentimentalism of those who attempt to conserve the beauties of town or country. For example I think it is quite unjust, a favouring of the rich & powerful when the Caledonian & G & S W Railways are allowed to span the Clyde with bridges constructed on principals of strict economical utility and as a consequence strict ugliness which a poorer shopkeeper would not be allowed to practice.[13] Observe I am not saying that such structures may not be much better left plain than decorated if that is the reason of their nakedness good & well, but

E 13   it / is not: politeness is absent, only the body of man is served and so the selfish expression of civil engineering is uncorrected by architecture. Another hateful specimen of this selfish spirit, though not arising from parsimony and one unsparingly condemned by Ruskin is the seclusion of fine buildings and beautiful grounds behind high ugly walls, as so often met with in our country walks, rather than low pleasing hedges which allow the wayfarer in some measure to share the pleasures of the rich. An evil example is the alhambra, bare almost repellent externally, but luxurious within; all a very excellent arrangement for the visitor who is pleasingly surprised by the change, but this happy feeling can never unfortunately be shared by the less fortunate outsider. In this as in other cases the motive gives a large portion of the value to an action, if vulgar, ostentatious parade is made externally that all may see & admire the great Babylon that has been built, then certainly whatever benefit the public may obtain, no credit is due to the exibitor. But this is not a common failing, rather in this country at least, there appears to be the feeling that to appear substantial and well to do, externally all must be

E 14   plain to the verge of rudeness. We are all familiar with the desirable / family residence "seen among trees & flowers – square as a band box door placed symmetrically in the centre with windows at the sides and above, these windows more over are equally important  no sign from these, which light a pantry or Drawing Room Bath or dressing Room – the house I said was square there fore light for the centre portion is got by a skylight which prevents the comfort as well as the appearance of a fine

13. Caledonian and Glasgow and South-Western Railways. Caledonian: the reference is to the Central Station viaducts, designed by George Cunningham of Blyth & Cunningham in 1876-8, one over Argyle St, rebuilt 1899-1907, and one over the Clyde, a lattice girder structure on piers of Dalbeattie granite, demolished except for the piers in 1966-7. Glasgow and South Western: the reference is to the original City of Glasgow Union railway viaduct designed by John Fowler and John F. Blair, a lattice girder structure built in 1864-70 by Thomas Brassey & Co. It was replaced in 1898-1902.

Hall window. The rooms have no pleasing projections giving variety to the view of nature seen from them and pleasing effects to the house itself no picturesque chimney stalks like what are to be found in old english work, no projecting eaves, no all substantial symmetry and cheerful as a prison or infirmary. Now all this has given legitimate and even desirable character to our national Architecture, yet there is another side to the matter. You may remember in George Elliots Scenes in Clerical Life", the squire rather more cultured than his fellows, returned from the grand tour and fully entering into the spirit of the Renaissance (17th Centy) with its love for what was Classical, has built a magnificent manor house impoverishing himself by using rarest materials manipulated by Italian workmen, in the erection of beautiful Halls which remain unfurnished, while the whole dwelling arrangements are of the most limited extent –
E 15    how the writer of the story / while not altogether justifying him, points to the action as far nobler than the seeking first of commodious Kitchen and winecellar accomodation. To put all all the ornamentation of a house outside, till as was said of a nobleman of the period, "that to get the benefit of his own dwelling he had to take lodgings across the street,"[14] is a generous form of absurdity, which the general public at least need not resent.

Architecture then we find must serve mind and body, let us see how it does so when posessing the 3 attributes considered necessary namely Strength of stability usefulness & Beauty

Stability. This quality or condition refers to good sound practical workmanship in all the materials, which materials must vary with the locality. Strength itself will be a criterion of the excellency of the archit. everything approaching the gimcrack or flimsy will condemn the building be it ever so lovely  Of course this does not mean that a summer house or conservatory be built like a fortress, but it demands that all noble ornament should be of the most enduring material, and placed in the most secure positions. So much is Archi dependent on this quality that it requires not only the real fact but the appearance and will prefer of
E 16    two / equally substantial materials the one which has most bulk  I think that you will admit that it is the want of apparent strength which is the chief blemish of modern street Archi. iron is much stronger than stone & so a thin clothes pole of metal is as strong as a much bulkier piece of stone or brick but the eye is distressed at huge lofty tenements resting to all appearance on nothing more stable than plate glass for the real actual supports are easily overlooked.

These two comparatively modern materials iron & glass though eminently suitable for many purposes will never worthily take the place of stone, because of this defect the want of mass. With the advent of the

14. This anecdote probably refers to 29 Great Burlington Street, London, built in 1723 for General George Wade to designs by the Earl of Burlington.

Crystal Palace and the many rosetinted hallucinations of that period arose the belief in the invention of a new style. At last common sence it was shouted prevails – no more connection with the works of the past – no more deference to the ideas of artists poets, or even the principals of beauty in Nature: for now we can pile up the hugest buildings with the least possible means of support, and that on most economical principals as design can be turned out of the foundry by repetition without limit, to the minimising of intellectual labor and so also to the payment of it.

E 17    But time has passed, and practical experience has / shown that apart altogether from any defect in stability or actual comfort the want of appearance of stability is fatal to the introduction of such a style for either domestic, civil or ecclisiastical buildings. These demand actual mass even if of a weaker material taking bulk for bulk. The leaning Tower of Piza though abundantly strong as has been proved by centuries, is yet tottering & insecure to all appearance some say so much so that to sleep under its tottering shadow would be almost impossible. Thus in this quality of Archi mind & body must be served|considered.[15] Egyptian remains will always impress the mind in a way Chinese flippery never will  The Alhambra gorgeous & refined in its ornament though it was, more beautiful than perhaps any other building, yet because its materials are but plaster, wood, porcelain & tile work, is yet of a lower type of Architecture than the far plainer but more enduring Country churches of England or Normandy.

Utility, Consider next the quality of utility.

From what was said before about the influence the individual or corporate body who requires the erection of a building possesses over its design ( – the potent influence of the employer – it may be believed that

E 18    this quality, is most reasonably considered the first and principal one / The highest types of architecture are no doubt seen in the temple & cathedral – take for instance the Parthenon and Salisbury – but architecture is not limited in its application to these, but includes every class of bdn. man requires. For in Greece while the Temple was certainly far before all other edificis in importance, and so had the greatest artistic care lavished upon it, the Theatres distinctly different in every requirement were yet noble monuments, while the private dwellings though singularly plain, were, there can be no doubt, as well as being comfortable – their primary object – substantial & at the same time pleasing to the eye, which is the same as saying the mind. Later on in Roman times the versatility of Archi is seen in its application to the ever increasing variety of buildings, the outcome of increased power & growing civilization, take the Baths of Caracalla, the private dwellings at pompei – the Triumphal Arches & the plain aqueducts the Palaces & the Tombs all of widely diverging purposes, yet

15. Mackintosh wrote 'served' first, then 'considered' above, without finally deleting either option.

fue will deny that all of them have been made things of beauty. And yet later still, with the birth of the new era, the Christian Church, though at first unpretending yet always suitable both in accomodation & design – rose the glory the glory of the Medieaval Cathedral, and with the demand of the churchmen for magnificent and at the same time lasting and

E 19    suitable buildings Archi / kept pace. Please note this fact, that from the Basilica all our Cathedrals sprung & the form of the cross was always kept for the plan, but beyond that arbitrary rule it was growing opulence alone which influenced the medieaval archi. not as has been absurdly believed, not nature. The pointed arch grew out of the semi-circular, nearly invariably to suite Convenience, rarely asthetic wants, and never to imitate a forest avenue: nor was the idea of painted windows ever taken from sun gleams among the branches. Yet this, with a vast amount of other absurd rigmarole, is believed by many indiscriminating admirers of nature, who unable to deduct a principal, would attempt a childish mimicry. The whole theory has been cleverly applied to an existing effect whose cause must be looked for elsewhere  to return  These cathedrals again were co-incident with powerful fortresses & Castles with whose appearance everyone is familiar, and also with Commercial Warehouses Colleges and many other forms of buildings such as the Manors & Barns of the low Counties of England among the most picturesque buildings extant, all these buildings were erected for particular purposes, and which particular purpose was in every case served, and yet redeemed from the selfishness of mere building by good architecture. I have got with me no

E 20    illust so must trust to your recollection / of such to notice that in all these different cases the Archi. while always preserving a certain continuity & similarity, was the decoration of the different practical requirements – that is to say, no beholder would mistake the general purpose of a building, I do not say that these varities could be equally beautiful, by no means, but the incumbent duty of making the best of each case and still preserving truthfulness to the necessities of the building was admitted & surely with happier results, than that of these modern antiquarian-sentimentalists, who, getting the half truth firmly embedded in their unpractical minds – that the Greek Temple & Medieaval Cathedral are worthy of all admiration & imitation, further it by erecting marvellous villas which only by an unfortunate chimney can be decided not to be a place of Pagan Worship or as in some cases I know of, monastic cloisters. These as houses might be comfortable and useful enough, and the Architectural adornment beautiful enough in its right place, which however was certainly not where its application prevented the reasonable purpose of the building being manifested.

And, widely as the nature of the buildings & nationality of the builders has differed, as greatly has the materials of construction. The huge

E 21    monoliths of Granite / obtained and used by the Egyptians, were rejected by the Greeks for their famed marbles. When however in Roman times

the arch replaced the lintel, because of the greater openings which had
to be spanned, smaller materials were found to be necessary, and so the
bricks they so well knew how to make, were admirably suited for their
purpose.[16] Later on when in N Italy the Lombards built uniformly with
bricks, the veneering of their walls with thin slabs of marble, was under
the geological conditions of the country perfectly legitimate and quite
artistic, while in the South of Italy, through the abundance of Stone a
more dignified and really more substantial type of building was attained,
and of course the design was influenced by the material but in both these
there was true Archi. Naturally both had the flat pitched tile roof and
narrow windows necessitated by a dry & sunny climate, which in more
northern latitudes gave place to the lofty roofs & large generous window
openings Here let me note in parenthesis, one of these curiosities of
popular criticism? so often encountered, namely, that Gothic as opposed
to Classic is quite unsuitable for present day requirements, it is gloomy?
monastic? the dim religious light its inseperable concomitant. This I admit
E 22   is true of Castles / & fortresses, but I should like to hear of the eastern
mosque or Classic Temple that has the whole side of an apartment one
huge window as many of our cathedrals have, while among greek
Temples it is the great disputed point among archiologists how light of
any kind was admitted at all. Some even holding that it was absolutely
excluded and artificial light employed. The accomodation for the worshipper in both cases was given but the different requirements of the
different forms of worship lead to different results. These two religions the
Pagan & Christian were however totally different. Yet take the instance of
a religion requireing similarity of ritual in different countries having
different climates and different building materials, and you will see that
utility which must in common sence be studied (& will be no matter what
the artistic fraternity say) is not inimical to Architecture but on the
contrary gives variety and character – take I say the Duomo – the
Cathedral – of Florence or any other Italian city erected for the Roman
Catholic service, and then see the identically same service accomodated in
France or England. In all these 3 countries, though the cross is taken of
course arbitrarily – a matter of sentiment not of necessity.) as the shape
for the plan to follow, how differently is it worked out, in Florence &
throughout Italy bricks are used, necessitating the arch  the light & heat
E 23   is so general that the windows are but mere slits; / the roof is hardly seen
on account of its flatness: while in England and France at least its northern portion, the churches are built of stone which readily permits a
bolder construction, hence vaulting (which is rarely used in italy) the
windows are ample to admit light, but the necessity is seized as a pretext
for decoration, hence glass staining (unknown almost in Italy) rain &

---

16. See Ruskin, 'The Lamp of Truth', *The Seven Lamps of Architecture*. Much of the
following passage appears to be based on direct observation.

snow must be provided against hence the high pitched leaded roofs.[17]

We have thus examples to show how dignified & beautiful a building may be when exactly fulfilling a utilitarian purpose as the ancient Temples of the Greeks did, with side walls unbroken by a single window – so dignified and beautiful in fact that one might wonder how any other requirement could result in anything like such perfection – yet other and widely different requirements did arise in other countries with different climates & materials, yet surely no one will say that the Cathedrals of N. Europe are anything less than perfection in their own degree. Yet the principals which governed both were identical – the practicing of which principals must vary with circumstances – but may always be resolved into the 3 we are considering namely — Strength – Utility – & Beauty.

E 24  There remains then the third quality Beauty to consider, / by far the most difficult to deal with as there are erroneous ideas regarding it to be removed and true & reasonable ones to be substituted. Yet there is no final standard of taste to which all may appeal, no code of laws to which every little detail may be submitted – no authoratative committee of taste to decide on the disputed points, for even the most learned in these matters diverge widely in their ideas of the beautiful  Many, because of the dissagreement among professors – which however is more upon matters of practice rather than principal  many foolish persons discredit the existance of any other way[18] of deciding than their own personal taste; you say a design is bad, they say it is good, well there is no more to be said, simply they like it. They mischievously take the proverb "There is no disputing about taste" which only applies to the palate or other sences, quite different from Taste which is another word for sound & cultivated sense, judgement & perception of fitness. Eastlake in his interesting book "Hints on [Household Taste]" says, Genius implies a creative & inventive power, which is the highest effort of the understanding  Taste is more properly the art of selecting & guiding the efforts of genius, and is the offspring of a sensative & delicate mind.[19] The common saying that "tastes are not to be disputed" owes its influence & general reception to

E 25  the error of imagining the faculty of [taste] too high [and] original / to submit to the authority of an earthly tribunal. It corresponds with the notion of these who consider it a mere phantom of the imagination, so devoid of of substance as to elude all criticism. "Those who most sternously assert the indisputable & uncertain nature of all tastes, do yet papably

17. The following line contains the puzzling instruction 'Page 23 omit here – '. Page 23 [E 25] contains the central passages of Mackintosh's discussion on taste, not relevant here. No subsequent instruction signals the end of the implied omission.

18. In the margin against the line beginning 'way of deciding ...' Mackintosh has written 'Law– '.

19. C. L. Eastlake, *Hints on Household Taste*, first published 1868. The precise quotation is unlocated, and may be a reformulation by Mackintosh of ideas found in Eastlake.

acknowledge a right & wrong in taste when they challenge the taste of others, an inconsistency with their maxisms which they are sure to commit. It is the consolation of those who have neither relish or preference in their minds for the objects of taste, to maintain the total impossibility of bringing the opinion of mankind to any rational

E 25a  standard / Perfect taste is the faculty of receiving the greatest possible pleasure from those material sources which are attractive to our moral nature In Its purity & perfection; but why we receive pleasure from some forms & colors, and not from others, is no more to be asked or answered than why we like sugar & dislike wormwood.

And the pleasure which perfect taste has in things which it finds true & good, is so great, that it cannot possibly be led aside by any tricks of fashion or diseases of variety; it cannot be cramped in its conclusions by partialities and hyprocrisies; its visions & its delights are too penetrating – too living – for any white washed object or shallow fountain long to endure or supply. It clasps all that it loves so hard that it crushes it if it be

E 25b  hollow. / The faculty of distinguishing good from bad in design is a faculty which most educated people – and especially ladies – conceive they possess. How it has been aquired few would be able to explain. The general impression seems to be, that it is the peculiar inheritance of gentle blood, and, independent of all training that while a young lady is devoting at school, or under a governess, so many hours a day to music, so many to languages & so many to general science, she is all the time unconcicnciously forming that sense of the beautiful which we call taste, that this sense, once developed will enable her unassisted by any special study or experience not only to appreciate the charms of nature in every

E 26  aspect, / but to form a correct estimate of the merits of Works in Archtec Painting, Sculpture etc. That this impression has gained ground so far as to be a posative conviction, may be infered from the fact that there is no single point on which well-educated women are more jelous of disparagement than in this  We may condemn a ladies opinion in polotics – criticise her handwriting – correct her pronunciation of Latin and disparage her favourite authors with a chance of escaping displeasure, but if we venture to question her taste in the most trivial matter we are sure to

E 26a  offend.[20] / So far as education does indeed tend to make the sences delicate and the perceptions accurate, and thus enable people to be pleased with quiet instead of gaudy colour, and with graceful instead of course form; and by long acquaintance with the best things, to discern quickly what is fine from what is common – so far acquired taste is an honourable faculty, and it is true praise of anything to say it is in "good taste" But nobody need begin this second volume sentence unless they are breathed like the Graeme –

---

20. 'The faculty of distinguishing ... sure to offend.' See Eastlake (n. 19) introduction.

> "Right up Ben Ledi could he press,
> And not a sob his toil confess."[21]

so far as this higher education has a tendency to narrow the sympathies and harden the heart, diminishing the intrest of all beautiful things by familiarity, untill even what is best can hardly please, and what is brightest hardly entertain, – so far as it fosters pride, and leads men to found the pleasure they take in anything, not on the worthiness of the thing, but on the degree in which it indicates some greatness of their own (as people build marble porticoes, and inlay marble floors, not so much because they like the colours of marble, or find it plesent to the foot, as because such floors are costly, and seperated in all human eyes from

E 26b   entrances of stone & timber): – so far as it leads people / to prefer graceful-ness of dress, manner, and aspect, to value of substance and heart, liking a well said thing better than a true thing, and a well-trained manner better than a sincere one, and a delicately-formed face better than a good natured one, – and in all other ways and things setting custom and semblance above everlasting truth; – so far finally, as it induces a sence of inherent distinction between class & class and causes everything to be more or less dispised which has no social rank, so that the affection, pleasure, and grief of a clown are looked upon as of no intrest compared with the affection & grief of a well bred man; – just so far, in all these several ways, the feeling induced by what is called a "liberal education" is

E 26c   utterly adverse to the understanding of noble art." / It is however a lamentable fact, that this very quality is commonly deficient not only among the generally ignorant, but also among the most educated classes in this country. How can it be otherwise? Even the simplest and most elementary principals of Archi – or any other form of art for that part, forms no part of early instruction, and the majority of the public are left completely uninformed about them. Many people will not take the trouble to balance an opinion but invariably fly to extremes; they would have and believe in the laws of art tabulated like Scientific formulae or codified like law, and because of the absence – the very impossibility of any dogmati-cally minute regulation which would exclude all national as well as

E 27    traditional characteristic and fail to take cognisance / of these varying circumstances which do so alter cases they decline to see or admit any principal whatever, and in taste become a law unto themselves. In the same way the young polititian or ecclisiastic will save himself a deal of cogitation and admissions of ignorance if from the first he will trustingly join the extreme section of a party, or of the church, statistics; facts; arguments; none of these move him if they are but advanced by his opponents.

Now in Archi there are two great styles Classic & Gothic which may in a general way be termed the styles of the lintel and of the Arch, and both

21. This is inaccurately remembered from Walter Scott's *The Lady of the Lake*, Canto 2 xxv: 'Right up Ben-Lomond could he press, / And not a sob his toil confess.'

these styles have their partisans whose bigotry to the candid mind is as childish as in the other cases I have named. I cannot hope to be quite impartial so rather than enquire into the respective merits of the beauty of each I shall attempt to give some principals of beauty which are common to both and to all true Architecture.

Truth[22] is certainly the chief quality, everyone will admit that all shams are detestable, but this admission does not prove that a just discrimination is made between truth in pictorial & truth in decorative art. In the former the truth is acknowledged when you can forget it is canvas

E 28    you / you are looking at, and imagine the object depicted is actually before you, while in the latter truth is only present when every material is shown on its own merits and mimics not the resemblance of any others. This it may be necessary in a brick wall to weather proof it – internally or externally it does not matter – with plaster or cement which may be done & no deceipt shown but the practice is detestible where it is scored over to delude into the belief that stone is used. I do not think though that there is any sham about marble veneering of a brick building, because everyone knows that it is so precious as to be used just as in mosaic, in thin slabs; the material is beautiful & is attached as an adornment is much in the same way as gilding, with which no one is for a minute deceived, as the value is so well known as to prohibit a picture frame or organ pipes being solid metal, only when gilding is applied to small articles, which might reasonably be expected to be bona-fide – such as jewellry – does it become a sham. Equally objectionable is all graining, marbeling, or painted granite  for that part a charming specimen of which can be seen on one of the bridges across the Kelvin which is a beautiful? granite erection at a distance, but which closer inspection shows to be only a hollow mockery.[23] And the dissapointment felt by most people when they find this is surely a sign that evyone desires truthfulness[24]  and bronzing of the low housepainter. I admit that the evil is lessened when the deception is quite apparent. I suppose that none are taken in by "oak" or "walnut" doors so plentiful in our houses, the fault then lies in taking for a model some thing which can be copied, or better still copying it without the

E 29    least / effort of the designing faculties. It is a poor spirit this apeing the posessions of richer people – doors & all woodwork must certainly be preserved, <u>and if it must be</u> by painting then it should be in even tint – if the yellowish tone of oak grained doors – or the dark brown of the walnut fraud be liked – then the same effect may be obtained in a rational manner by harmonious arrangement; a still better way is to use stains

22. *Cf.* the discussion of architectural deceits in Ruskin, 'The Lamp of Truth' (n. 16). Mackintosh's text is a mixture of abridgement and personal observation.

23. The bridge no longer exists and remains so far unidentified.

24. Mackintosh's example of painted granite work, 'for that part ... evyone desires truthfulness', is an afterthought noted in the margin, interrupting his list of unacceptable sham decorative techniques.

which permit the true grain of the wood to be seen. Paint I say is no deception, for in wood, iron, plaster & sometimes even stone it is necessary for comfort, but there is no need for paltriness with it, the "massive" pillar – of lath & plaster is not improved by mimicing rare marble. Cast iron can be a useful & at the same time beautiful object, but it is not improved when with imitation rivet heads it tries to pass for handwrot metal work or by paint for bronze. All these instances are but the auxaliries of architecture, but unhappily tricks as gross are to be met with in architecture itself. In italy as we have seen the roofs are pretty flat, yet it is no uncommon thing to see gables that are simply masks, not the decoration & expressions of the necessities of the buildings, but to meet the supposed requirements of the Gothic style they are lofty & steeply pitched, so that only a view from another point of sight than that intended by the architect discloses the sham. St Pauls has an upper storey to give the effect of

E 30    what a Classic Temple / required to be to accord with the public taste during the Renaiscence, which storey is quite independent of the church, and not only so, but which actually falsifies the structure.[25] But even if this positive evil be not reached truth requires that rather than expend time & trouble in covering up what may often mistakenly be considered irredeemably commonplace & vulgar, if that object be an absolutely essential one, the time should be employed in trying to render it if not actually beautiful at least inoffensive  Such an object is the roof which is quite as essential as the walls and should get all due credit. True, covered with lead it may be almost flat & so hidden entirely from view, partly by the balustrade, which in a truly affecting way is generally provided as if promenading on our house tops were a general custom. Now I think that the French Chateau gain half their effect from the steeply pitched slated roof, giving a picturesque sky-line even without the rather expensive gable. The effect of the roof so treated may be to a certain extent seen in the Central Station & Stock Exchange.[26] These are quite plain & only of a shape required by truth, not to press another principal which is an element in Beauty, namely, that Cons. should be decorated, not dec. con. This principal is one of the most important & yet most commonly violated of any in Archi.[27] It was included to a certain extent in the consideration

E 31    of utility, where Architecture is declared to be the rightful / accompanyment, of whatever kind of building is essential to man, wherever situated. This may now be considered as the same principal applied in more

25. *Cf.* James Fergusson, *History of the Modern Styles of Architecture* (3rd edn, London 1891) p. 38.

26. Central Station, Glasgow, by George Cunningham and John Hawkshaw, completed 1879, extended 1901-7. Mackintosh is probably referring to the high roofs of the Central Station Hotel, designed by R. R. Anderson as railway offices in 1879, and reconstructed as a hotel in 1880-6. Stock Exchange, St. George's Place, Glasgow by John Burnet Sen., 1875-7.

27. See Scott (n. 3). A repetition of the statement quoted earlier [E 9].

minute detail. Then the salient & most requisite features should be selected for ornamentation, so from this it must appear, that, windows & doors being about the most important of modern requirements, round these should any ornament be sought. Yet note how this is forgotten in a type of building you are all acquainted with – the classic churches in vogue 20 years ago, such as Dundas St Station,[28] Daily Mail Office[29] & Bridge St Station[30] all churches once & many others throughout the city – which you will note depend for Architectural effect on the application of flat colomes attached to the wall in imitation of the temple style, while the windows & doors are simply holes in the wall – observe I am not complaining of plainness when little money can be got but of missapplic-ation of money when obtained. Now examples of a contrary & preferable application may be seen in the Conserv. Club.[31] Bank of Scotland & Merchants House[32] and others when you will see that the wall surface is plain & the decoration consists of columns at the sides & rich pediments above the windows & doors. These particular examples are in the style of the Renaiscence followed in Florence, Rome, & Venice – the practice was

E 32 in that style first & most beautifully applied / by a painter – Raphael in the Pandolfen Palace.

However, not only in that style, for the principal was well known & appreciated by the Cathedral Builders where also you find a perfectly plain wall & most elaborate windows. Still, for the same reason of fitness there are exceptions to this principal also thus I think it quite reasonable that all Buttresses should be left absolutely plain that their strength & purpose may be the more apparent, that is dispense with ornament not with design and it is this same cause which makes the lowre portion of a building plain & solid, while as the building becoms lighter as it gets higher, so does the decoration increas, for it would be rather rediculous to see minute delicate work at the base surmounted by cyclopean masonry, yet I confess a trifle more of this might be worth attempting so that our walls in narrow streets might present some ornament at eye level. Yet one other powerful element in Beauty is Association or Tradition, which will modify the force of laws which in the abstract are admitted to be

28. Presumably Queen Street Station, Glasgow. The reference appears to be to West George St Independent Chapel, designed by James Gillespie Graham in 1819, demolished 1975.

29. North British Daily Mail Offices, previously the Unitarian Church, 102-104 Union St, Glasgow; demolished *c.* 1898.

30. Mackintosh was in error in believing this had been a church. Built as the station to designs by James Collie in 1840-1, with a Greek Doric portico to answer Euston; de-molished 1971. See Colin Johnston & J. R. Hume, *Glasgow Stations* (Vermont 1979).

31. 112-14 West George St and 46-50 Renfield St, Glasgow, now the Scottish Widows Building, by David Bryce, 1868-9.

32. The west side of George Square, comprising the Bank of Scotland by J. T. Rochead (1868), Bank of Scotland Chambers by James Sellars (1874) and the Merchants' House by John Burnet (1874-7), built as a unified composition.

correct & true and grant a certain [left blank] to local or national customs or to practices sanctioned by high authority. When Burns in his "Cotters Saturday Night" after enumerating some of our favourite psalm tunes bursts out "compared wae this Italian trills are tame".[33] as a piece of musical criticism it may not hold true world-wide yet it is a very sufficient

E 33     reason / & obvious truth to Scotsmen, so in the same manner there are many decorative features in Scotch Archi, which might well be replaced by others of antiquity yet just because we are Scotch & not Greek or Roman we reject. For example there is the quaint old Scotch gate pillars with the spire resting on 3 or 4 stone bullets – the curious Balls often seen at stairs, such as the old College one now at Gilmorhill and very many other features which give a historical caracter to the buildings they adorn for they tell of a time when Scot. was much more friendly with france than with England and so our castles much more resembled the French Chateau than the Manor of our neighbour country. In fact I think we should be a little less cosmopolitan & rather more national in our Archi, as we are with language, new words & phrases will be incorporated gradually, but the wholesale introduction of japanese senta[nces] for example would be denounced & rightly by the purist.

Attention to national chacteristics was well shown by Sir G. Scott when erecting St Marys Cath Edin. for an English Service with of course the typical plan & arrangement of that church, he yet took the ornaments peculiarly Scotch as seen at Holyrood, Kelso &c as his models. only in the spire of which unhappily Scotland has no good examples did he take an English model[34] Still of course this conservatism is often made a cloak &

E 34     excuse for / mediocrity in design & the senseless & unceasing repitition of features which have only their age to recommend them, & so Variety & Novelty if not carried to far are qualities both allowable & desirable, but by ignorance often clamoured for most unreasonably. Archi. being as old almost as mankind is not a new art, so there is hardly any form that is applicable for construction that has not been tried: A house is composed of walls & roof – well for a roof you must either have the Dome (the noblest form of all) the pitched roof or the properly flat one  in walls there must be windows & doors – well these openings can only be spaned by the lintel or arch – if the latter there is no form which has not been used – semi-cir – pointed – horseshoe & ogee. Civil engin. is quite a modern science & so got plenty of scope and is never weary of assuming that archi is effect & cant originate & yet when it does attempt to ornament it simply copies & that in the most unreasonable way. For instance you will see in many bridges iron Balusters with moulded parapet|cornices[35] –

33. Robert Burns, *The Cotter's Saturday Night*, vs 13.

34. Built 1874-9 and 1890-1. Kelso is a slip for Jedburgh. The design of the spire with its pronounced entasis is based on that at Chartres Cathedral.

35. Mackintosh wrote 'parapet' first, then 'cornice' above, without deleting either option.

suitable enough in a building when in the proper situation, but are manifestly degraded when mimiced by cast metal which only forms a hollow shape mouldings being repeated in the cornice whose only beauty consisted in their usefulness when the material was stone The common sence way of using cast iron there & elsewhere is to have patterns of the E 35     most elaborate & beautiful design / impressed on each plate, in a manner which in stone would be unsubstantial as well as wasteful & extravigant but which can be economically accomplished with a material which is run into a mould.

But novelty & variety might be attained were Archi as regards the patronage of the rich & cultured on the same grounds as Painting & Sculpture – which it is not — the young struggling painter is seized with a noble conception, if he have but the skill to embody it, he can get color & canvas for a few shillings & when the work is finished he submits it to the public patronage and if looked at impartially it stands or falls on its own self-evident merits. The poor sculptor can also, t[hough] not quite so redily if he chose a heroic subject, at a very small expense prodcce, even though it be in clay, a finished work. But the Architect afflicted with genius, without a corresponding quantity of wealthy connection, submits his inspirations with drawings with far less shadow of resemblance to the realty, than that posessed by the scribbles in an academy catalogue – for the rudest strocks of black ink may at least indicate the relative positions of what may on the canvas be intended for glorious ethereal clouds, for the picter has but one point of view, while a building must be considered internally & externally as altering with every step you take. Now this E 36     necessity of giving a prophetic view / of a non-existing structure requires <u>some</u> little artistic skill & so this alone demolishes the popular idea that the practical man is the right architect to employ. These drawings then can always give but a very poor idea of what the reality will be.

Now I do not in the slightest degree make a moan about this handicapping under which Architecture labors compared with the other fine arts, for unfortunate though it may be it is unavoidable & just because professionalism is checked & made subservient to the public idea of what is fit & proper, it is a fair question for you to consider that what may be lost in abstract perfection of beauty, may not be compensated for by the presence of qualities appreciable by the many.

As I said before the history of nations is written in stone, but it certainly would be a difficult task to read a history from the architecture of this nation at the present time  We do not build as the ancients did who in each succeeding building tryed to carry to further perfection the national type  No. We are a world acquainted people who cast aside all prejudice and build now in Greek if we love the Classic, now in Norman if we doat on the romantic, or if we have travelled show their [our] ill regulated admiration for foreign beauties by reproducing Swiss Chateau, &c &c in the most inappropriate positions

E 37     It is to increas your intrest in these that I have ventured to bring the
subject of Archite. before you to-night, and have refrained as far as
possible from taking into consideration styles, for they are only too apt to
be taken as receipts which ensure certain results without requiring any
effort of sensible discrimination. Not that I would slight or ignore styles &
say with many why not unite the beauties of all in one modern style, for
each style has an expression peculiar to itself – an expression which
would only be weakened by the introduction of any other, as Sir J.
Renolds said of the same question of style applied however [to] Sculpture,
"a statue in which you endeavor to unite stately dignity youthful elegence
& stern valor must surely posess none of these to any eminent degree.[36]
The expression which is plainly observable in the different styles, has led
to the establishment by some critics of a distinct element in Beauty –
namely that a building should be Phonetic, that is explain its purpose or
illustrate history.[37] Thus a Temple should aim at sublimity, a villa at
domesticity, a Palace of Justice at dignity & so forth. Well I think that a
building can not really be phonetic, merely expressive, for it is generally
only association of ideas which has given these attributes any standing.
This is analogous to the rules of criticism for either sculpture or music.
Though these arts are popularly considered self explanitory & altogether
independent of the catalogue yet of the former Renolds says "I suspect
E 38     that it will be found, / on close examination, by him who is resolved not
to see more than he really does see, that the antique figures are distinguishable by ther insignia rather than by any variety of form or beauty.
Take from appolo his Lyre & from Bacchus his Thirsus & vine leaves &
Meleager the Boar Head & there will remain little or no difference in their
characters  In a Juno Minerva or Flora the idea of the artists seems to
have gone no further than representing his idea [of] perfect beauty & then
adding the proper attributes, with a total indifference to which they gave
them. Thus John de Bologna, after he finished a group of a young man
holding up a young woman in his arms, with an old man at his feet,
called together his friends, to tell him what name he should give it, and
they was agreed to call it the Rape of the Sabines, & this is the celebrated
group which now stands before the old Palace at Florence.[38] The figures
have the same general expression which is to be found in most of the
antique sculpture: & yet it would be no wonder if future critics, should
find out delicacy of expression which was never intended & go so far as to

36. Sir Joshua Reynolds, *Discourses on Art*, ed. Robert R. Wark (2nd edn, New Haven
1981) discourse 5, p. 79.
37. 'Phonetic' is a term derived from James Fergusson, *An Historical Inquiry into the True
Principles of Beauty in Art* (London 1849) pt 2 sect. 8, pp. 115-24.
38. Mackintosh had described Giambologna's *Rape of the Sabines* (1583) as 'a stupid
thing' in his Italian diary [B 20 May].

see in the old mans countenance the exact relation which he bears to the woman who appears to be taken from him[39]

Music again is not one whit more expressive than stolid Archi.

E 39    "programme music" as it is called is understandable enough / when we know or are told by a description of the pieces what is intended to be represented, but without this forewarning it is somewhat difficult by intuition to guess that quavering trills among the high notes of a piano or orchestra, or a pounding scramble among the lower denote in turn "Sunrise in Arcadia or "the moon rising behind the trees of a churchyard with vampires flitting around the open grave of a maiden. Again to quote Ruskin. "A building which recorded the Bible history by means of a series of sculptural pictures, would be perfectly useless to a person unaquainted with the Bible beforehand: on the other hand the text of the old & new Testaments might be written on its walls and yet the building would be a very inconvenient kind of book, not so useful as if it had been adorned with inteligible and vivid sculpture. So again the power of exciting emotion must vary or vanish, as the spectator becomes thoughtless or cold: & the building may be often blamed for what is the fault of the critic or endowed with a charm which is of the spectators creation. It is not therefore possible to make expression any fair criterion of excellence in a building, untill we can fully place ourselves in the position of those to whom the expression was originally adressed & untill we are certain that we understand every symbol, and are capable of being touched by every

E 40    association / which its builders employed as letters of their language"[40] This appeal of Ruskins is just adressed to the public that it may take [more] of [an] intelligent intrest in archi than at present It does, that is if you would admire old buildings you must put yourself in the place of those contempory with their erection – this can only be done by the educated (and that means at no far distant date everyone) and un-doubtedly such an intrest if applied to modern work would ensure better Architecture than that prevailing. Artists (I mean of course Architects) must be as select in those whom they desire to please as in those whome they desire to imitate. Without the love of fame they can never do any-thing excelent: but by an excessive & unsatiable thirst after it they will come to have vulgar views, they will degrade their style & their taste will be entirely corrupted.

It is almost certain to be the lowest style which will always be most popular as it falls within the compass of ignorance itself. So I have tried to show what principals rule in Architecture, & how these are very greatly influenced by the public in the shape of the all potent employer, – "for

39. 'I suspect that it will be found [E 37] ... taken from him.' Reynolds (n. 36) discourse 10, pp. 181-2.

40. John Ruskin, 'The Virtues of Architecture', *The Stones of Venice*, ch. 2. This passage and the preceding one on music are repeated in the later lecture on architecture [F 6-8].

E 41

living to please, we must also please to live" sometimes as we have seen
by the literary art critic & also & most powerfully by the poet or novelist,
who without formulating any rules / yet give expression to the ideas of
the general cultured mind – such writers as Scott  Tennyson, G Elliot
Dickens & others describe the different effects which most move them the
romantic the grandoise or the picturesque proving that as well & almost
to a great a degree, pleasure to the mind is desired besides comfort and
protection to the body, and this double service is accomplished by
Architecture

CHARLES RENNIE MACKINTOSH

# F. *Architecture* (1893)

F 1  Architecture
Feby 1893.

Although the invitation to write this paper on Architecture came in simple form it were surely unjust to the thoughts of our hosts if we did not interpret it less as a piece of courtesy to ourselves than as a graceful act of homage to that great queen mother of all the arts which we so unworthily represent.

In reading this essay I must ask for indulgence, although I offer no apology, in the first place for reading an essay on this subject to an audience chiefly composed of pecture painters and secondly for an attempt to set out from an architects point of view the basis of certain ideas common to the architecture of many lands & religions, the purposes behind structure & form which may be called the true[1] principals of architecture and for an attempt to deal with a subject that could only be

F 2  rightly handled by one having the equipments of a wide / scholarship – while I can only claim that there should come of regular apprenticeship & long practice in any art or craft a certain instinct of insight not possessed by mere outsiders though never so learned.

I say this in the hope that writing thus on my own art, may be sufficient excuse for any appearance of affectation & presumption in quoting unfamiliar matter at second hand, for I must say at once what will be sufficiently apparent as I proceed that my knowledge of books is only that of the general reader.

In such a wide field I have thought it well to concentrate my attention on some few definite points, and I fear in doing this there may be some unnecessary insistence & repitition, a tendency to over prove, and an attempt to explain too much, on the one hand to burden with what is

F 3  obvious, on the / other to weaken by unfounded conjecture. What then is architecture?

Architecture is the world of art and as[2] it is everything visible & invisable that makes the world, so it is all the arts & crafts & industries that go [to] make architecture

The history of architecture as usually written with its theory of utilitarian origins from the hut & the tumulus, and further developments in that way – the adjustment of forms to the conditions of local circumstances – the clay of Mesopotamia – the granite of Egypt and the

1. Mackintosh scored out 'esoteric' and substituted 'true'.
2. Mackintosh here scored out 'it is the people who make the world the'.

marble of greece – is rather the history of building, of architecture it may be in the sence we so often use the word, but not the architecture which is the synthesis of the fine arts, the commune of all the crafts.[3] See how

F 4     architecture has the biggest programme, the widest range / of sympathy & action of all the arts – it is more practical – it demands more technical workshop knowledge, it deals with a greater number of materials – of subjects – of fellow workmen than any other art, except perhaps music. At least this is being more generally admitted for the day is happily passing away when architecture may be deemed a thing of quantities of dillitanteism & drains.

As the pigments are but the vehicle of painting so is building but the vehicle of <u>architecture</u>, <u>which</u> is the thought behind form, embodied and realised for the purpose of its manifestation & transmission.

Architecture then interpenetrates building not for the satisfaction of the simpler needs of the body but the complex ones of the intellect. I do not mean that we can thus distinguish architecture & building in those

F 5     qualities in which[4] / they meet & overlap but that in the sum & polarity of them all – these point to the response of future thought   those to the satisfaction of present need.

And so although no hut or mound however early or rude but had something added for thoughts sake yet architecture & building are quite clear and distinct ideas the soul & the body.

Of the modes of this thought we must again distinguish, some were unconcious & instinctive, as the desire for symmetry smoothness, sublimity and the like merely aesthetic qualities, which properly enough belong to true architecture and others were direct & didactic, speaking by a more or less perfect realisation, or through a code of symbols accompanied by

F 6     traditions which explained them.[5] Which traditions & symbols / must be thoroughly understood & appreciated be fore you can interpret the true meaning of the Architecture, and this is equally true of all the arts.

As Renolds says of sculpture, "I suspect that it will be found on close examination by him who is resolved not to see more than he really does

---

3. The eight-page introduction to W. R. Lethaby's *Architecture, Mysticism and Myth* (London 1891), with minor amendments to punctuation and phraseology, provides the greater part of Mackintosh's text from F 3-18. 'The history of architecture ... all the crafts.' Lethaby p. 1.

4. On the verso of F 4 are draft notes on Mackintosh's 1891 Italian tour:
Left Glasgow on March 21st 1891.
In order to fulfill the conditions laid down by the thomson Trustees I left Glasgow on 21st March of this year for Italy. I made Naples my first resting place. I stayed here 3 or four days and found the museum the principal attraction from an artists point of view owing to the fine collection of relics from Pompei especially the frescoes which are very beautiful.
The Trustees of the thomson memorial having honoured me with the Scholarship for 1891, I left Glasgow for Italy on March 21 to fulfill the conditions of the said Scholarship.

5. 'And so although ... traditions which explained them.' Lethaby (n. 3) pp. 1-2.

see, that the antique figures are distinguishable by their insignia rather than by any variety of form or beauty  Take from Appolo – Bacchus and other antique figures[6] their various symbols & there will remain little or no difference in their caracters  In a Juno Minerva or Flora the idea of the artists seems to have gone no further than representing his idea of perfect beauty & then adding the proper attributes with a total indifference to which they gave them.[7]

Music again is not a whit more expressive – programme music as it is called is understandable enough when we know or are told by a descrip-

F 7   tion of the / piece what is intended to be represented but without this forewarning it is somewhat difficult by intuition to guess that quivering trills among the high notes of an orchestra or a pounding scramble among the lower denote in turn "Sunrise in Arcadia" or the moon rising behind the trees of a churchyard with vampires flitting around the open grave of a maiden".[8]

Again to quote Ruskin "A building which recorded the Bible history by means of a series of sculptural pictures, would be perfectly useless to a person unacquainted with the bible beforehand, – on the other hand the text of the old & new testament might be written on its walls and yet the building would be a very inconvenient kind of book, not so useful as if it had been adorned with intelligible & vivid sculpture or painting. So again the power of exciting emotion must vary or vanish as the spectator

F 8   becomes thoughtless or cold, & a building may / be often blamed for what is the fault of the critic, or endowed with a charm which is of the spectators own creation. It is not therefore possible to make expression any fair criterion of excellence in a building untill we can fully place ourselves in the position of those to whom the expression was originally adressed & untill we are certain that we understand every symbol and are capable of being touched by every association which its builders employed as letters of their language.[9]

The main purpose & burthen of sacred Architecture – and all architecture when temple, tomb, or palace was sacred in the early days – is thus inextracably bound up with a peoples thoughts about god & the universe

Behind every style of architecture there is an earlier style in which the germ of every form is to be found except such alterations as may be

F 9   traced to new / conditions or directly innovatory thought in religion, all is the slow change of growth and it is almost impossible to point to the time of the invention of any custom or feature.

6. Mackintosh scored out '& Meleager' and substituted 'and other antique figures'.

7. This quotation from Sir Joshua Reynolds is reused from the earlier lecture: see E 38, n. 39.

8. This paragraph also appears at E 38-9. It is at least in part obviously not original, but its source has not been traced.

9. John Ruskin, 'The Virtues of Architecture', *The Stones of Venice* i ch. 2 §2. This passage is also quoted at E 39. The following paragraph resumes the Lethaby text.

As Herbert Spencer[10] says of ceremonial generally, "Adhering tenaciously to all his elders taught him the primitive man deviates into novelty only through unintended modifications. Every one knows that languages are not devised but evolve: and the same is true of usages.

It has rightly been the habit of historians of Architecture to lay stress on the differences of the several styles and schools of successive ages, but in the far larger sence all architecture is one, when traced back through the streams of civilizations as they followed or influenced one another. For instance argue as the archeologists may, as to whether the columns

F 10    at / Beni Hassan are rightly called proto Doric it is a fact to be read as in an open book that a greek Temple & an Egyptian temple are substantially at one when we consider the infinite possibilities of form – if disassociated from tradition  It has often been pointed out how early examples of stone construction still repeat the forms of the manner of buildings in wood that went before and so is it always.

How long the steamship retained survivals of the sailing ship & how the vocabulory of the coach road still answers for the railway

What then are the ultimate facts behind all Architecture which has given it form?

Mainly three.

The similar needs & desires of men  Secondly on the side of structure, the necessities imposed by materials & the physical laws of their erection

F 11    & combination / and thirdly on the side of style, nature. It is this latter that we need to think most about, the influence of the known & imagined facts of the universe on Architecture, the connection between the world as a structure & the building – not of the mere details of nature & the ornaments of architecture important though they are – but of the whole – the Heavenly temple & the earthly tabernacle. Let us get beyond the hodman & the builder – what I would ask is the connection between the Kingdom of heaven & the matter of fact mortar, tee squares & trowels. Architecture in the true sence occupies itself in reality with a temple built without sound of hammer axe or tool or iron, the temple of the skies in point of fact. It will be necessary not only to examine Architecture in the monuments, but the contemporary statements which relate to them the

F 12    stories about the buildings / & even the mythology of architecture for such a mythology there is.[11]

But of course such an exam. is impossible tonight. If we trace the artistic forms of things made by man to their origin, we find a direct

10. Herbert Spencer (1820-1903): English sociologist and philosopher, and early advocate of the theory of evolution.

11. 'The main purpose and burthen of Sacred Architecture [F 8] ... for such a mythology there is.' Lethaby (n. 3) pp. 2-4. In the penultimate sentence, Mackintosh substitutes 'Architecture in the true sence' for Lethaby's 'Esoteric masonry', and omits Lethaby's phrase 'the Macrocosmos' after 'temple of the skies'.

inspiration from if not a direct imitation of nature. The thought behind
a ship is a fish – the Egyptians & greeks giving their ships two eyes to
enable it to see its way across the pathless sea. Tables & chairs like the
beasts are quadrupeds. The lions leg & foot of modern furniture comes to
us from Assyria & Egypt.

And so with everything – where else indeed should we go for the
highest imagination. The commonplaces of poetry in which the world is
likened to a building – heavenly vaults – or azure dome – gates of sunrise
& the rest are survivals of a time when the earth was not a tiny ball
projected at immesureable speed through infinite space, one among other
F 13    fireflies of the night / but was stable & immovable the centre of the
universe the floor on which the sky was built. The whole a chamber
lighted by the sun moon & stars.

So the ceremonial of religion during the great building ages in Chaldea
Egypt & India was going through the phase of nature worship in which
the sky the sun & the sea were not so much veiled as afterwards to the
Greeks untill they became persons not things: but open and understood.
Astronomical observation was closely associated as part of the cultus. In
all this there is enough to dispose us to receive evidence of a cosmical
symbolism in the buildings of the younger world. and it is now generally
admitted that the intention of the temple (speaking of the temple idea as
F 14    we understand it), was to set up a / local reduplication of the temple not
made with hands, the worlds temple itself, a kind of model to scale, its
form governed by the science of the time. It was a heaven an observatory
an almanac  Its foundation was a sacred ceremony the time carefully
chosen by augury and its relation to the heavens defined by observation.

Its place was exactly below the celestial proto type, like that it was
sacred like that strong, its foundations could not be moved if they were
placed four square to the walls of the firmament, as are still our churches,
and was it not to be like the heavenly sanctuary that Solomon built the
temple without the sound of tools?

I do not necessarily claim that this was the origin of all structures set
F 15    apart for a purpose in a sence sacred: / nor possibly in every case was this
the first interpretation of some of the symbols. Customs have many
explanations. I claim that given the idea of a universe & universe gods,
the phase here set out was a necessary one: and at this stage certainly
every where preceded the age, when works, worthy the name of architecture were produced – buildings which enshrined ideas – it is here we shall
find the formative factor in their design.[12]

We need not suppose however that temples were a sum of these
symbols in all cases, if in any: but that from this common book of archi-

12. 'If we trace [F 12] . . . in their design.' Lethaby (n. 3) pp. 4-6, with minor editing out
of further examples.

tecture, each took what he would, little or much sometimes openly, sometimes with more or less translation, sometimes at first hand, often as a half remembered tradition[13]

F 16     Old architecture lived because it had / a purpose. Modern architecture, to be real, must not be a mere envelope without contents.

As Cesar Daly says, if we would have architecture excite an interest real & general, we must have a symbolism immediately comprehensible by the great majority of spectators. But this message cannot be that of the past  terror, mystery, splendeour. Planets may not circle nor thunder roll in the temple of the future. No barbaric gold with ruddy bloom; no jewels, emeralds half a palm over, rubies like an egg, and crystal spheres, can again be used more for majic that for beauty. No terraced temples of Babylon to reach the skies no gold plated palaces of Ecbatana seven walled. no ivory palaces of Ahab. nor golden houses of Nero with cor-

F 17     ridors a mile long; no stupendeous temples of Egypt at first / all embracing then court and chamber narrowing and becoming lower, closing in on the awed worshipper and crushing his imagination; these all of them can never be built again, for the manner and the materials are worked out to their final issue. Think of the Sociology and Religion of all this, and the stain across it "each stone <u>cemented</u> in the blood of a human creature. These colossal efforts of labor forced on by an irresistable will, are of the past, and such an architecture is not for us nor for the future.

What then will this art of the future be?

The message will still be of nature & man, of order and beauty, but all will be sweetness, simplicity, freedom, confidence, and light: the other is past and well is it, for its aim was to crush life: the new, the future,

F 18     is to aid life / and train it, "so that beauty may flow into the soul like a breeze".[14]

This much about ancient architecture will (and although I have only instanced one period and that very early, all architecture in successive ages up till the end of the 15th Century when we may say architecture ceased to be – was as vividly & inseperably the expression of the religious or social thoughts of the times) – I hope prove two things firstly that what are called Architectural styles were not made purposely as many people imagine – some say I like gothic – some I like classic – but you cannot surely believe that Architecture changed from classic to gothic because the old architects were sick of classic. No Architecture changed or rather evolved because the religious & social needs & beliefs changed, and when you consider as I said before how no change can be definitely pointed out

F 19     you will understand how the[15] / changes of Architecture were only the

13. 'We need not suppose ... half remembered tradition', Lethaby (n. 3) p. 6.

14. 'Old architecture [F 15, end] ... like a breeze".' Lethaby (n. 3) pp. 7-8. César-Denis Daly (1811-93): French architect and architectural editor and writer.

15. On the verso of F 18 Mackintosh has inscribed: '26A Begin at Page 53 XIX. The worth of a diamond is simply the understanding of the time it must take to look for it

expression & embodiment of the natural unconcious evolution of mans thoughts caused by the changes of civilization and things around him.

And this leads on to the second point which I hope this essay so far will help to emphasize – namely all great & living architecture has been the direct expression, of the needs & beliefs of man at the time of its creation, and how if we would have great architecture created this should still be so. How absurd it is to see modern churches theatres, Banks, Museums, Exchanges Municipal Buildings, Art Galleries &c &c made in imitation of greek temples. I am quite concious of the dignity of greek temples when built in greece 1000 years ago as temples, but to be imported into this

F 20   country and set up for such varied purposes, they must / surely loose all their dignity. And yet these are the modern buildings most people admire – perhaps even some of you dispute the loss of dignity – well let us admit that an art gallery copied from a greek temple has the same charm & dignity as its original  I would ask whether the dignity is still retained if we reduplicate the design and make it into a small black marble clock & put it on a black marble chimney piece as is so often done. There are many such buildings in Glasgow but to me they are as could & lifeless as the cheek of a dead chinaman  Dignity in architecture is the same as natural dignity — the very frankness of some natures is the essence of all thats dignified – which frankness if copied by one not natually frank immediately becomes impudence not dignity. It is absurd to think it is the duty of the modern architect to make believe he is living 4 – 5 – 6

F 21   hundred or even 1000 / years ago – and that his mission is to exercise on the forms found associated with a certain decade.[16] – no all the past is one art and all for us. And I am glad to think that now there are men such as Norman Shaw – John Bentley, John Belcher  Mr Bodley  Leonard Stokes and the late John D Sedding – names most of you will never have heard before but for all that quite as great if not greater artists than the best living painters  men who more & more are freeing themselves from correct antiquarian detail and who go streight to nature. We must clothe modern ideas, with modern dress – adorn our designs with living fancy. We shall have designs by living men for living men — something that expresses fresh realization of sacred fact – of personal broodings of skill – of joy in nature in grace of form & gladness of colour[17]

F 22   You will ask now why I read you this paper on Architecture – 'Do I want you all to be architects – No certainly not. But I do want you all to take an intellegent interest – to show some appreciation for Architecture

---

before it is to be found; and the worth of an ornament is the time it must take before it can be cut'.

16. 'It is absurd . . . a certain decade.' W. R. Lethaby, 'J. D. Sedding', *Builder* 61 (1891) p. 271.

17. J. D. Sedding, 'Design', in *Arts and Crafts Essays* (London 1893): 'We must clothe . . . living fancy', p. 412; 'We shall have . . . gladness of colour', p. 410. Mackintosh must have been aware of this chapter from its earlier quotation in Lethaby's obituary of Sedding (n. 16).

& not despise it as is too often now the case. I want you all so far as possible to be artists – and just so far as you are capable of any true and noble art, so far will your sympathetic appreciation of architecture go.

You ask how are you to judge architecture. just as you judge painting or sculpture – form, colour, proportion all visable qualities – and the one great invisable quality in all art, soul.

These are the essential qualities of all true architecture, and of the various subordinate arts that were used – in the days when there was

F 23    true art – for / its further enrichment as a work of art, and if you who are trained side by side with the architect, for as I heard Mr Newbery[18] say the other evening  and I apologise for taking the liberty of repeating it  the education of all artists must be conducted on one grand principal all must be educated alike – with one common aim —

I say if you who are trained to observe & admire beauty of line of proportion & of colour can see nothing in any architecture to admire then you may be sure there is something seriously wrong – with you.

I do not say you shall be capable of creating architecture – but you should be capable of adding whatever of your own art the architect may require for the thorough realization of his creations, and to do this of course you must be able to think & feel with him, so that when he

F 24    has / built his building and says to you paint this panel – you may so thoroughly understand and feel[19] the spirit of the work that you will fill your panel as part of the whole not as a panel distinct & seperate nothing more than a painting. To get true architecture the architect must be one of a body of artists posessing an intimate knowledge of the crafts, and no less on the other hand the painter & sculptor & other craftsmen must be in direct touch & sympathy with architecture. There must be a real communion, a common understanding & a working together towards the highest & best aim.

And I do contend that what architecture there is at the present time does not get the attention it deserves, from painters & other artists.

In reading a book or poem you do not glance at the title page & then convince yourself that you know all about it and have learned all it has to tell  no, every word may be beautiful, every line full of meaning & interest, and so you read through the book finding new cause for rapture & delight in every page.

The same in painting – every touch of the brush has its work to do & may make or mar the picture, every square inch of canvas is full of

F 25    beautiful combinations of colour, and / exquisite touches of drawing  all these must be studied carefully before you can say you know the picture.

Again in nature, you may go mad over some grand lanscape but nevertheless every tree – aye every leaf – every blade of grass & even

18. Francis H. Newbery (1853-1946): Director of Glasgow School of Art, 1885-1917.
19. Mackintosh scored out 'appreciate' and substituted 'feel'.

"every wee modest crimson tipped flower" demands and I hope receives its share of admiration.

And why a piece of architecture should be passed with only a passing glance – if even that – bestowed upon it is beyond my comprehension, the more so, when you consider that the fairy tale which it embodies is told in an even more obscure & indirect manner than in painting, in literature or in music. every form of an architectural composition, every feature every detail will command your attention

It may be that the details beautiful though they are, are overshadowed if not totally smothered by the grand tout ensemble – you may profess a sneaking regard for the grand mass as a whole – you may make this an F 26 excuse for your neglect of the minor / beauties, but believe me there never was an artist who took a thorough & true delight in the grander beauties of nature & art but who also took delight in every small atom of beauty which went to make the whole grand.

And still you ask what is the connection between Architecture & painting. Everything. Every artist whether architect or painter knows that natuer is not to be copied but exalted, that the loftiest order of art selecting only the loftiest combinations is the perpetual struggle of humanity to approach the gods The great painter or Architect embodies what is possible to man it is true – but what is not common to mankind. The idea of beauty is the artists own mind. This idea is inborn but has to be developed by intense study. But that study has been of the ideal that can be raised from the positive & the actual into grandeur and beauty. The F 27 commonest model becomes / full of exquisite suggestion to him who has formed this idea. A venus in flesh & blood would be vulgarized by the imitation of him who has not.[20]

Beauty in art is created by the idea of beauty in the artists own mind, and in every art whether it be expressed in marble, colour, or sound, the servile imitation of nature is the work of small minded men. But this you cannot get people to understand When a traveller beholds in Persia or India the ruins of temples & palaces the ignorant inhabitants inform him they were the work of magicians. What is beyond their own power the ignorant & vulgar cannot comprehend to be lawfully in the power of others But if you mean by magic that quality which takes architecture above building & painting beyond paint that quality which alone can raise the work of man to something beyond mechanism that quality which ever could or ever can give a human soul one ray of pleasure, F 28 that / perpetual research amongst all that is most latent & obscure in nature – I answer we must all profess that magic and that he who does so, comes but nearer to the fountain from which all true art springs And you who would be a painter is not there a majic also in the art you

20. Mackintosh here scored out 'And you ask, if you have all this sence of beauty why cannot you all be architects'.

would advance, must you not after long study of the beautiful that is and has been, sieze upon new and airy combinations of a beauty that is[21] to be.

See you not that the grander art of every Artist, ever seeking for the truth abhors the real, that you must sieze nature as her master not lackey her as her slave.

You demand mastery over the past a conception of the future.[22]

Has not the art that is truly noble for its domain the future and the past. You would conjure the invisable beings to your charm. and what is

F 29    Art / but the fixing into Substance the "invisable'

Are you discontented with this world? This world was never meant for Jenius to exist it must create another. (the invisable) What magician can do more? What science can do as much[23]

There are two avanues for the little passions & the drear calamities of earth, both lead to heaven & away from hell, Art & Science  But art is more godlike than Science  Science discovers. Art creates. You have faculties which may command art, be contented with your lot  The astronomer who catalogues the stars cannot add one atom to the universe the poet can call an universe from the atom, the chemist may heal with his drugs the infirmities of the human form – the Architect the painter or the Sculptor fixes into everlasting youth forms devine which no disease can ravage and no years impair. Renounce these wandering fancies which lead you to believe that architecture is not an art. I will

F 30    admit that much that is done now is / not art neither is it architecture – for to whom should an architect look for help & encouragement in his war against ignorance & ugliness if not his fellow artists  We mean to stand to architecture in its widest sense – we plant our feet in traditional tracts, we will not relinquish one item of the time honoured programme of our art as practiced in days of old.

I will admit an architects art is apt to represent a good deal more survival than revival. Practicing a calling which is bound more or less to appeal to tradition & precedent – and whose responsabilities seem to increas every day the tendancy of an architect is to carry on his work with a stolidity & lack of enthusiasm that accounds for much that is tame & stogy in his productions  But as I said before we now have men of high mettled genius and unspoiled ardour  here with them we have the pick of things  here we have design that is not survival but that is alive with individuality and revolutionary motive  And if you are not content with

F 31    what there is of architecture / you can recall the old womans laconic reply to Southley[24] who wishing to be civil remarked as he passed her on

21. Mackintosh here scored out 'and has been'.
22. A marginal note reads 'must you not after long study'.
23. Imprecise notations mark off the previous three sentences which Mackintosh may have intended to insert elsewhere.
24. Robert Southey (1774-1843): English poet and historian.

the road that it was dreadful weather – "Any weathers better than none"
says she and so methinks any design better than none.

I say again renounce these wandering fancies I ask you to look upon
all the arts going hand in hand as one — our pencil is our wand  we
may, raise Utopias fairer than Condorcet dreams of[25] – I press not for
your decision but what man of genius – and you are every one a genius –
ever asked for more to cheer his path to the grave than honour & love &
glory –

25. Marie Jean Antoine Nicolas Caritat Condorçet (1743-94): French mathematician
and philosopher, author of *Esquisse d'un Tableau des Progrès de l'Esprit Humain* (1793-4),
written when in hiding during the Terror.

75. C. R. Mackintosh: Finial, Glasgow School of Art (*c.* 1898-9)
A flowering from the 'green leaf' of reality.

ROBERT MACLEOD

# *Seemliness*

I have chosen as my theme "Seemliness" but the theme will often be lost in my wanderings, will sometimes be only faintly heard in the variations. [G 1]

The occasion for this lecture is not known for certain, but that Mackintosh was addressing a body of fellow artists, and perhaps teachers, is clear from the text. The most likely occasion is that suggested by John Archer: a lecture to the Northern Art Workers' Guild in Manchester, on 6 January, 1902.[1] Whatever the circumstances it is clear that the title was of Mackintosh's own choosing, even if, as he confesses himself, its central significance is less than clear.

This was a generation whose public prose was conditioned by the outpourings of Ruskin on the one hand, and the Sabbath art of homiletics on the other. Preaching, persuasion, the call to high endeavour were of its essence. The lamps of sacrifice, truth and power burned brightly, if erratically, and the resonances of the Grand Old Man of Coniston, though the voice was silenced, still hung on the air. It may well be that the Mackintosh lectures were very much more effective in the speaking than in the reading; there is clearly a good deal of scope in their manner to allow for transformation through speech and an assured platform manner, and even the propensity for self-deprecatory introductions could be more engaging in the flesh than on paper.

Be that as it may. Their flavour is of their time, and if the medium was for Mackintosh a little alien, the substance of what he had to say is nonetheless important to us for its direct bearing on his work. This is particularly, if less obviously, true of this lecture.

Here the borrowings are not as obvious, not to say blatant, as in some of the earlier papers, although in this connection there is an interesting passage in Ruskin's *Seven Lamps of Architecture* which may have some bearing on Mackintosh's attitude to precedents, borrowings and dependencies.

... it is at least interesting, if not profitable, to note that two very distinguishing characters of vital imitation are, its Frankness and its Audacity: its Frankness is especially singular; there is never any effort to conceal the degree of the sources of its borrowing. Raffaelle carries off a whole figure from Masaccio, or borrows an entire composition from Perugino, with as much tranquillity and simplicity of innocence as a young Spartan pickpocket; and the architect of a Romanesque basilica gathered his columns and capitals where he could find them, as an ant picks up sticks. There is at least a presumption, when we find this frank acceptance, that there is a sense within the mind of power capable of transforming and renewing whatever it adopts; and too conscious, too exalted, to fear the accusation of plagiarism, – too certain that it can prove, and has proved, its independence ...[2]

If anyone was in such a position in his community at this time, it was Mackintosh. He was at the height of his powers, in the very middle of that relatively brief span of architectural activity which made his reputation. He had proved his independence, and demonstrated the capacity to accept architectural precedent, form and tradition, and to transform it.

It is indeed about transformation that Mackintosh is speaking in this paper, if not directly about borrowing. He postulates an opposition between 'the advocates of individuality, freedom of thought and personal expression on the one hand and the advocates of tradition and authority on the other' [G 2]. Clearly the villains are the latter (including establishment villains) 'retarding [the cause of our art] by feebly im[it]ating some of the visable and superficial features of beautiful old works and neglecting the spirit the intention the soul that lies beneath' [G 2].

Thus far the argument could be just the typical 'young bohemian versus old establishment' complaint. But it quickly moves onto a different and altogether more interesting plane. 'I want to speak on the possible improvement in the design of everything' [G 2-3]. The argument here is a significant step beyond the Morris declaration that art is simply the expression of 'joy in the making'. It is much closer, indeed, to the kind of vision Mackintosh was sharing with Fritz Wärndorfer and the founders of the Wiener Werkstätte.[3] It has to do with individual expressiveness, with taste, with the active pursuit of 'beauty'.

In the conventional Arts and Crafts view, there was a kind of determinacy in the design-making process: if a thing were well designed for overt purpose and made with skill, it would have an inevitable and entirely appropriate beauty. But this was not how Mackintosh perceived the world – or indeed, how he designed. Beauty, propriety, seemliness were a product of, as he described it, 'a discriminating thoughtfulness' [G 3] with respect to shape, decoration, design. He was much too familiar with the bewildering plethora of choices that lies within the most function-driven design problem to suppose a simple determinism deriving from the tangible. No, his concern here was with 'the intangible – with the qualities that are excited by ambition and instinct, not the product of learning or accumulated knowledge  not so much with the technical as with the etherial the indefinable side of art' [G 3]. The issue here, of the indefinable characteristics and aspirations of the 'true' artist, lies at the very centre of Mackintosh's work, and there is no doubt that this essay represents his most articulate attempt to convey his own understanding of his motives.

Mackintosh and his friends had already felt the disapprobation of the Arts and Crafts disciples six years before. Mackintosh, Herbert MacNair and the Macdonald sisters – 'The Four' – had exhibited by invitation at the Arts and Crafts Exhibition Society in London in 1896. While it is almost certain that the widespread disquiet aroused by their modest contributions was due to the visual associations with Aubrey Beardsley and the aesthetic movement, visual influences that had been now well left behind by Mackintosh himself,

76. C. R. Mackintosh: Music Room for Fritz Wärndorfer, Vienna (1902)
In 1903 Mackintosh wrote to Wärndorfer on the proposal to found the Wiener
Werkstätte, 'every object which you pass from your hand must carry an
outspoken mark of individuality, beauty and most exact execution'.

nonetheless there remained a difference. The ethereal was very much, even
if indefinable, a central issue.

In line with the Ruskinian view, Mackintosh began with the belief that
the artist is born, not made: 'this appreciation must be inborn, it can be
cultivated, but it cannot be acquired it must be a personal one' [G 5]. This
particular declaration of faith – for that is all it can ever be – created then, as
it does today, serious problems in articulating the nature of the artist, and
also the nature of the art itself. But, in fact, Mackintosh was rather more
specific in his description of the particular facility with which the artist must
be born: 'a kind of instinct, a synthesis, or integration of myriads of details
and circumstances of which he cannot be directly concious but the appreciation of which makes the master in every profession' [G 5]. The cultivation
of this basic gift of instinct came with commitment to the work of the craft.
Was there just a hint here of the diversion of purpose and intent between
John Keppie and himself which was to culminate eventually in Mack-

intosh's departure? 'The Architect must become an art worker, and be content to forego the questionable distinction & pleasure of being respected as the head (perhaps the founder) of a large and successful business' [G 6].

This particular issue, the role of the architect in relation to the execution of the architectural work, was of course very topical. It had reached fever pitch some ten years before on the presentation of the first Registration Bill to Parliament in 1891, and the public debate on that occasion had culminated in a book of essays entitled *Architecture, a Profession or an Art*, edited by Norman Shaw and T. G. Jackson. It is fair to say that almost all architects of real distinction at the time were opposed to the idea of professional registration, with its inevitable formalising and distancing of the act of design from the act of execution, of the designer from the builder, and with the imposition of a regulated system of examination and control. Although the registration of architects in the United Kingdom did not occur until 1931, these formalising mechanisms were well under way, and the constraints of increasingly formal contractual relationships governing the execution of buildings were an ever more demanding reality of Mackintosh's working life.

At this point in the lecture the polemical outpouring was clearly reaching its emotional climax: 'The man with no convictions – no ideals in art, – no desire to do something personal something his own, no longing to do something that will leave the world richer his fellows happier is no artist The artist who sinks his personal convictions – who lives not up to his ideals is no man' [G 7]. The self-deprecating introduction to the lecture was one thing; here is the tyrannical core of the artist whose will may not be diverted, whose detailing may not be compromised, whose purpose may not be thwarted. But 'something his own'? In what sense and to what degree is the building, executed by others for the use of yet others, his own?

There are of course glib and ready answers to such a question. Yet the reality of building design and realisation means the active participation of many more than the solitary artist/architect, and the purposes of building as well as their expense are those of others than the artist. But the reality of this tension at the heart of the designing of buildings had much to do with Mackintosh's own difficulties within the practice of Honeyman & Keppie, and certainly within the process of realising his buildings.

The following section of the lecture is of particular interest in retrospect, for it appears that Mackintosh was convinced that the 'manner' – it can hardly be called either a school or a style – of work of the known friends with whom he was associated, both at home and increasingly abroad, was a growing trend. It is of even more interest to see how he characterised it: 'The focus of the true art of our country of the world is being gradually but surely accepted – and that focus will eventually proove to be the work of the individual worker – will proove to be the emancipation of all artists from the stupid forms of education which stifles the intellect paralizes the ambition and kills emotion' [G 11].

The irony of the history that subsequently unfolded was that the very characteristics which he so applauded, those which won him international acclaim and which lent such diversity and vitality to much of the work of the turn of the century, were stopped in their tracks within a decade or so – not just by the advent of war, but by the very 'forms of education' which Mackintosh so deplored. His prophecy was wrong, but he identified his enemy very clearly.

As he was speaking, the 'stupid forms of education' were emerging in Britain almost for the first time. The normal pattern of architectural education until this time was the system of 'articled pupillage', a form of apprenticeship, which had developed over two centuries, and which during the nineteenth century had begun to be supplemented by evening classes in the newly emerged local art schools. This was the pattern of education to which Mackintosh himself had been subjected, and which, it must be said, had served him very well indeed. But the kind of education to which it is assumed he was referring was the model of full-time study, as had been introduced at the University of Liverpool and University College, London, some ten years earlier, and whose effect was now, as he spoke, being seen.

The urge towards full-time University education for architects was part of the general push by the profession to establish its own credibility in society. But the departure from the much less structured articling system, where a good deal of the education of the aspirant could be almost by osmosis, and where the habits and traits of successive generations of designers can be seen almost as family legacies, changed forever the approach to design. For there was only one precedent extant for the teaching of design – the method of the Ecole des Beaux Arts. Methods of composition, rules about relationships, formulae for the ordering of elements, precedents for everything, were contained in a developed system, refined over centuries, and supported by comprehensive textual material.

Such an eminently teachable system, and one into which the great heroes of the English Renaissance could be happily absorbed, was naturally irresistible. Yes, certainly, in dull hands it could be seen to stifle the intellect, paralyze the ambition, and kill emotion. But it was safe, comprehensible, assessable, and ultimately it prevented men like Mackintosh from ever obtaining the opportunities by which they could realise their own altogether wilder, more glorious visions.

In the recognition that Mackintosh's visions were less convention-bound, however, it must not be assumed that tradition played no part in them. Throughout the paper he is contrasting superficial imitation with the understanding of substance, and, at least by implication, with the need to study and understand the old works – 'the spirit, the intention, the soul that lies beneath'.

As Mackintosh was during this year engaged in the preparation for the Liverpool Cathedral competition entry, it is a wholly appropriate example of the way in which he could entirely submerge himself in a proposal in

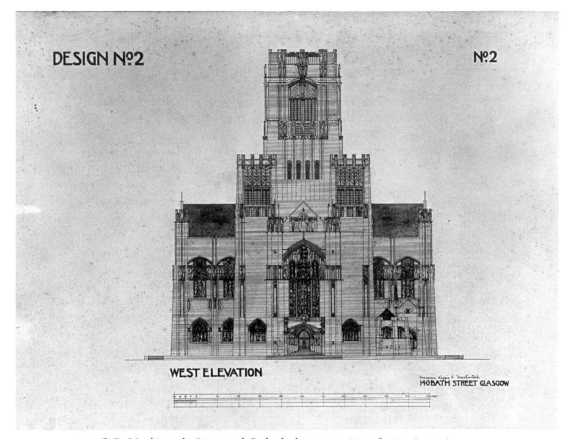

DESIGN Nº2                                                                    Nº2

WEST ELEVATION

HOBATH STREET GLASGOW

77. C. R. Mackintosh: Liverpool Cathedral – competition design (1902)

traditional form, organisation, and liturgical order, and yet imbue it with a kind of lyrical tension and quality all his own. Having thus accepted the form, he transformed it, but was that simply done by imagination? He would not have said so: 'He must posess technical invention in order to create for himself suitable processes of expression – and above all he requires the aid of invention in order to transform the elements with which nature supplies him – and compose new images from them. All good work is thoughtful and suggestive – carefully reasoned – and characterized no less by wide knowledge – than by closeness of observation and instinctive appropriateness' [G 14].

The reliance on reasoning, knowledge and invention may sound unusual to a generation raised on a much more self-justifying and indeed self-indulgent view of art. But in Mackintosh's view art was firmly bedded in life. His analogy here is direct. 'Art is the flower – Life is the green leaf' [G 14]. But the flower was not to be something alien – or even wilful – that was imposed on the leaf: 'Let every artist strive to make his flower a beautiful living thing – something that will convince the world that there may be –

there are things more precious – more beautiful more lasting than life. But to do this you must offer real living – beautifully coloured flowers – flowers that grow from but above the green leaf' [G 15]. In other words art and life partook of the same substance, were measured by the same criteria. Art was the outgrowth and the transformation.

This was to a certain extent conventional Arts and Crafts description, particularly with the use of the term 'invention'. And it was conventional Arts and Crafts prescription as well, for it was addressed to all the applied artists. But in reality Mackintosh had already demonstrated in his work the release of a degree of imagination (or invention) far beyond the confines of that ultimately limited movement.

There are in this essay all of the basic clues as to how Mackintosh perceived the basis of his art: it was to be couched in an understanding of the spirit of the great works of the past; supported by wide knowledge of the material problem; guided by close observation of the forms of nature; transformed by invention; constrained by instinctive propriety. But it was to the flower that every craftsman must be impelled.

This compulsive thrust towards individuality, at the time of the emergence of the greatest era of collectivism the world has ever seen, could not but fail. There was no societal basis on which it could succeed. We look back on these works where each repetitive element in a design, be they the great knots of wrought iron on the Art School, or delicate carved flowers in panelling – and Mackintosh was by no means unique in this – was varied individually within a theme, and we wonder. What kind of dedication, what attitude to time, what attitude to money prevailed? The kinds that were already out of phase with their time, and daily becoming more so. It was on precisely this rock that the social impulse of the Arts and Crafts movement foundered. It was only wealth and leisure that could afford such indulgence.

So this paper can be seen not only as a manifesto of Mackintosh's attitude to his art, but as a declaration of an approach, an attitude, which was finally to isolate him within his generation. For architecture is a public and a social art, and is finally dependent on the specific demands of patrons, and the collective skills of the participants in the building process: with neither of these sets of people could Mackintosh's urge towards expressive individuality be eventually reconciled. His vision was a moving one for his time, but there was no way that it could be of his time.

NOTES

1. John H. G. Archer, 'Edgar Wood', in Patrick Nuttgens, ed., *Mackintosh & His Contemporaries* (London 1988).

2. John Ruskin, *The Seven Lamps of Architecture*, ch. 5 § 5.

3. Peter Vergo, *Art in Vienna* (London 1975) p. 132.

CHARLES RENNIE MACKINTOSH

# G. *Seemliness* (1902)

G 1    Seemliness.

It was with timidity and misgivings that I agreed to accept your very generous invitation to come here and address you tonight. Timidity, because I have already had the pleasure of meeting some of your distinguished members and admiring them as men and as artists both in language and in line, misgivings because that so long as you only desired me to come here, so long as you only assumed that I had anything to say, for just so long would you be spared that feeling of acute disappointment which I am sure will be the result of my appearance here tonight.

I have chosen as my theme "Seemliness" but the theme will often be lost in my wanderings, will sometimes be only faintly heard in the variations.

I want to speak to you only as artists, and if anything I say has already been said by any of you, I sincerely hope it will not loose anything on

G 2    that account, but will because[1] / it is in a sense reiteration in a sense mutual agreement, help us all to greater strength and courage, to present a braver front   a more determined opposition in the great struggle that must always (I am afraid) continue to be waged by the advocates of individuality, freedom of thought and personal expression on the one hand and the advocates of tradition and authority on the other – the men of our own profession (some of them by the inexplicable irony of fate in high and exalted positions) who because of their own imbecility imagine they are conforming to a high convention or carrying on a laudable tradition, who imagine they are helping on the cause of our art whereas they are retarding it by feebly imating some of the visable and superficial features of beautiful old works and neglecting the spirit the intention the soul that lies beneath.

G 3    I want to speak on the possible improvement / in the design of everything, on the possible improvement in the education and work of architects and craftsmen as artists. To insist on some artistic intention being evident in the making or adornment of each article of everyday use

Mackintosh's graphic designs of the early 1900s often create patterns through the unconventional placing and breaking of words: compare fig. 7. In the 'Seemliness' manuscript he has made pronounced use of gaps and dashes of varying size, and while these occasionally punctuate sub-paragraphs, their role is primarily decorative. For clarity's sake no attempt has been made to replicate this in the transcription. The increasing freedom of the sentence structure, particularly in the second half of the script, also reflects Mackintosh's involvement in his argument.

   1. Dated at foot of page 'Xmas 1902'.

or requirement, an[2] appeal for a discriminating thoughtfulness in the selection of appropriate shape – decoration – design for everything no matter how trivial. I do not propose or presume to tell you how this is or may be done. But as my own thoughts and aspirations sometimes prompt a desire in myself, so, I hope that my thoughts though faintly expressed may arouse in some of you, a desire an definite purposeful ambition. to do this, to strive always and constantly to make everything of the best that passes through your hands. I do not for a moment propose to deal with the tangible qualities of our art, but rather with the intangible – with the qualities that are excited by ambition and instinct, not the product of learning or accumulated knowledge  not so much with the technical as with the etherial the indefinable side of art

G 4    We have all heard and I have no doubt spoken ourselves about the bad taste, want of thought, lack of appreciation – the vulgarity of the public – of the ordinary man in the street, but I do not think it will do any of us any harm to turn our attention for one night to the qualities and attainments, to the serious desires and longings of the majority of presumably highly educated artists and designers. I do not ask any to lower their ideals of what art is or should be, nor do I say that what I advocate so poorly will raise anyones ideals to a higher level their ambitions to a nobler sphere (although I strongly hope and suspect it will)  I only want each individual to know or seek to know when the requirements of a thing – are fulfilled and when presented in beautiful form, without violating the elements of usefulness on the one hand and appropriate beauty on the other

G 5    I may be only repeating oft expressed ideas, but I hope that even the repetition of those ideas, may arouse in some of you further desires to renew resolves which circumstances may have dulled, may suggest some slight interest, which interest if carefully nourished, may develop into real earnest endeavour, may lead to some new and personal achievements in the arts which we all so much desire to further. The architect the art worker depends very greatly for his success upon a kind of instinct, a synthesis, or integration of myriads of details and circumstances of which he cannot be directly concious but the appreciation of which makes the master in every profession. But this appreciation must be inborn, it can be cultivated, but it cannot be acquired it must be a personal one and expressed without resorting to the remote accessories in use elsewhere,

G 6    the commonplace acquirable / accessories which mark the feeble mind the mind imbued with the stolidity of stupidity, the mind that thinks it follows but as a fact only abuses all precedent all tradition all custom. The subject of such appreciation is almost inexhaustible for the questions of an artists

---

2. In the right hand margin, Mackintosh has inscribed 'See original XXX', probably a cross-reference to an earlier draft.

knowledge his learning must inevitably merge into that of his perceptions, his visions his divinations. The Architect must become an art worker, and be content to forego the questionable distinction & pleasure of being respected as the head (perhaps the founder) of a large and successful buisness – the art worker must become an architect. Architecture must no longer begin and end with the mechanical possibilities of the tee square the set square the pencil bows the deviders; the undoubtedly meritorious work of those necessary instruments may be likened to the alphabit, the grammer, of language, the artistic and beautiful phrasing of literature, to the more precious adornments of a building, and that is just
G 7    where the real work of an architect / as an artist should and must begin if the architect is to be appreciated as an artist, if his work is to be given to the world and understood by its people as the great mother art, the all embracive the comprehensive embodiment of all the arts. But to do this requires conviction

The man with no convictions – no ideals in art, – no desire to do something personal something his own, no longing to do something that will leave the world richer his fellows happier is no artist    The artist who sinks his personal convictions – who lives not up to his ideals is no man

The only true modern individual art in proportion in form and in colour, is produced by an emotion, produced by a frank and intelligent understanding of the absolute and true requirements of a building or object – a scientific knowledge of the possibilities and beauties of material, — a fearless application of emotion and knowledge a cultured intelligence
G 8    and a mind artistic yet not too indolent to / attempt the solution of these problems that have not before arisen — not too indolent to attempt the task of clothing in grace and beauty the new forms and conditions that modern developements of life — social – commercial and religious insist upon –

It is delightful to see thought and feeling and aspiration dressed in the bright raiment of present day art  On the whole I am inclined to believe that much of the work of today – the work of many individual artists – will take its place in the world of art – and the magic of time may be permitted to play on its present reputation as earnest individual work.

I refer to the examples we all know of living strenuous work – not the work that is carved in the image of emptiness and inanity – this we also know. we know it because it is so smeared and blurred with stupidity – so invaded and dominated by the spirit of dulness – so liable to swoon into
G 9    meaninglessness – that / to come to the work of some of our present day architects and designers is like an escape into the mountain air from the stagnant vapours of a morass. Many people question you as to whether the pleasure extractable from art work at all counterbalances the seeming bother of doing it. But I think there can be no two answers to such questions – All artists know that the pleasure derivable from their work is their lifes pleasure – the very spirit and soul of their existance. But you

must be independant – independant independant, dont talk so much – but
do more – go your own way and let your neighbour go his. Don't meddle
with other peoples ideas when you have all your work cut out of you in
trying to express your own — Shake off all the props – the props tradition
G 10   and authority offer you – and go alone  crawl – stumble – stagger – / but
go alone — You cannot learn to walk without tumbles and knocks and
bruises, but you will never learn to walk so long as there are props. The
props of art are – on the one hand – the slavish imitation of old work
no matter what date or from what country – and on the other hand the
absurd and false idea – that there can be any living emotion expressed in
work scientifically proportioned according to antient principals – but
clothed in the thin fantasy of the authors own fancy. — The artists
motto should be I care not the least for theories for this or that dogma –
so far as the practise of art is concerned – but take my stand on what I
myself consider my personal ideal. — And I am sure that no one of any
gifts of reasoning – will question the value of a high ideal — a strong
G 11   ambitious conviction – / as compared with the greatest knowledge of
scientific theories of formulae. —

   The focus of the true art of our country of the world is being gradually
but surely accepted – and that focus will eventually proove to be the work
of the individual worker – will proove to be the emancipation of all artists
from the stupid forms of education – which stifles the intellect paralizes
the ambition and kills emotion   And as you are careful and anxious
about the art you yourself produce –  as each new achievement gives you
pleasure and happiness — as you are jealous of every thought you think
– so also be jealous and happy in your seeking for, and assisting in the
encouragement of each youth of promise in your world — any youth
whose work may – no matter how slightly – suggests promise of further
things — like the first flowers of spring – who may be likened to the seeds
and bulbs which if carefully nurtured and tended may grow to be beautiful things — whereas if neglected or discouraged their ultimate worth
G 12   may be lost to the world for ever. Each / spateful of earth carelessly
thrown away – may contain the germs of the most beautiful flower the
world has yet seen – and each years group of students may contain a
new Heaven born jenius – What is – in an artist the most important – the
essential faculty – The artist may have a very rich psychic organisation –
an easy grasp and a clear eye for essentials – a great variety of aptitudes –
but that which characterizes him above all else – and determines his
vocation is  the exceptional developement of the imaginative faculties –
especially the imagination that creates – not only the imagination that
represents — The power which the artist posesses of representing objects
to himself explains the halucinating character of his work — the poetry
G 13   which pervades them – and their tendancy towards symbolism – But / the
creative imagination is far more important. — The artist cannot attain to
mastery in his art unless he is endowed in the highest degree with the

faculty of invention. In analizing the work of today, it will be found that this essential faculty is mostly conspicuous by its absence — it will be found that the art of the years that are past – recently past  is lacking as to style or character – and lacking in substance as to matter — It will be found profoundly and hopelessly wearisome – the authors neither recognized arts limitations – acquiesed in its offices – nor apprehended its distinctions – it is thin – light   artificial – revealing no personality.

What one misses in most of the work I refer to is – the large rythm that undulates through that of the great masters antient and modern – the sustained note of informing purpose – the deep vibration of some unifying undertone / now rising to accent and emphasis – now sounding faintly, beneath the multifareousness of accompanying motives – but always visable to an attentive sense as – the basis if not the burden of the theme with variations – the ensamble which every artists work – no matter how trivial, should constitute. Reason informed by emotion – expressed in beauty – elevated by earnestness – lightened by humour – that is the ideal that should guide all artists.

G 14

He must posess technical invention in order to create for himself suitable processes of expression – and above all he requires the aid of invention in order to transform the elements with which nature supplies him – and compose new images from them. All good work is thoughtful and suggestive – carefully reasoned – and characterized no less by wide knowledge – than by closeness of observation and instinctive appropriate-ness — Art is the flower – Life is the green leaf / Let every artist strive to make his flower a beautiful living thing – something that will convince the world that there may be – there are things more precious – more beautiful more lasting than life. But to do this you must offer real living – beautifully coloured flowers — flowers that grow from but above the green leaf — flowers that are not dead – are not dying – not artificial – real flowers springing from your own soul – not even cut flowers – you must offer the flowers of the art that is in you – the symbols of all that is noble – and beautiful – and inspiring — flowers that will often change a colourless cheerless life – into an animated thoughtful thing.

G 15

How Beautiful the green leaf – how beautiful life often is – but think of the stupendeous possibilities of the flower thus offered – of art. And it has been more towards art perhaps - more towards the flower I hope – that I have tried to tempt your imagination tonight – tempted your imagination to the fact – that the craftsman of the future must be an artist – not what they too often are just now artistic failures[3] / men and women who are not intellectually fit to be architects painters or sculptors  And it is by advocating this and insisting upon it that all the applied arts will once again take their proper and dignified place in the world of artistic produc-tion – it is only then that they will command that respect which we all so

G 16

3. On the verso of G 15 is a semi-legible note: 'artificial. appreciate. as before [?]'

much desire — it is only then that craftsmen will begin to love and think highly of their own efforts their own art — and it is only then that the possible utility and beauty of every article of everyday use and personal adornment – will be be realized — will be designed thoughtfully to suit its every purpose — will be designed beautifully to please artist and owner alike. it is only then that artists will thoroughly understand and appreciate the possible application and beauty of each material he is called upon to handle. – that all the varied problems and materials the world has to offer will be understood – and thoroughly valued because of the artistic possibilities that is in them.[4]

G 17     unuttered utterances[5]

The little man playing the lion, who is surprised because he is not successful.

Carved in the image of emptiness and inanity

lacking the hushed reserve that is always felt in nature the precious reserve that only true art posesses.

Let us look upon the result of the worlds artistic achievements as the beginning the morning of our lives – not the grave of our aspirations the death knell of our ambitions.

The artists may gather from  A close and careful study of old work a great deal that will refine his tastes, that will help him to a more adaquate appreciation and therefore a fuller enjoyment of art and nature and life

4. On the verso of G 16 is inscribed: 'motives that prompted all my work not any isolated item'.

5. These aphorisms occupy the last page of the manuscript.

# Appendix 1:
# Correspondence relating to the Italian Tour

*This correspondence between Mackintosh and John Shields, Secretary of the Alexander Thomson Memorial, is reproduced by kind permission of the Glasgow Institute of Architects. Shields' letters are drafts, often written on the verso of Mackintosh's originals, and retained as file copies for the Memorial Trust.*

---

2 Fir Park Terrace,<br>
Dennistoun,<br>
Glasgow.

Dear Sir

As I intend starting on my travels about the beginning of March I would need to make arrangements about getting my money. I dont know whether it is a fast rule that you only give half the money at a time. If it is, it will be rather hard on me as I intend staying away for at least nine months  If you could fix a time I should like to see you and have a talk over my arrangements

Trusting that you and Mrs Shields are keeping well

Yours faithfully<br>
Chas. R. McIntosh[1]

---

6 Nithsdale Road,<br>
Pollokshields. 13th. Feby 1891

Mr Chas R. McIntosh
2 Fir Park Terrace
Dennistoun

Dear Sir,

I am pleased to learn that you intend to commence your tour about the beginning of March, will you kindly let me have a short statement of the places you intend to visit? I earnestly hope that you will greatly benefit by your lengthened absence from Glasgow

The half £30 of the prize will be paid to you as soon as you have made arrangements to start but I am sorry to say that the Trustees have not the power to pay the second £30 until your return.

When I have your statement (asked for above) I shall arrange with Mr. Gordon & Mr. Watson to meet you, before setting out – these gentlemen were appointed to do so along with[2]

Yours truly<br>
John Shields

---

2 Fir Park Terrace,
Dennistoun,
Glasgow.

Dear Sir

Kindly let me know when it will be convenient for the Committee to
meet me and I will then submit my tour

Yours truly
Chas R McIntosh

6 Nithsdale Road.
Pollokshields. 23rd Feby 1891

Dear Sir,

I have arranged with Mr Gordon and Mr. Watson to meet you in Mr.
Gordon's office, 124 Bath St on Friday 27th instant at twelve o'clock
noon to receive your notes of proposed tour, and consider them
    on talking over with these gentlemen the question of paying the second
half of the prize money  it has been proposed that you might send the
sketches & drawings required by the Regulations at the end of three
months, and, if these are found satisfactory, the balance may then be
remitted to you.
    Hoping this will meet your views. I remain

Yours truly
John Shields

Mr. Chas. R. McIntosh
2 Firpark Terrace
Dennistoun

The "Alexander Thomson," Memorial.

Glasgow. 27th. Feby 1891. Received from John Shields, Secretary to the
Trustees, the sum of Thirty pounds sterling, being the first half of the prize
of £60 awarded to me on 18th. Septr 1890, in the competition decided at
that date.

£30

Received payment
Chas R McIntosh

2 Fir Park Terrace,
Dennistoun,
Glasgow.
2nd March 1891

Dear Sir

Since I saw you the other day Mr Newbery of the School of Art has asked me if he can have my drawings to send with the other School of art work to South Kensington[3] You might let me know if I can have the loan of them for this purpose  Mr Anderson sent his you will perhaps remember and got a Silver Medal for them

Yours sincerely
Chas. R. McIntosh

6 Nithsdale Road
Pollokshields 2nd March 1891

Dear Sir,

When getting away your drawings from the Corporation Galleries, Mr. Newbery asked them for the exhibition at South Kensington, and I promised that he would have them on condition that they were carefully returned – he was to let me know when they would be required. I shall assume your application to be on his account and if you will take the trouble to call on Mr. John Thomson (Thomson & Sandilands) West Regent St. in whose keeping your drawings are, and shew him this letter you can have them. I presume all the drawings from the Glasgow School of Art will go up together, and be returned together, – I forget whether I told you that Mr. John Thomson is now associated with me in the Secretaryship.

As I have to make a minute of our meeting in Mr. Gordon's office on Friday, will you kindly send me a copy of the plan of your tour?

I shall be very pleased to hear from you at any time in your journeyings, and with best wishes for a successful and happy tour, and a safe return. I remain,

Yours truly,
John Shields.

Mr. Chas. R. McIntosh
2 Fir Park Terrace
Dennistoun.

Cremona 14th June 1891.

Dear Mr Shields,

I have now been away nearly 3 months. I have been to Palermo, Monreale, Naples, Pompei Paestum, Amalfi, Rome, Orvieto Siena, Pisa, Pistoya, Bologna, Ravenna, Ferrara Venice, Verona Mantua and now I am at Cremona When I get to Milan my Italian tour will be completed. Instead of coming direct home I would like to spend some time in the south of France. To do this I will need some more money, and I write to see if I can have the remaining half of my prize I would send home my drawings to you, but I think they might get spoiled in some way, the post people are so careless.

I can assure you however that I have been working concienciously during my tour. I hope this will be enough to warrant you in sending me the money.

I will be at Milan in eight or ten days from now when I hope to hear from you. My address will be Albergo Biscione & Bellevue Milan.

I am
yours sincerely
Chas. R. McIntosh

Callander 22nd June 1891

Dear Sir,

Your letter of the 14th. has been sent on to me here where I am staying at present

I hope that you will believe that I shall do all that I can for you but I will require to go to Glasgow before getting money, and, besides having to act under the Rules and Regulations of the Trust I have to consider my responsibility to the Trustees –

I would advise you to send on the drawings at once, taking all necessary precautions for having them safely forwarded, as I am doubtful whether the Trustees have power to remit the balance of the prize money until this is done

I shall be here till Wednesday when I return to Glasgow, and my new address there is 98 Kenmure St Pollokshields

Believe me,
Yours truly
John Shields

Mr. Chas. R McIntosh
Albergo Biscioni & Bellevue
Milan. Italy

Hotel Biscione & Bellevue
Milan
27th June 1891.

Dear Sir

I have just arrived here this morning and found your letter waiting for me. I hope you will be able as you expect to arrange the matter with the Trustees I will wait till I hear from you and then if <u>necessary</u> I will send on my sketches and let them take their chance of arriving safely.

I will be in Milan for some days then I go to Pavia & Genoa.

Hoping that you will let me know as soon as possible I am

Yours in haste
Chas. R McIntosh.

John Shields Esq
98 Kenmure St. Pollokshields

---

98 Kenmure St
Pollokshields Glasgow 30th. June 1891

Dear Sir,

Yours of 27th. was received yesterday evening. This forenoon I saw Mr. Gordon. – Mr. Watson is from home.

Mr. Gordon and I are decidedly of opinion that the sketches which you have prepared must be sent to the Committee named by the Trustees to be examined and approved before the second half of the prize money can be paid. as we are obliged to give account of our actions not only to the Trustees of the A. Thomson Memorial, but to the Council of the Glasgow Institute of Architects

I suppose that there will be a system of registration for documents transmitted by the Post Office in Italy, as there is here – whereby through paying a small additional fee the safety of your sketches will be ensured, and I think it likely that in Milan there will be some official who acts as representative for Great Britain whose good offices in this matter will be available, if asked for. The Committee will expect that the utmost precaution is exercised in providing for their safe delivery to me here, and I undertake to bear any expense which may be incurred by so doing.

Believe me, Yours truly
John Shields

Mr. Chas R McIntosh
Hotel Biscioni & Bellevue, Milan, Italy.

Hôtel & Restaurant Milan
Certosa
12 July 1891.

Dear Sir

Your letter has been forwarded to me here. If I had known there would be any trouble about sending out the money I should not have written for it. As it is I can only express my sorrow at having given you so much trouble and that I will wait till I come home for the balance of my prize

I am
Yours faithfully
Chas. R. McIntosh.

---

2 Firpark Terrace
Dennistoun 12th Aug.

Dear Sir

Will you kindly let me know, when the Committee can see my sketches

I am
Yours faithfully
Chas. R. McIntosh.

---

98 Kenmure St.
Pollokshields, 13th. Augt 1891.

Dear Sir,

I have arranged for a meeting of Trustees on Thursday next, 20th instant, in the Religious Institution Rooms, Buchanan St, the room will be taken for the day.

Will you kindly have your sketches hung on the walls in the forenoon of that day?

Hoping that you have greatly profited in your professional studies by your tour

I remain
Yours truly
John Shields

Mr. Chas. R McIntosh,
2 Firpark Terrace,
Dennistoun.

2 Firpark Terrace
Dennistoun
17th August 1891.

Dear Sir

I will have my drawings hung in the rooms mentioned in your letter of the 17th on Thursday morning. If I am to be at the meeting you will kindly let me know at what hour you propose having same. I am
Yours faithfully
Chas. R. McIntosh

John Shields Esq.

98 Kenmure St
Pollokshields, 18th Augt 1891

Dear Sir,

I thank you for undertaking the hanging of your drawings.

Since last writing you I have taken the room No. 10, up two stairs (Religious Institution Rooms, 200 Buchanan St), from 1 till 4 on Thursday afternoon, 20th Augt and as the meeting is called for 3 P.M. I hope there will be ample time for getting the drawings hung before the meeting.

Mr. W. J. Anderson was not asked to be present when his drawings were being examined, and I read the manuscript memoir description of his tour to the Trustees at the meeting – if you have prepared one, as provided for by the conditions of competition, will you please have it forward along with your drawings? and you might come, say at 3 15 P.M. on Thursday, and as soon as the examination is over, you could be called in to the meeting – this, of course, is altogether in your option

The people in the Religious Institution have expressly stipulated that "the drawings will be put on the walls with small drawing pins"

Yours truly,
John Shields

Mr. Chas R McIntosh,
2 Firpark Terrace,
Dennistoun.

Glasgow, 20th. Augt. 1891.[4] Received from John Shields, Secretary to the Alexander Thomson Memorial Trust. The sum of Thirty pounds Stg. being the second half of the prize of Sixty pounds awarded to me in the Competition for the Travelling Studentship decided in Sept 1890.
£30
20 August 1891.
Chas. R. McIntosh

John Honeyman & Keppie,
Architects.
140 Bath Street,
Glasgow,
18th Dec. 1891

Dear Sir

I am going in for the Pugin Studentship this year, and I would feel
much indepted if you as Secretary of the Thomson Memorial would
supply me with a testimonial saying whether I gave satisfaction during
my Thomson Tour[5]

Trusting you are keeping well

I am yours faithfully
Chas. R. Mcintosh

P.S. My drawings go off on Tuesday morning so you might let me have
this by Monday. C.R.M.

---

98 Kenmure St. Pollokshields
19th. Decr 1891.

At the meeting of Trustees held on 18th. Sept. 1890, the prize for the best
set of drawings in the competition for the Travelling Studentship was
awarded to Mr. Charles R. McIntosh, thereafter he made a lengthened
tour in Italy – on his return to Glasgow in terms of the conditions of
competition he submitted the sketches which he had made, and the
Trustees at their meeting on 20th. Augt 1891 approved of these sketches.

John Shields Secretary.

98 Kenmure Street
Pollokshields. 19th Dec. 1891

Dear Sir,

Herewith is sent certificate which I hope will serve the purpose asked
for

I may remind you that at the meeting of Trustees on 20th. Augt
you were requested to send a copy of one of the drawings which were
exhibited that day – When you have prepared it you can send it to Mr
John Thomson I.A. West George St who is now Associate Secretary[6]

Yours truly
John Shields

Mr. Chas. R. McIntosh
at Messrs. John Honeyman & Keppies.
140 Bath St.

---

2 Firpark Terrace,
Dennistoun,
Glasgow.

Dear Sir

I got your letter for which I tender my most sincere thanks.

Yours truly
Chas. R. McIntosh

---

NOTES

1. C.R.M. did not adopt the style and spelling 'Charles Rennie Mackintosh' until the mid 1890s. Rennie was his mother's maiden name. The new spelling of his surname was probably influenced by his friendship with the Macdonald sisters. It was shortly after his marriage to Frances Macdonald in 1899 that J. Herbert McNair adopted the spelling 'MacNair'.

2. Thomson Trustees John Gordon and T. L. Watson, respectively President and Council member of the Glasgow Institute of Architects, were members of the Memorial sub-committee responsible for the 1890 Studentship competition.

3. Mackintosh's Public Hall designs won a silver medal at South Kensington. William James Anderson's drawings of Thomson's Queen's Park Church, Glasgow, had won the previous Studentship.

4. At the meeting of 20 August 1891 the minute book records, 'The Trustees expressed their opinion that the second clause of the Trust should be more strictly adhered to in future – "That the Studentship or prizes shall be awarded for the furtherance of the study of Ancient Classic Architecture as practised prior to the commencement of the third century of the Christian era and with special reference to the principles illustrated in the works of the late Alexander Thomson"' – a comment prompted by Mackintosh's obvious preference for the later periods of art and architecture.

5. Mackintosh unsuccessfully submitted a selection of Italian drawings for the 1892 Pugin Studentship.

6. This drawing has not been identified.

# Appendix 2:
# Memoir on the Italian Tour

*This memoir by Mackintosh is the tour account required by the Studentship regulations and read at the meeting of 20 August 1891. It is reproduced with the kind permission of the Glasgow Institute of Architects.*

The Trustees of the "Alexander Thomson Memorial" having honoured me with the Scholarship for the year 1891, I left Glasgow for Italy on March 21, in order to fulfill the conditions of said scholarship

My first resting place in Italy was Naples where I spent four or five days. I found the Museum the principal attraction from an architects point of view, owing to the very extensive collection of fragments from Pompei, the frescoe decorations being specially worthy of study.

In naples there are various churches more or less interesting, but none of outstanding merit. There are some very good monuments to be seen here. The exterior of the Theatro S Carlo is a very good piece of work. At the Certosa di S. Martino behind naples there is also some very good work to be seen.

From Naples I visited Pompei & Paestum both very interesting and instructive places, but unfortunately the wet weather at this time made sketching almost impossible.

I next went to Palermo in Sicily  The exterior of the Cathedral (the interior has been modernised) and the interior of the chapel of the Royal Pallace being particularly good.

The church and cloisters at Monreale (about 2 miles from Palermo) are also very beautiful. The mosaic decoration in the interior of the church being wonderful.

Palermo is altogether a very interesting town for an architectural student  From Palermo I returned to Naples and then proceeded to Rome, where I spent a fortnight, studying principally the Ruins, the magnificent decorations in the Sixtine chapel by Mich. Angelo, / the various rooms decorated by Raphael, and the wonderful collection of statuary, architectural fragments &c in the Vatican Museum.

From Rome I went to Orvieto where I was much impressed by the rich colouring and beautiful composition of the Cathedral facade. The interior is also very beautifully proportioned. I went from Orvieto to Siena which, being beautifully situated, with its interesting cathedral, its many beauti ful pallaces, and pictures by Sodoma, is one of the most instructive places in Italy.

My next stoppage was at Florence, where the attractions for an architectural student are many and varied

The cathedral with Brunellesco's / famous Dome and Campanile by
Giotto, (which for quiet dignity and beauty of detail cannot be surpassed)
the Battisterio with the Ghiberti doors, the Uffizi and Pitti Galleries
with their unrivalled collections of pictures &c, the churches of S Croce,
S Maria Nuova, S. Badia, S. Miniato and S Lorenzo, the various exquisite
Pallaces (in the Florentine style) and the works of Mich. Angelo, Donatella and Della Robbia all combine to make Florence one of the finest
towns in Italy.

After Florence I visited Pisa, (where the cathedral Battisterio, Campo
Santo & leaning Tower are very interesting) Lucca, Pistoya (where the
Battisterio is particularly nice) and Bologna, but did not stay any
length of time till I came to Ravenna which town I found particularly
interesting / and instructive

The mosaic decorations at S Apollinare Nuovo, and S Apollinare in
Classe, and the plan and general conception of S Vitale being specially
good. I visited Ferrara on my way to Venice.

The various features of Venice are so well known to every one that it
is quite superfluous to enumerate them here. I stayed three weeks at
Venice but even that time was quite insufficient for a careful study of the
many beautiful architectural features of this charming city.

I next visited Padua where the church of S Lorenzo and the bronze
reliefs in S Antonio by Donatella are the principal attractions /

Vicenza was our next resting place which town is made interesting by
the works of Paladdio

From Vicenza we went to Verona where the various phases of Architecture from the early Roman Period are very plentifully illustrated  The
churches of S. Annastasia the Duomo, and S Zeno being particularly
good, and also the Tombs of the Scaligers.

After Verona I visited Mantua Brescia and Bergamo, and found many
interesting and beautiful things in each place. From Bergamo I went
to Como where the Cathedral, and the churches of S Abbondio and S.
Fedele are the principal Architectural attractions

Milan the next town I visited, I found to be interesting in many ways.
The cathedral though / perhaps overdone has many good points, and the
churches of S. Ambrogio & S Maria del Grazie (near which is da Vinci's
Last Supper) are both worthy of very careful study.

I next visited the Certosa di Pavia, my appreciation of which, will, I
hope be gathered from the sketches I made there.

Chas. R. McIntosh

# Select Bibliography

This bibliography cites the principal texts in which Mackintosh's architecture and its historical context are discussed. For a bibliography of his other work as a designer and artist see Macleod (1983) and Nuttgens.

Roger Billcliffe, *Architectural Sketches & Flower Drawings by Charles Rennie Mackintosh* (London 1977)

William Buchanan, ed., *Mackintosh's Masterwork: The Glasgow School of Art* (Glasgow 1989)

Jackie Cooper, *Mackintosh Architecture: The Complete Buildings and Selected Projects* (2nd edn, London 1980)

Andor Gomme and David Walker, *The Architecture of Glasgow* (2nd edn, London 1987)

Thomas Howarth, *Charles Rennie Mackintosh and The Modern Movement* (3rd edn, London 1990)

Hiroaki Kimura, 'Charles Rennie Mackintosh', *Process Architecture* 50 (Tokyo 1984)

Robert Macleod, *Style and Society* (London 1971)

Robert Macleod, *Charles Rennie Mackintosh: Architect and Artist* (2nd edn, London 1983)

Andrew MacMillan, *Some Designs by Charles Rennie Mackintosh*, exhibition catalogue, Architectural Association (London 1981)

Patrick Nuttgens, ed., *Mackintosh & his Contemporaries* (London 1988)

Nikolaus Pevsner, *Pioneers of the Modern Movement* (3rd edn, London 1960)

Nikolaus Pevsner, 'Victorian and after', *Studies in Art, Architecture and Design* ii (London 1968)

Nikolaus Pevsner, *Some Architectural Writers of The Nineteenth Century* (Oxford 1972)

Nikolaus Pevsner and J. M. Richards, eds, *The Anti-Rationalists* (London 1973)

Pamela Robertson, *Charles Rennie Mackintosh: The Architectural Drawings*, exhibition catalogue, Hunterian Art Gallery (Glasgow 1990)

Alastair Service, ed., *Edwardian Architecture and its Origins* (London 1975)

# Illustration Sources and Acknowledgements

H.A.G. = Hunterian Art Gallery, University of Glasgow

1. H.A.G.; 2. Dr Thomas Howarth; 3. Scottish National Portrait Gallery; 4. Scottish National Portrait Gallery; 5. W. R. Lethaby, *Architecture, Mysticism and Myth* (1891); 6. The British Architectural Library, R.I.B.A., London; 7. H.A.G.; 8. Bruce Hanson; 9. *The Bailie* (1898): Mitchell Library Glasgow; 10. Victoria & Albert Museum; 11. Glasgow Art Gallery and Museum; 12. R. W. Billings, *The Baronial and Ecclesiastical Antiquities of Scotland* (1845-52) ii; 13. D. MacGibbon and T. Ross, *The Castellated and Domestic Architecture of Scotland* (1887) ii; 14. Glasgow School of Art; 15. MacGibbon and Ross (1887) ii; 16. *Deutsche Kunst und Dekoration* (1905); 17. The Trustees of Sir John Soane's Museum; 18. Royal Commission on Ancient Monuments, Scotland; 19. Trevor Graham; 20. H.A.G.

21. Wilma Paterson; 22. *The British Architect* (1890): Mitchell Library Glasgow; 23. H.A.G.; 24. Dr Thomas Howarth: photo courtesy of Roger Billcliffe; 25. Glasgow School of Art; 26. H.A.G.; 27. H.A.G.; 28. Wilma Paterson; 29. Dr Thomas Howarth: photo courtesy of Roger Billcliffe; 30. Charles Rennie Mackintosh Society, Glasgow; 31. Hans Karlinger, *Die Kunst der Gotik* (1926); 32. Glasgow School of Art; 33. Dr Thomas Howarth: photo courtesy of Roger Billcliffe; 34. Dr Thomas Howarth: photo courtesy of Roger Billcliffe; 35. *The British Architect* (1892): Mitchell Library Glasgow; 36. Glasgow School of Art; 37. H.A.G.; 38. Dr Thomas Howarth: photo courtesy of Roger Billcliffe; 39. H.A.G.; 40. H.A.G.

41. H.A.G.; 42. H.A.G.; 43. Dr Thomas Howarth; 44. Royal Commission on the Historical Monuments of England; 45. Annan; 46. Royal Commission on the Historical Monuments of England; 47. H.A.G.; 48. The British Architectural Library, R.I.B.A., London; 49. Royal Commission on the Historical Monuments of England; 50. *The British Architect* (1892): Mitchell Library Glasgow; 51. H.A.G.; 52. H.A.G.; 53. *The British Architect* (1892): Mitchell Library Glasgow; 54. *Annual Architectural Review* (1891); 55. H.A.G.; 56. *The Builder* (1892): Mitchell Library Glasgow; 57. *The British Architect* (1892): Mitchell Library Glasgow; 58. H.A.G.; 59. *The British Architect* (1889): Mitchell Library Glasgow; 60. H.A.G.

61. *The Bailie* (1893): Mitchell Library Glasgow; 62. Country Life; 63. Renfrew District Museums Service; 64. *Academy Architecture* (1893); 65. Royal Commission on the Historical Monuments of England; 66. *Academy Architecture* (1892); 67. *Academy Architecture* (1895); 68. *Academy Architecture* (1894); 69. *Academy Architecture* (1895); 70. *Academy Architecture* (1890); 71. *Academy Architecture* (1893); 72. Royal Commission on the Historical Monuments of England; 73. *The British Architect* (1893): Mitchell Library Glasgow; 74. *Academy Architecture* (1893); 75. Glasgow School of Art; 76. *The Studio* (1912); 77. H.A.G.

# *Index*

to come to the work of some of our
present day architects and designers
is like an escape into the mountain
air from the stagnant vapours of a
morass.                    Many people
question you as to whether the pleasure
extractable from art work at all
counterbalances the seeming bother of
doing it.           But I think there can
be no two answers to such questions —
All artists know that the pleasure
derivable from their work is their lifes
pleasure —    the very spirit and
soul of their existance.        But
you must be independant — independant
independant — dont talk so much —
but do more —    go your own way
and let your neighbour go his.
Dont meddle with other peoples ideas
when you have all your work cut
out of you in trying to express your
own _____                Shake off
all the props —      the props tradition
and authority offer you —    and go alone
Crawl —    stumble —   stagger —